Self-Sufficiency and Sustainable Cities and Regions

The concept of self-sufficiency involves the notion of sustainable, circular, and carbon-neutral cities. This book examines how urban planning can lead to greater self-sufficiency.

It sheds light on how urban and regional circular and self-sufficiency development can effectively contribute towards the ultimate goals of the United Nations (UN) Agenda 2030 and the European Union (EU) Green Deal. It not only embraces the scientific fields of regional and urban studies but also addresses environmental sustainability-related and regional resilience aspects, such as renewable energy production, sustainable mobility, and the circular economy. This book offers a full toolkit of knowledge on how to effectively implement planning approaches for circular and self-sufficiency development at both urban and regional levels. It begins by presenting a theoretical framework and debate on urban and regional planning approaches that can effectively make cities and regions circular and self-sufficient in certain development domains, such as producing intra-city electric energy, sustainable mobility, and promoting a circular economy. Further, it advances a range of policy development proposals aiming at providing a comprehensive introduction to contemporary thinking about how cities and regions can design innovative planning and governance processes and, where appropriate, build capacity to implement systemic and integrated climate-neutral policies, building on existing place-based territorial capital and experiences developed by local and regional networks. The chapters are written by established authors in their respective domains.

This book will thoroughly prepare students and provide knowledge to academics, researchers, and policymakers in the fields of urban and regional planning/development and studies, environmental sustainability, regional resilience, human geography, economic development, and public/EU/UN policies.

Eduardo Medeiros is a geography professor, an integrated research fellow in Setúbal Polytechnic Institute – RESILIENCE – Centre for Regional Resilience and Sustainability, and an associated research fellow in DINÂMIA'CET-IUL, Instituto Universitário de Lisboa.

Regions and Cities
Series Editor in Chief
Joan Fitzgerald, *Northeastern University, USA*

Editors
Roberta Capello, *Politecnico di Milano, Italy*
Rob Kitchin, *Maynooth University, Ireland*
Jörg Knieling, *HafenCity University Hamburg, Germany*
Nichola Lowe, *University of Minnesota, USA*

In today's globalised, knowledge-driven and networked world, regions and cities have assumed heightened significance as the interconnected nodes of economic, social and cultural production, and as sites of new modes of economic and territorial governance and policy experimentation. This book series brings together incisive and critically engaged international and interdisciplinary research on this resurgence of regions and cities, and should be of interest to geographers, economists, sociologists, political scientists and cultural scholars, as well as to policy-makers involved in regional and urban development.

About the Regional Studies Association (RSA)
The RSA is the global community for regional and urban research, development and policy. As a learned society for regional studies, it provides an authoritative voice for researchers, students and practitioners from disciplines including economics, geography, political science, planning, urban sociology, transport planning and other fields. The RSA delivers its charitable aims through knowledge exchange and policy engagement activities, its portfolio of journals and publications, its programme of conferences and events and its worldwide territorial and research networks. The RSA also runs a grant funding programme and recognises good practice in regional studies through its awards. It is an inclusive, diverse and environmental responsible organisation. For more information go to http://www.regionalstudies.org

There is a **30% discount** available to RSA members on books in the ***Regions and Cities*** series, and other subject-related Taylor and Francis books and e-books including Routledge titles. To order, simply email Luke McNicholas (Luke.McNicholas@tandf.co.uk), or phone on +44 (0)20 701 77545 and declare your RSA membership. You can also visit the series page at www.routledge.com/Regions-and-Cities/book-series/RSA and use the discount code: **RSA225**

155 Questioning Planetary Illiberal Geographies
Territory, Space and Power
Edited by Jason Luger

156 Inequalities, Territorial Politics, Nationalism
Edited by Donatella della Porta, Michael Keating and Mario Pianta

157 Spatial Justice and Cohesion
The Role of Place-Based Action in Community Development
Edited by Matti Fritsch, Petri Kahila, Sarolta Németh and James W. Scott

158 Self-Sufficiency and Sustainable Cities and Regions
Planning for Sustainable, Circular and Carbon-Neutral Development
Edited by Eduardo Medeiros

For more information about this series, please visit: www.routledge.com/Regions-and-Cities/book-series/RSA

Self-Sufficiency and Sustainable Cities and Regions

Planning for Sustainable, Circular and Carbon-Neutral Development

Edited by
Eduardo Medeiros

LONDON AND NEW YORK

Designed cover image: 3000ad

First published 2025
by Routledge
4 Park Square, Milton Park, Abingdon, Oxon OX14 4RN

and by Routledge
605 Third Avenue, New York, NY 10158

Routledge is an imprint of the Taylor & Francis Group, an informa business

© 2025 selection and editorial matter, Eduardo Medeiros; individual chapters, the contributors

The right of Eduardo Medeiros to be identified as the author of the editorial material, and of the authors for their individual chapters, has been asserted in accordance with sections 77 and 78 of the Copyright, Designs and Patents Act 1988.

All rights reserved. No part of this book may be reprinted or reproduced or utilised in any form or by any electronic, mechanical, or other means, now known or hereafter invented, including photocopying and recording, or in any information storage or retrieval system, without permission in writing from the publishers.

Trademark notice: Product or corporate names may be trademarks or registered trademarks, and are used only for identification and explanation without intent to infringe.

British Library Cataloguing-in-Publication Data
A catalogue record for this book is available from the British Library

Library of Congress Cataloging-in-Publication Data
Names: Medeiros, Eduardo (Geography professor), editor.
Title: Self-sufficiency and sustainable cities and regions : planning for sustainable, circular and carbon-neutral development / edited by Eduardo Medeiros.
Description: Abingdon, Oxon ; New York, NY : Routledge, 2025. |
Series: Regions and cities | Includes bibliographical references and index.
Identifiers: LCCN 2024027385 (print) | LCCN 2024027386 (ebook) |
ISBN 9781032807102 (hardback) | ISBN 9781032807119 (paperback) |
ISBN 9781003498216 (ebook)
Subjects: LCSH: Sustainable urban development. | Regional planning—Environmental aspects. | Sustainable development.
Classification: LCC HT241 .S44 2025 (print) | LCC HT241 (ebook) | DDC 307.1/216—dc23/eng/20240820
LC record available at https://lccn.loc.gov/2024027385
LC ebook record available at https://lccn.loc.gov/2024027386

ISBN: 978-1-032-80710-2 (hbk)
ISBN: 978-1-032-80711-9 (pbk)
ISBN: 978-1-003-49821-6 (ebk)

DOI: 10.4324/9781003498216

Typeset in Times New Roman
by codeMantra

Contents

List of figures	*ix*
List of tables	*xi*
Editor	*xiii*
List of contributors	*xv*
Foreword	*xxi*

Introduction   1
EDUARDO MEDEIROS

PART I
Public policies towards urban and regional self-sufficiency   5

1   **Transforming EU Cohesion Policy into a territorial self-sufficiency policy**   7
EDUARDO MEDEIROS

2   **Urban sustainable development via self-sufficiency planning approaches. A theoretical discussion**   23
MARCO ANTONIO SÁNCHEZ TRUJILLO AND
MARÍA ÁNGELES HUETE GARCÍA

3   **Just Transition governance via self-sufficiency regional development**   36
LEFTERIS TOPALOGLOU

PART II
Urban planning for self-sufficient cities   57

4   **Intra-city renewable energy production**   59
KARNA DAHAL

viii *Contents*

**5 Urban stewardship and net zero: The case of the London
    Landed Estates**   77
PATRICIA CANELAS

6 Intra-city clean smart and sustainable mobility   94
NIKOS GAVANAS

PART III
Regional planning for self-sufficient cities   117

**7 Solutions to achieve electricity self-sufficiency in regional
    planning: comparing São Paulo and Ceará's Brazilian States**   119
FLÁVIA MENDES DE ALMEIDA COLLAÇO, JOÃO M. M. PAVANELLI,
MARIAH PIRES CARRAMILLO AND MÔNICA CAVALCANTI SÁ DE ABREU

**8 Promoting local autonomy through the circular economy:
    rethinking regional development**   137
SÉBASTIEN BOURDIN

9 Clean, smart, and sustainable regional mobility   149
ELOÍSA MACEDO AND JORGE M. BANDEIRA

Conclusion   170
EDUARDO MEDEIROS

Index   *175*

Figures

1.1	General levels of regional and urban self-sufficiency	10
3.1	Critical drivers and parameters that enhance renewable energy self-sufficiency and justice. Source: Own Elaboration	49
3.2	Policy recommendations that can enhance renewable energy self-sufficiency and justice. Source: Own Elaboration	50
4.1	Global reduction of energy-related carbon emissions until 2050: Current plans vs. energy transformation	62
6.1	The vicious cycle of congestion	95
6.2	Priorities of sustainable urban mobility and related SDG Targets	97
6.3	Steps of the SUMP process	100
6.4	The trinary system of Curitiba, Brazil	103
6.5	The Superblock concept in Barcelona, Spain	104
7.1	Methodological main steps	120
7.2	Electricity historical generation by source in Ceará State	125
7.3	Ceará's historical self-sufficiency performance	126
7.4	Electricity historical generation by source in São Paulo State	128
7.5	São Paulo's historical self-sufficiency performance	129
7.6	São Paulo and Ceará's historical self-sufficiency performance (2013–2021)	130

Tables

1.1	Main policy priorities of ECP programming periods	14
6.1	List of SDG Targets related to sustainable urban mobility dimensions and priorities	98
6.2	Criteria for the selection of examples	101
6.3	Revisiting the "alternative approach to sustainable mobility"	109
7.1	Ceará supply, demand and self-sufficiency historical performance in GWh	126
7.2	São Paulo Supply, Demand and Self-sufficiency historical performance in GWh	129
8.1	The nine guiding principles of the circular economy and their application at regional and local level	141

Editor

Eduardo Medeiros is a geography professor, an integrated research fellow in Setúbal Polytechnic Institute – RESILIENCE – Centre for Regional Resilience and Sustainability, and an associated research fellow in DINÂMIA'CET-IUL, Instituto Universitário de Lisboa. He has a PhD and post-PhD in Geography – Regional and Urban Planning, and around 200 publications, including more than 60 published papers in international journals, 12 books, and 25 book chapters. His research interests are focused on EU Cohesion Policy, Territorial Impact Assessment, Territorial Cohesion, Territorial Development, Territorial Cooperation, Environmental Sustainability, and Spatial Planning. He is a DG REGIO, URBACT III, and EU b-solutions expert, a member of the scientific advisory panel of ESPON and the European Commission Sounding Board of the Cohesion for Transitions Community of Practice, and a contributor to the Reflection Group on the future of Cohesion Policy. He is also a Regional Studies Association Fellow and a Fulbrighter. He coordinated several international policy evaluation projects and was a member of DG REGIO, ESPON, and FCT projects. He was invited as a project adviser and to write reports and position papers for DG REGIO, the World Bank, and the European Parliament. He was invited to be a keynote speaker by several International Universities and EU institutions (European Commission and Committee of the Regions). He is a member of the scientific and editorial committee of several journals and a peer reviewer of around 50 journals. He was a final jury of the New European Bauhaus Prizes 2022. He is the lead expert in the Main Area of Governance in the Preparatory Action 'New European Bauhaus Knowledge Management Platform' and organiser of four workshops of EURegionsWeekUniversity.

Contributors

Jorge M. Bandeira is an assistant researcher at the Centre for Mechanical Technology and Automation at the University of Aveiro (PhD in Mechanical Engineering). His current research focuses on traffic and emissions modelling, eco-navigation, traffic assignment and network optimisation, and Cooperative Intelligent Transportation Systems Impacts and mobility data. He has authored and co-authored several scientific and technical papers in the field of sustainable mobility. He has been the PI and leader of several consortia, including the European projects. Since 2018, J. Bandeira has also taken on the role of Vice Coordinator of the TEMA mobilising project 'Technologies for Well-Being'. He also serves as an evaluation expert for international funding programmes, including COST action and Horizon 2020. The team he leads in interregional cooperation projects was recently honoured in the 'Territories, Economy and Culture' category of the annual awards given by the University of Aveiro.

Sébastien Bourdin is a professor of Economic Geography at EM Normandie Business School. He is also the chairholder of the European Chair of Excellence 'Circular Economy and Territories'. With a PhD in Geography and an Accreditation to Supervise Research, his expertise lies in Territorial Development, Regional Inequalities, and Energy Transition. He is also a specialist in European issues, including Cohesion Policy and Public Policy Evaluation. In his research, he combines quantitative methods, such as Spatial Econometrics and Modelling, with qualitative methods to offer a comprehensive perspective. Sébastien Bourdin has successfully led numerous research projects on contemporary subjects, including Renewable Energies and the Circular Economy.

Patricia Canelas is Course Director and a lecturer for the Master's in Sustainable Urban Development at the University of Oxford and a fellow of Kellogg College. Prior to her academic roles, Patricia worked as an architect and urban planner and continues to work in policy making and analysis. Her research and teaching seek to advance knowledge on the dynamic relationship between the public, private, and civic sectors involved in the governance of value creation and capture through the built environment. This includes exploring how the different sectors share responsibilities, how and why roles and responsibilities shift, the fundamental values of each sector, their knowledge sources, and the relative power of each side. She has been involved in international research projects in China, the US, Portugal, the Netherlands, Denmark, Scotland, and England.

Mariah Pires Carramillo is a graduate student in Environmental Management at the School of Arts, Sciences and Humanities of the University of São Paulo (EACH – USP). Currently, she works as a sustainability analyst at a company focused on the energy transition. In 2022, she completed undergraduate research into the Brazilian energy sector, focusing on governance, technology, and the environment.

Flávia Mendes de Almeida Collaço is a visiting professor at the Technology Park (PARTEC) and at the Faculty of Economics, Administration, Actuarial Sciences, and Accounting (FEAAC) at the Federal University of Ceará (UFC). Undergraduate in Public Policy (2012) from the School of Arts, Sciences, and Humanities (EACH) at the University of São Paulo (USP), holds a Master's and PhD degrees in Energy from the Graduate Program in Energy at the Institute of Energy and Environment (IEE), also at USP. Flávia´s research focuses on Renewable Energies and Energy Transition, Energy Systems Modelling, Public Policies and Energy Planning, Green Hydrogen Nexus, Water Uses and their Socio-environmental Impacts, Circular Economy, Climate Justice, and Climate Change, as well as Cities and Sustainability.

Karna Dahal is a researcher and EU project manager at Vaasa University of Applied Sciences (VAMK), where he teaches renewable energy. He worked as a postdoctoral researcher at the University of Eastern Finland (UEF) (2021–2023) and Chalmers University of Technology in Sweden (2019–2021) and received his PhD in Energy Transition and Carbon Neutrality from the University of Helsinki (2015–2018). He is the author of 16 scientific papers, including articles and proceedings. He is currently leading an Erasmus⁺ funded project called H2Excellence, which is about fuel cells and green hydrogen. He has worked in multidisciplinary fields. Recently, he worked on the topics of fine particles and small-scale solid fuel combustion technologies at UEF and in the field of alternative fuels and propulsion technologies at Chalmers. He has also developed a kitchen grease filtration (UV/Turbo) system with the application of the UV/TiO_2 technique.

Mônica Cavalcanti Sá de Abreu is Full Professor for Business Management and Logistics at the Federal University of Ceará, Brazil. She holds a PhD in Industrial Engineering from the Federal University of Santa Catarina, Brazil, and was Visiting Researcher at the University of Cambridge, England. Her research interests encompass societal grand challenges, corporate social responsibility, environmental management, circular economy, renewable energy, and climate change policies and strategies. She is an author of several studies and publications in various international journals, including *Business Strategy and the Environment*, the *Journal of Cleaner Production*, the *Journal of Management*, *Environmental Science and Policy*, *Energy Policy*, the *Journal of Business and Industrial Marketing*, and the *International Journal of Human Resource Management*, *Competition and Change*, *Science and Total Environment*, among others.

Nikolaos Gavanas is Assistant Professor of the Department of Planning and Regional Development, School of Engineering, University of Thessaly, where he teaches Transport Planning and Traffic Engineering, and Director of the Research Unit for Infrastructure, Technology Policy and Development, and served as a policy officer at the European Commission's Directorate-General for Research and Innovation (2017–2020) and as member of the Sectoral Scientific Committee (TES) of Environment, Energy and Sustainable Mobility of the National Council for Research, Technology and Innovation (ESETEK) (2020–2022). He is the author of more than 20 articles in peer-reviewed scientific journals, three books, and eight chapters in collective volumes and editor of two collective volumes.

María Ángeles Huete García is a professor in the Department of Sociology at the Pablo de Olavide University in Seville. She has conducted research stays at the University of Chicago (United States), Odense (Denmark), and Essex (England). Her research focuses on the analysis of governance systems in the field of urban policies, participating in competitive research projects at the national and international levels. Her work has been published in journals such as *Local Government Studies* and *European Planning Studies and Regional Studies*. Her research trajectory linked to the analysis of urban public policies focuses on the study of urban development initiatives from the perspective of the EU and Latin America. Currently, she leads a research line on urban and metropolitan development. In this line, she has coordinated various panels on urban regeneration at national and international congresses. She serves as Secretary of the Urban Sociology Committee of the Spanish Federation of Sociology (FES) and Board Member of the Comparative Studies on Local Government and Politics (RC05) of IPSA. She is a collaborating researcher at the Institute of Latin American Studies at the University of Salamanca, of which she is the director of the journal *América Latina Hoy.*

Eloísa Macedo is an assistant researcher at TEMA – Centre for Mechanical Technology and Automation (University of Aveiro) and LASI – Intelligent Systems Associate Laboratory (PhD in Mathematics). E. Macedo's research has been focused on data-driven analysis of traffic-related impacts and solutions for sustainable mobility. She has authored/co-authored books, book chapters, and more than 40 peer-reviewed research contributions to sustainable mobility and

xviii *Contributors*

data-driven analysis fields. E. Macedo has a vast experience in management and coordination and leading tasks in both R&D and interregional cooperation projects. She was also recently recognised as University of Aveiro representative for the PO5 line – 'Mobility as a service' of the CRUSOE Network Working Group on 'Mobility and Intelligent Transport'.

João M. M. Pavanelli is a graduate in Marketing from the University of São Paulo (2012), and has experience in consulting for different companies in different markets (mainly covering strategy, sales, and branding projects). In 2016, he completed the Master's in Sustainability (MSc in sciences) at the University of São Paulo, focusing on the influence of formal and informal institutional aspects on preferences for modes and sources of generation in the Brazilian electricity sector and in 2022 the doctorate (Doctor of Science) focusing on institutional changes in the Brazilian and Nigerian electrical industries. His research interests include institutional changes, energy transitions, collective action, and history of national and regional electrical industries.

Marco Antonio Sánchez Trujillo is a PhD candidate and researcher at the Department of Sociology, Universidad Pablo de Olavide, Sevilla. He is also a member of the UPO-Metropoli research group at the same university. His research focuses on urban sustainability, exploring the environmental, social, and economic aspects of urban development, and how these principles are manifested in specific public policy instruments such as urban agendas. He has made several contributions to this field and has published several papers in journals and editorial platforms such as Springer. Additionally, he has presented his research findings at various international congresses and seminars.

Lefteris Topaloglou is an associate professor at the Chemical Engineering Department of the Polytechnic School of the University of Western Macedonia in the field of 'Energy Transition & Development Transformation Policies'. Since May 2023, he holds the position of the director of the Institute of Energy Development and Transition to the Post-Lignite Era, UCRI TEMENUS of the University of Western Macedonia. At the same time, he is the head of the Laboratory of Energy Transition and Developmental Transformation – ENTRA Lab of the Department of Chemical Engineering. His basic degree is in political science and international studies. He obtained a Master's degree (MSc) in 2001 in the field of regional development and spatial planning. His PhD thesis, which he completed in 2008, is entitled: 'Borders and European Integration: Space, Economy & Politics', focusing on the nature of borders and the dynamics of the border phenomenon. His research interests are currently focused on the just energy transition, spatial justice, approaches based on place-based analysis, and issues related to the governance of the energy transition. His teaching experience began in 2001 and continues uninterrupted until today, both in undergraduate and postgraduate programmes. His research experience is related to a total of

28 research projects, most of which involve European Commission multiannual funding (FP5, FP6, FP7, HORIZON, ESPON) on borders and just transition. In three of these research projects, he is the scientific manager. His scientific work involves co-editing of books, publications in collective volumes, publications in scientific journals, and a significant number of publications in scientific conferences with review and proceedings.

Foreword

The European Union (EU) Policies, and especially EU Cohesion Policy, have played a critical positive role in supporting the transition to climate-neutral and sustainable EU regions and cities over the past decades.

In this stance, the European Green Deal solidified the EU's commitment to transform Europe into a modern, resource-efficient, and competitive economy, via setting out concrete and ambitious goals in EU legislation to mitigate and adapt to climate change, and protect vulnerable groups leaving no one and no region behind and reconciling economic prosperity with a sustainable use of environmental resources.

EU climate policies will bring deep structural changes, and its implementation will entail grand challenges. To be successful in such transformations, all citizens and stakeholders need to be involved. In this context, recently, the European Commission supported the Cohesion for Transitions (C4T) Community of Practice initiative. In short, the C4T Community of Practice is a community-based platform that aims to support EU Member States and regions to make a better use of EU Cohesion Policy to tackle climate change. C4T engages national, regional, and local cohesion and sustainability transitions practitioners in sharing experience and good practices, creating partnerships and jointly identifying solutions. C4T also provides technical assistance to facilitate the development and/or implementation of sustainability transitions and ensure a swift implementation of Cohesion Policy resources to act where most needed in the fight against climate change.

In this context, this book, by presenting the case for self-sufficient urban and regional planning, adds another valuable and relevant contribution to the design and implementation of effective environmentally sustainable projects, programmes, and policies. Equipping regions and cities with additional tools, such as the concept of self-sufficiency, to increase their resilience to climate change impacts and the sustainability of their processes bears utmost importance towards achieving the EU Green Deal and the United Nations 2030 Agenda' goals.

Dr. Luis A. Galiano Bastarrica (University of Seville – Spain)

Introduction

Eduardo Medeiros

The concept of self-sufficiency entails the notions of a sustainable, circular, and carbon-neutral city. This monograph is concerned with explaining how urban and regional planning can lead to greater self-sufficiency. Alongside, this book sheds light on how urban and regional circular and self-sufficiency development can effectively contribute towards sustainable, circular, and carbon-neutral urban and regional development and the ultimate goals of the United Nations (UN) Agenda 2030 and the European Union (EU) Green Deal. It not only embraces the science fields of regional and urban studies but also addresses environmental sustainability-related and regional resilience scientific aspects: renewable energy production, sustainable mobility, and circular economy. These three main book topics are debated as main sources of greenhouse gas emissions and environmentally unsustainable processes globally. In essence, this monograph offers a full toolkit of knowledge on how to effectively implement planning approaches for circular and self-sufficiency development at both urban and regional levels. In particular, it advances a range of policy development proposals aiming at providing a comprehensive introduction to contemporary thinking about how cities and regions can design innovative planning and governance processes and, where appropriate, build capacity to implement systemic and integrated climate-neutral policies towards circular and self-sustainability in critical development policy domains, building on existing place-based territorial capitals and experiences developed by local and regional networks.

This book is divided into three main sections. The first presents a theoretical framework and debate on urban and regional planning approaches that can effectively make cities and regions circular and self-sufficient in certain development domains such as producing intra-city electric energy, sustainable mobility, and promoting a circular economy. This section starts with a chapter written by Eduardo Medeiros, which presents a conceptual proposal of the general levels of regional and urban self-sufficiency. In concrete, he proposed that the first level of self-sufficiency entails the production of food, water, and energy, as the key pillars of the development of any civilisation. Hence, in almost every way, a self-sufficient city or region needs to be self-sufficient in all these three pillars. For that, in the context of a carbon-free economy, significant advances need to be made in the areas of intra-city food (vertical farms) and renewable energy production, as

DOI: 10.4324/9781003498216-1

2 *Eduardo Medeiros*

well as the implementation of clean water recycling systems. The second chapter, written by María Ángeles García, explores the concept of urban self-sufficiency planning as an intrinsic part of sustainability and strategic environmental transition processes. Aiming at providing relevant information on the theoretical foundations of self-sufficiency planning for sustainable urban development, this chapter develops the importance of integrating various dimensions such as energy, water, food, waste management, and transportation to foster resilient and self-reliant urban systems. The last chapter of this section explores the concept of self-sufficiency at the regional level instead. More particularly, it develops the rationale for a just transition governance model via self-sufficiency regional development supported by the principles of environmental sustainability, social justice, and economic resilience.

The second section presents concrete examples of policy implementation of urban self-sufficiency in concrete policy arenas (energy, mobility, and circularity). Here, Chapter 4, written by Karna Dahal, is focused on the analysis of renewable energy production in cities to combat climate change and achieve their carbon-neutral goals. This analysis highlights the need for supporting renewable energy production within public and private buildings whilst highlighting the importance, feasibility, and challenges of renewable energy production in cities to achieve their energy targets and climate goals. Instead, Chapter 5 sheds light on hard governance-related processes (legislation and the development of metrics, guidance, best practices, standards, and certifications) which can mandate the decarbonisation process of the built environment in urban areas. Ultimately, the author (Patrícia Canelas) scrutinises the potential implications of practices preceding policies and the potential for the industry to influence future regulatory frameworks. The last chapter (6) of this section, written by Nikos Gavalas, reflects on emerging urban planning visions of implementing clean, smart, and sustainable mobility systems, as a key pillar to implementing urban self-sufficiency and addressing the current ecological and socio-economic challenges.

Finally, the third section presents a similar analysis of the previous section, but with a focus on the regional scale of self-sufficiency. Chapter 7, written by two Brazilian authors (Flávia Collaço and Mônica Cavalcanti de Abru), introduces the importance of fostering self-sufficiency in renewable energy production at the regional level, in response to current societal needs for a free-carbon economy. Crucially, the authors call for a general implementation for the formulation of coherent and integrated public policies, which are necessary to cope with the effects of climate change and for the promotion of both demand-side and supply-side pathways for self-sufficiency. In a complementary manner, Chapter 8, written by Sébastien Bourdin, develops a regional planning conceptual framework embracing the importance of moving from linear to circular economic models in which resources are reused, recycled, and reallocated, reinforcing the sustainability policies of cities and regions. The main goal is to highlight the economic, social, and environmental benefits of implementing circular economy policies at the regional level and to demonstrate how to contribute to regional self-sufficiency processes. The last chapter of this book (8) is written by Eloísa Macedo and Jorge M. Bandeira. These authors present a case for fostering clean, smart, and sustainable regional mobility, by describing relevant domains and initiatives that can bring insights for supporting policy development and driving policy change for a more clean, smart, and sustainable regional mobility.

In essence, this monograph addresses the crucial role of urban and regional planning for circular and self-sustainability in three policy areas: energy, mobility, and circularity. Hence, its main themes are centred on analysing urban and regional development, as well as planning processes and policies, and the potential benefits of a circular and self-sustainability policy approach towards sustainable, circular, and carbon-neutral urban and regional development. In short, the textbook has the following main objectives:

- Provide academics, students, and policymakers a thorough understanding of the potential positive benefits of transitioning into urban and regional planning for circular and self-sustainability vis-à-vis mainstream urban and regional planning approaches.
- Introduce academics, students, and policymakers, theoretical thinking, and a range of policy strategies essential to implementing effective urban and regional circular and self-sufficiency planning approaches.
- Highlight the potential role of the cities and regions to effectively achieve the EU Agenda 2030 main goals via self-sufficiency planning approaches, by supporting sustainable, circular, and carbon-neutral urban and regional development.
- Offer a roadmap for urban and regional planning theories and strategic policy guidelines, by providing evidence-based narratives of how cities and regions can effectively implement circular and self-sufficiency planning strategies in the domains of intra-city energy, sustainable and smart mobility, and circular economy.
- Fill a gap in existing literature on the concept of urban and regional self-sufficiency and how cities and regions have and can contribute towards empowering effective sustainability innovation and become generators of sustainability policy and practice.
- Provide a wealth of updated analysis on ongoing projects exploring the use of intra-city renewable energy, smart and sustainable mobility, and circular economy-related processes in cities and regions.
- Set the agenda for future work on planning for urban and regional circularity and self-sufficiency development.

Considering these goals, this monograph fills up a gap in the available literature on urban and regional planning and environmental sustainability development studies, by focusing on the specific role of circular and self-sufficiency policy approaches on three main policy domains: energy, mobility, and circularity. Indeed, since the publication of the Brundtland Report, an increasing global concern has united countries to pursue a sustainable development path on their political agenda, due to an increasing realisation of the persistent deterioration of the human environment and natural resources. This was meant as a development process to meet the needs of the present, without compromising the ability of future generations to meet their own needs. However, despite some positive developments in promoting environmentally friendly policy development measures (i.e., increasing the use of renewable energy sources), many parts of the world still face tremendous challenges in solving the continuous deterioration of natural resources. Curiously, and despite increasing global urbanisation trends and the realisation that urban areas are largely responsible for the ongoing ecological and climate crisis, long-term existing pro-environmental sustainability political rhetoric continues not to be matched by action on the ground, which corresponds to the scale and urgency of the task at hand. Indeed, much of the global, European, and national environmental policy development strategies seem to continue an incremental ecological modernisation technocracy of the past, which has failed to deliver far-reaching, rapid, effective, and unprecedented systemic changes in all aspects of society required to avert the worst consequences of global climate warming, many of which are now irreversible.

Critically, cities are major consumers of resources and producers of waste. As such, urban resources must be better managed to lessen cities' and regions' global ecological impact and to transform cities in resource efficient, ecologically regenerative, and adaptive engines. In this context, this book provides the reader with a quite complete set of theoretical and practical knowledge on how cities and regions can accelerate a needed transformation into an effective sustainable development process by following a circular and self-sufficient planning approach, in key policy domains such as energy, food, and mobility. From a policymaking perspective, the collected evidence can serve as a pool of best practices that could be replicated elsewhere. Critically, this book introduces a novel concept (urban and regional self-sufficiency) which is intended to be gradually adopted by future local, regional, national, and transnational territorial development strategies to effectively implement the United Nations Agenda 2030. This is the ultimate goal of this book, to serve as an effective vehicle to instil academics, policymakers, and practitioners to the need to focus on concrete urban and regional self-sufficiency as a concrete and viable solution towards an effective sustainable development path.

Part I

Public policies towards urban and regional self-sufficiency

1 Transforming EU Cohesion Policy into a territorial self-sufficiency policy

Eduardo Medeiros

1.1　Introduction

In 1987, the Brundtland Report (Brundtland, 1987) placed the goal of uniting countries to pursue a sustainable development path on the political agenda, due to an increasing realisation of the persistent deterioration of the human environment and natural resources. This was meant as a development process to meet the needs of the present, without compromising the ability of future generations to meet their own needs. However, despite some positive developments in promoting environmentally friendly policy development measures (i.e., increasing the use of renewable energy sources – Atkinson, 2007), many parts of the world still face tremendous challenges in solving the continuous deterioration of natural resources. Curiously, and despite increasing global urbanisation trends and the realisation that urban areas are largely responsible for the ongoing ecological and climate crisis (UN, 2022), long-term existing pro-environmental sustainability political rhetoric continues not to be matched by action on the ground, which corresponds to the scale and urgency of the task at hand. Indeed, much of the global, European, and national environmental policy development strategies seem to continue an incremental ecological modernisation technocracy of the past, which has failed to deliver far-reaching, rapid, effective, and unprecedented systemic changes in all aspects of society required to avert the worst consequences of global climate warming, many of which are now irreversible (Daly, 2023). Critically, cities are major consumers of resources and producers of waste. As such, urban resources must be better managed to lessen cities' global ecological impact and to transform cities in resource-efficient, ecologically regenerative, and adaptive engines (Williams, 2023).

In this context, urban and regional planning for self-sufficiency provides a vision and a policy framework for environmentally transformative, circular, and sustainable development (May & Marvin, 2017). Curiously, there is not much literature specifically dedicated to proposing concrete solutions to implementing self-sufficient cities and regions. Here, the work of Guallart (2010) is an exception, even though it is mostly centred in analysing the potential benefits of networks of self-sustainable cities for the future of mankind, and not so much analysing, with a practical urban planning lens, the implementation of such a vision for an individual

DOI: 10.4324/9781003498216-3

city, but more on how such cities can define conditions in the urban environment that will allow the urban areas of the 21st century to be inhabited in networked self-sufficiency. As such, much of the state-of-the-art related to the rationale of planning for a self-sufficient city and region is associated with the concept of sustainable cities and regions. Here, for instance, Orttung (2019) suggests that a sustainable city should meet the needs of current residents without compromising the capacity of future generations to live at a similar or better level, by solving critical sustainability challenges and by stimulating the process of development sustainability solutions.

By acting as generators of sustainability policy and practice, sustainable cities should address climate change challenges by, for instance, repurposing urban spaces towards deeper civic needs and truly resilient communities (Fields & Renne, 2021), via policy measures that can effectively solve issues of pollution and quality of urban life (Hodson & Marvin, 2017). In almost every way, the rationale for implementing a sustainable city plan would gain from supporting smart city planning, which can be seen as one useful approach to an evolutionary transformation in urban infrastructure and management, by focusing on optimising coordination and planning through information technology systems and real-time data (Young & Lieberknecht, 2019). This smart-cities rationale can be linked to a circular urban development approach (Williams, 2023) to increase urban planning effectiveness in implementing self-sufficient cities in several policy areas, to produce more resource-efficient, ecologically regenerative, and resilient cities.

The United Nations (UN) 2030 Agenda's (UN, 2016) ambitious and transformational vision for the world embraces measures specifically focused on cities. Amongst these are the recognition of the need for sustainable urban development and planning to minimise the impact of cities on the global climate system. More importantly, however, this Agenda defines one main goal dedicated to cities (11): "make cities and human settlements inclusive, safe, resilient and sustainable". This goal encompasses several policy domains such as housing, transport, road safety, integrated and sustainable planning, cultural and natural heritage, risks, waste management, green spaces, and social inclusion, among others. However, there are no specific mentions of the potential advantages of 'Planning for Self-Sufficient Cities' as a potential integrated policy avenue for implementing the UN Agenda 2030 goals more effectively, by recognising cities as core intervention areas to accelerate an intended green transformative transitional development path.

Likewise, a UN World Cities Report (UN, 2020a), while revealing that urban areas are, by now, home to 55% of the world's population (68% expected by 2050), does not shed light on the potential benefits of promoting urban planning processes towards implementing self-sufficient cities, as a more effective policy measure to tackle climate and environmental-related challenges faced by humankind. Crucially, the latest UN World Cities Report (UN, 2022) asserts that the vision of sustainable and equitable urban futures will not be guaranteed unless cities and subnational governments take bold and decisive actions to address both chronic and emerging urban challenges. Hence, within a global rise of urbanisation trends, coupled with increasing global environmental sustainability and urban liveability concerns, this chapter discusses the potential advantages for public policies and specifically European Union (EU) Cohesion Policy (ECP) to be more effective in achieving the UN 2030 Agenda via the 'Planning for Self-Sufficient cities and regions policy rationale' in four main critical human survival domains: access to basic nourishment, clean water, clean energy, and green mobility (public transports).

A particular focus of the self-sufficiency policy approach in this chapter will be placed on the urban domain since cities are more and more seen as the engines of development. Here, even though the notion of a 'Self-Sufficient City' is not necessarily new, it has been mostly approached from an architectural and urban networking prism (Guallart, 2010) and has not yet gained currency within ongoing EU, national, regional, and urban development/planning strategies. For instance, the EU Green Deal aims at placing "sustainability and the well-being of citizens at the centre of economic policy, and the sustainable development goals at the heart of the EU's policymaking and action" (EC, 2019: 3). It does not propose, however, an effective integrated approach for dealing with some of its main policy goals, such as supplying clean affordable and secure energy and a healthy and environmentally friendly food system, as well as accelerating the shift towards sustainable and smart mobility. Instead, the rationale for implementing the concept of a 'Self-Sufficient City Plan' embraces a rationale for a more effective and integrated approach for using public funding to face the potential future failure of critical resources, environmental shocks, and consequent social unrest.

Mostly supported by desk-based research of policy documents as well as recent scientific literature on primary analytical domains of the concept of urban and regional self-sufficiency (energy, water, food, and mobility), the next topic discusses the most relevant components of this novel policy concept. The following topic provides a summarised view of the implementation of strategic visions of ECP over the past decades to better understand how it has contributed to promoting sustainable urban and regional development. The last topic before the conclusion presents a series of policy recommendations for transforming ECP into a key policy vehicle to support the implementation of the policy rationale of self-sufficient cities and regions in future programming periods.

1.2   The concept of urban and regional self-sufficiency

What is a self-sufficient city or region? In simple terms, it is a city or region that is fully independent of the outside world in providing the most basic needs for the survival of its dwellers. Since these needs are vast and complex, the chapter is primarily focused on four critical human needs: constant access to basic nourishment, clean energy, clean water, and sustainable mobility. This concept can then be applied to larger cities or regions and be tailor-made to its urban/regional development/planning specificities. Indeed, with increasing technological innovations, cities and regions can soon become self-sufficient in energy (via implementing renewable energy production solutions) and food production (via implementing vertical farming food production-based solutions), as well as have the capacity to fully recycle drinking water and to implementing a sustainable and smart mobility system (public transports).

It goes without saying that, in current times, a fully self-sufficient city or region is still a far cry from reality. Crucially, in an ideal scenario, urban and regional self-sufficiency would require complete independence from other territories to fulfil not only basic or 'level 1' survival needs (access to potable water, nourishment, and energy) for their inhabitants but also the remaining modern standard of living-related needs (Figure 1.1). Given the policy implementation complexity and challenges involved in making all urban areas and regions fully independent in all levels of self-sufficiency, it is recommended that this proposed policy transition process follows several distinct stages. The first stage of self-sufficiency embraces three basic human survival needs (access to basic nourishment, potable water, and energy) and sustainable mobility. Understandably, all the main components of self-sufficiency presented in Figure 1.1 are largely interdependent. Water, energy, and inter-city/regional food production require the construction of infrastructure which, instead, requires processed raw materials from mining, quarrying, and forestry, sometimes not available in certain regions.

Again, in this self-sufficiency complex policy implementation context, it is proposed that the first policy stage to implement public policies towards self-sustainability should focus on supporting the following policy domains:

A *Self-sufficiency to access potable water:* Fresh and clean water is a vital element for human direct and indirect survival (Tortajada & Ong, 2016). On average, human beings use around 40 litres of freshwater a day for drinking, cleaning, and cooking. It is also estimated that urban areas use around 11% of global freshwater withdrawals (NG, 2022). Hence, a self-sufficient city, or region, needs to be fully independent in accessing the needed amounts of fresh and clean water, not only to fulfil their inhabitant's needs but also to support local

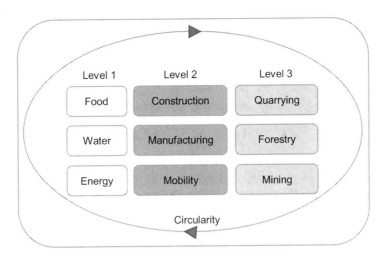

Figure 1.1 General levels of regional and urban self-sufficiency.

Source: Own elaboration.

and regional economic activities. This implies that in territories that do not receive the necessary amount of fresh and clean water, water cleaning/recycling facilities/systems and reservoirs are built (Wester & Broad, 2021).

B *Self-sufficiency to access basic food supplies:* In a world facing systematic food insecurity (NG, 2022), the challenge for urban/regional food self-sufficiency in basic nourishment needs inevitably requires intra-city/regional food production systems via, for instance, "controlled environment agriculture (CEA), also referred to as vertical or indoor soil-less farming" which "encompasses numerous technologies, including hydroponics, aeroponics, and aquaponics. Vertical farming requires only a small plot of land and can be carried out indoors, allowing for the cultivation of food in urban and industrial spaces, and leading to shorter supply chains" (FAO et al., 2023: 128). Since humans rely mostly (80%) on plant sources for food energy (calories), vertical farming at large scale is a potential solution for basic human nourishment (Beacham et al., 2019), coupled with producing plant-based meat alternatives (Tyndall et al., 2022) as well as integrated vertical farming with aquaculture (Hasimuna et al., 2023). At the regional level, future food production systems will rely both on vertical farming and controlled-environment agriculture (Benke & Tomkins, 2017).

C *Self-sufficiency to access renewable energy:* Human activities run on energy. But while the world has, over past decades, weaned itself off fossil fuels, the total renewable energy power capacity has grown substantially in past years, following national policies supporting this clean-energy capacity, mostly in developed countries (NG, 2022). Crucially, a self-sufficient city or region needs to be fully independent in producing its full energy needs, mostly in the form of electricity, via renewable sources of energy. By now, this is possible in the context of an urban area (Hess & Gentry, 2019; Medeiros, 2020a). Recent data shows that "renewable energy is largely made up of wind and solar power and bioenergy, and also includes geothermal power. Renewables expand rapidly over the outlook, offsetting the declining role of fossil fuels. The share of renewables in global primary energy increases from around 10% in 2019 to between 35–65% by 2050, driven by the improved cost competitiveness of renewables, together with the increasing prevalence of policies encouraging a shift to low-carbon energy" (BP, 2023: 19).

D *Self-sufficiency to foster smart and clean mobility:* Despite not being one of the three basic pillars of policy self-sufficiency, clean mobility can easily be aligned with them, in particular to implementing intra-city self-sufficiency mobility, as this can be seen as a key policy domain of urban sustainable development (EC, 2020). The use of non-motorised transport systems as a goal towards more sustainable transport services and green, pedestrian-friendly urban areas (UN, 2020b) can be regarded as a major milestone in achieving urban self-sustainability in the energy sector (Freeman & Quigg, 2009). Besides favouring energy-green transition processes, sustainable urban mobility planning contributes to addressing urban inhabitants' requirements in dealing with air pollution, accessibility, congestion, and safety by increasing the share of sustainable (mostly public) transport modes and active mobility (Hartl et al., 2023).

12 *Eduardo Medeiros*

Indeed, environmental sustainability is a critical dimension of both territorial development and territorial cohesion processes (Medeiros, 2016, 2019, 2022), at all territorial levels. In all aspects, urban areas are engines of territorial development and catalysts for innovation and creativity. However, successful urban development strategies can only be achieved through an integrated approach (Urban Agenda, 2016). Hence, the sound implementation of self-sufficient city planning offers a fresh and ground-breaking perspective on urban sustainable development, as it embraces critical policy areas to make cities completely independent from the outside world in delivering basic survival needs for their inhabitants. As seen, these include basic nourishment, energy, and water, coupled with intra-mobility (public transport) needs. Concerning the production of electric energy in cities, a wealth of literature confirms their potential for self-sufficiency via, for instance, increasing the production and use of solar energy (Medeiros, 2020). As the EU Green Deal (EC, 2019) concludes, the power sector must be based largely on renewable sources, and the clean-energy transition should involve and benefit consumers, supported by a rapid decrease in the cost of renewables. The policy goal towards a transition to global climate neutrality would also benefit from the production of food in urban vertical farms to reduce the carbon-footprint, environmental pollution, and degradation (Carolan, 2022). Incentives promoting investments such as green infrastructure into cities should also contemplate constant access to fresh water in cities which can be systematically recycled following the rationale of a circular, climate-neutral, and sustainable economy (Mouritse, 2019). This needed clean-energy transition also requires a better understanding of cross-cutting urban and regional planning issues such as intra-urban mobility through clean solutions across all public transport modes (Cohen-Blankshtain & Rotem-Mindali, 2016).

1.3 EU Cohesion Policy past and present mainstream strategic development visions

ECP was formally initiated in 1989 with the underlying policy rationale to correct regional development asymmetries (the territorial cohesion rationale – see Medeiros, 2016) in the presently known EU. Since then, the EU has expanded its territory dramatically, not only to already highly developed Nordic countries (Sweden and Finland) but mostly to Eastern Europe, marked by below-EU socio-economic development average indicators (EC, 2001). Moreover, since 1986, when the 'Single European Act' was introduced, and dramatically influenced the first ECP phase (1989–1939), many other EU strategic development visions affected the strategic design of subsequent ECP programming periods. For instance, the 'Agenda 2000' (Hall & Rosenstock, 1998) influenced the 2000–2006 programming period of ECP, and the 'EU Growth and Jobs Agenda' of 2005 affected the design of the 2007–2013 ECP programming period (EC, 2014). Similarly, the 2014–2020 ECP programming period was influenced by the 'EU Europe 2020 Agenda' (Budd, 2013), whereas the current ECP programming period (2021–2027) was supported by an integrated strategic development vision covered in several EU strategic documents and visions: (i) The European Green Deal; (ii) A Europe fit for the digital age; (iii) An economy that works for people; (iv) A stronger Europe in the world; (v) Promoting our European way of life; and (vi) A new push for European democracy.

Table 1.1 summarises the changes in the main policy priorities over all the six ECP phases in which it is possible to verify the widespread financial support to all the main territorial development domains, which include economic competitiveness, social cohesion, environmental sustainability, territorial governance/cooperation, and spatial planning (see Medeiros, 2019). As expected, environmental sustainability and research and innovation-related issues have gained increasing attention from more recent ECP programming phases from a policy strategic standpoint. However, systematic financial crises have shifted ECP funding towards socioeconomic development goals which were initially destined to fund other policy goals, and in particular from environmental sustainability-related goals. Moreover, several studies have demonstrated how ECP funding for supporting environmentally sustainable related projects is still largely ineffective (see Medeiros et al., 2022; Medeiros & Valente, 2023).

As seen, ECP has been acting as a key EU financial instrument to promote development and cohesion processes over the past 35 years (EC, 2022). However, as a recent analysis has demonstrated, there is not a clear correlation between ECP investment and territorial cohesion trends at the national level in the EU. Instead, capital cities in each EU Member State continue to present above-average national socioeconomic trends when compared with the remaining surrounding regions (Medeiros et al., 2023). Hence, there is a case to question the effectiveness of ECP mainstream policy rationale in investing in a wealth of policy development themes, even though less socioeconomic developed regions have received the bulk of ECP funding over the past decades (EC, 2017). Taking a concrete case, Portugal has received ECP funding support since 1989 and still has four out of its seven regions (NUTS 2) in the group of less EU socioeconomic developed regions (Medeiros et al., 2023).

Understandably, ECP funding is limited given the EU socioeconomic lagging regions' development needs. The question is if ECP can be more effective by following a completely different policy implementation rationale? We think so. It is, however, undeniable that ECP provided concrete and tangible support to all EU regions in improving regional accessibility, human capital, economic activities, research and innovation, environmental sustainability, employment, integrated approaches to development, territorial cooperation, good governance, information and communication technologies, tourism, cultural activities, institutional capacity, a green and digital transition (EC, 1996, 2001, 2004, 2007, 2010, 2014, 2017, 2022). In the domain of environmental sustainability, for instance, ECP has financially supported projects aiming: (i) increasing energy efficiency; (ii) boosting renewable sources of energy; (iii) reducing greenhouse gas emissions; (iv) achieving low-carbon-transport mobility; (v) reducing the impact of climate change in flooding, coastal erosion, etc.; (vi) improving the environment via improved water quality, reduced waste production, and improved air quality (EC, 2022). In more

14   *Eduardo Medeiros*

Table 1.1 Main policy priorities of ECP programming periods

Programming period	Main development vision(s)	Specific/thematic priorities
1989–1993	– Territorial cohesion – Economic competitiveness – Social cohesion – Rural development – Territorial connectivity – Territorial cooperation	– Promoting the development and structural adjustment of regions whose development is lagging behind; – Converting regions seriously affected by an industrial decline; – Combating long-term unemployment; – Facilitating the occupational integration of young people; – (a) Speeding up the adjustment of agricultural structures and (b) Promoting the development of rural areas.
1994–1999	– Territorial cohesion – Economic competitiveness – Social cohesion – Rural development – Territorial connectivity – Territorial cooperation	– Promoting the development and structural adjustment of regions whose development is lagging behind; – Converting regions or parts of regions seriously affected by an industrial decline; – Combating long-term unemployment and facilitating the integration into the working life of young people and of persons exposed to exclusion from the labour market, promotion of equal employment opportunities for men and women; – Facilitating adaptation of workers to industrial changes and to changes in production systems; – Promoting rural development by (a) speeding up the adjustment of agricultural structures in the framework of the reform of common agricultural policy and promoting the modernisation and structural adjustment of the fisheries sector, (b) facilitating the development and structural adjustment of rural areas; and – Development and structural adjustment of regions with an extremely low population density (as of 1 January 1995).
2000–2006	– Territorial cohesion – Economic competitiveness – Social cohesion – Territorial connectivity – Territorial cooperation – Research & innovation	– Promoting the development and structural adjustment of regions whose development is lagging behind; – Supporting the economic and social conversion of areas facing structural difficulties, hereinafter; and – Supporting the adaptation and modernisation of policies and systems of education, training, and employment.

(*Continued*)

Transforming EU Cohesion Policy   15

Table 1.1 (Continued)

Programming period	Main development vision(s)	Specific/thematic priorities
2007–2013	– Territorial cohesion – Economic competitiveness – Social cohesion – Territorial cooperation – Territorial connectivity – Research & innovation	– Convergence: aims at speeding up the convergence of the least-developed Member States and regions defined by GDP per capital of less than 75% of the EU average; – Regional competitiveness and employment: covers all other EU regions to strengthen the regions' competitiveness and attractiveness as well as employment; and – European Territorial Cooperation: based on the Interreg initiative, support is available for cross-border, transnational, and interregional cooperation as well as for networks.
2014–2020	– Territorial cohesion – Economic competitiveness – Research & innovation – Environmental sustainability – Social cohesion – Administrative capacity – Territorial cooperation – Territorial connectivity – Integrated development	– Strengthening research, technological development, and innovation – Enhancing access to, and use and quality of, information and communication technologies – Enhancing the competitiveness of SMEs – Supporting the shift towards a low-carbon economy – Promoting climate change adaptation, risk prevention, and management – Preserving and protecting the environment and promoting resource efficiency – Promoting sustainable transport and improving network infrastructures – Promoting sustainable and quality employment and supporting labour mobility – Promoting social inclusion, combating poverty and any discrimination – Investing in education, training, and lifelong learning – Enhancing the capability of public authorities and efficient public administration. – European Territorial Cooperation
2021–2027	– Territorial cohesion – Economic competitiveness – Territorial connectivity – Research & innovation – Environmental sustainability – Social cohesion – Administrative capacity – Integrated development	– A more competitive and smarter Europe – A greener, low carbon transitioning towards a net zero carbon economy – A more connected Europe by enhancing mobility – A more social and inclusive Europe – Europe closer to citizens by fostering the sustainable and integrated development of all types of territories – European Territorial Cooperation

Source: Own elaboration based on several sources.

16   *Eduardo Medeiros*

detail, for the 2013–2020 ECP phase, €68 billion were devoted to 'greener Europe' policy goals,

> targeting: increases in energy efficiency and renewable energy; improvements in environmental infrastructure; the development of the circular economy; mitigation of, and adaptation to, climate change; risk prevention; biodiversity; and clean urban transport. The funding represents 19% of the total available under cohesion policy for the period.
>
> (EC, 2022: 278)

In past years, we have presented in articles, events, and reports several potential avenues to improving the effectiveness of ECP, either in its general implementation or in specific ECP policy themes like European Territorial Cooperation (see Medeiros, 2023). In essence, we have proposed that future ECP phases should maintain what has worked well so far, but that it should become more simplified as possible in its implementation process. Moreover, territorial cooperation should see its funding largely increased where transnational cooperation should have a major role in promoting EU territorial cohesion processes (Medeiros, 2017). In addition, for increasing territorial cohesion, the policy rationale for implemented territorial cohesion cities should be followed (Medeiros & Rauhut, 2020), and territorial impact assessment methodologies should be used from the ex-ante to the ex-post policy evaluation phases to assess the main impacts of ECP (Medeiros. 2020b). Finally, ECP overall budget should be significantly improved as well as the project selection process which should benefit the general interest and not private interests. However, this chapter advances a less-mainstream policy transition avenue to implementing future ECP programming phases supported by the 'Self-Sufficient Cities and Regions', not only at the national but also at cross-border and transnational EU territorial levels.

1.4   Projecting a future of EU Cohesion Policy supporting a Territorial Self-Sufficiency Policy

By 2023, the European Commission established a group of high-level specialists on the future of ECP, to maximise its effectiveness in tackling the multiple challenges identified in the eighth Cohesion Report. Due to the widespread policy focus of ECP, nine meetings were organised to discuss mainstream strategic development processes that have already been around ECP meanders for several decades: (i) developing the European growth model; (ii) enhancing resilience regions; (iii) supporting specific development needs; (iv) developing place-based policies; (v) discussing the development trap in Europe; (vi) complementing EU policy instruments; (vii) reassessing conditionality principles; (viii) revising the delivery mode mechanisms; and (ix) enhancing the policy capacity to respond to sudden shocks and crisis. Although all these discussions are relevant for improving ECP implementation process in the future, in our view, they do not present a novel paradigm to effectively achieve ECP main policy goal: territorial cohesion at the EU and national levels.

The paramount question is: can territorial cohesion be achieved and, if so, how? From a theoretical standpoint, territorial cohesion can be achieved at all territorial levels (Medeiros, 2016). In practice, this policy goal is extremely difficult to attain in the EU, especially at the national level (Medeiros et al., 2023). A concrete theoretical avenue to effectively achieving territorial cohesion trends at the national level is the already mentioned 'Territorial Cohesion Cities' policy rationale, supported by the idea that medium cities are the drivers of the development of socioeconomically less developed regions, and thus ECP investment should primarily invest in such cities to invert systematic territorial exclusion processes at the national level (Medeiros & Rauhut, 2020). In this section, however, we propose a complementary policy approach in which ECP should also allocate the bulk of its investment to urban areas located in socioeconomically less developed EU regions, but with an underlying self-sufficiency policy rationale. In practice, a self-sufficiency ECP policy rationale would be developed based on the following main strategic guidance principles:

- ECP main policy goal should continue to be the attainment of European Territorial Cohesion. Hence, the bulk of ECP investment should be concentrated in medium towns located in socioeconomically less developed EU regions.
- ECP main policy goal should focus on supporting place-based and integrated investments facilitating urban and regional self-sufficiency policy approaches in the first level of self-sufficiency development (water, food, and energy), as well as in green mobility. Alongside, the goal of European Territorial Cooperation should be supported but with cross-border and transnational planning (Medeiros et al., 2023b) focus on urban and self-sufficiency as well.
- In the domain of food self-sufficiency, ECP should focus on supporting investment in large-scale vertical farms (Martin et al., 2023) across the EU, mainly located in urban areas. ECP support to vertical farming should also be coupled with intra-city/regional aquaculture systems (Popp et al., 2018) and develop low-cost alternative plant protein (Chardigny & Walrand, 2016) as a more sustainable and healthy replacement for animal food production. All these ECP investments in self-sufficiency food production need to be powered by renewable sources of energy. This policy goal contributes to attaining the environmentally sustainable EU Greed Deal policy goals.
- In the domain of water self-sufficiency, ECP should focus on supporting investment in water cleaning, recycling, and desalination facilities (Silva, 2023) when appropriate via a place-based approach and fuelled by renewable sources of energy. The ultimate goal is to make urban areas and regions self-sufficient in accessing potable water sources at any given time, no matter the weather conditions, not only for people but also for economic activities (Kehoe, 2023).
- In the domain of energy self-sufficiency, ECP should focus on supporting investment in renewable sources of energy such as solar and wind, with a place-based approach (in some territories tidal, geothermal, hydroelectric, biomass, etc. – might make more sense to be explored) (Nitsch, 2018). ECP investment in renewable energy production should be concentrated in urban areas to explore

18 *Eduardo Medeiros*

existing infrastructure to place, for instance, solar panels (Medeiros, 2020; Ulpiani et al., 2023).

- In the domain of mobility self-sufficiency, ECP should only finance sustainable, smart, and affordable mobility-related infrastructure (Mantero, 2023) fuelled by renewable sources of energy. This includes support for the production and use of electric/hydrogen-powered vehicles for private and public mobility, as well as a green and smart high-speed railway network that can effectively replace many current regional flights and thus contribute to achieving EU Green Deal goals (Xiaolin & Kai, 2022).

1.5   Conclusion

Transforming our world to advance territorial development while easing planetary pressures via a low-carbon economic development path has been slow to catch on in practical terms, despite systematic global policy strategies supporting this policy avenue. In the EU, ECP has been the most financed policy for many years and has been used to support all territorial development dimensions, including environmental sustainability processes, with more or less efficacy, depending on the territory. Given the vital importance of ECP to promoting territorial development processes in the EU, this chapter proposes an alternative strategic approach to implement this policy, not only to achieve its main policy goal (territorial cohesion at all territorial levels) but also to increase its efficacy and efficiency in attaining the EU Green Deal goals to transform the EU into a modern, resource-efficient, and competitive economy. We call this proposed strategic vision 'Planning for Self-Sufficient Cities and Regions', which is further developed in all the remaining chapters of this book.

From a conceptual standpoint, a self-sufficient city or region is required to be fully independent from the outside world in providing the most basic needs for the survival of its dwellers. According to the proposed levels of urban and regional self-sufficiency in this chapter, the first or primary level of self-sufficiency considers three main policy areas: basic nourishment, access to clean water, and clean and renewable sources of energy. Hence, the proposed policy rationale supporting the implementation of future programming phases of ECP should consider the allocation of the bulk of available investment to foster the self-sufficiency of EU urban areas and regions in these three policy areas via the support of food production via vertical farming, the support to the production of renewable sources of energy, and the support to water cleaning infrastructure allowing constant access to clean water no matter the climate variations. A special emphasis should be given to the investment in these three policy areas in urban areas and in particular in the ones located in less-developed EU regions following the Territorial Cohesion Cities policy rationale.

Besides the concentration of the ECP funding in the domains of controlled environment agriculture, clean and renewable energy production, and clean water recycling, this policy should also include a fourth policy domain in its list of priority investments: sustainable mobility. Again, significant investment in green mobility is required to transform the current EU economy largely supported by fossil fuels into a green economy fuelled by renewable sources of energy, mostly produced within urban areas (i.e., solar). For this strategy to work, ECP also needs to robust its financial capacity as the challenges ahead to transform the EU into a no net emissions of greenhouse gases territory, and a space supported by socioeconomic development processes decoupled from resource use by 2050, is a major policy challenge. In our view, this proposed ECP strategic design following the planning for urban and regional self-sufficiency policy rationale would contribute to accelerating the needed green economy transformation envisioned by the EU Green Deal. Moreover, the implementation of this proposed policy rationale has the potential to contribute towards a more cohesive EU territory at all territorial levels, which has been one of the main failures of ECP.

References

Atkinson, A. (2007) Cities after oil: 'Sustainable development' and energy futures, *City*, 11(2): 201–213, https://doi.org/10.1080/13604810701422896

Beacham, A. Vickers, L. & Monaghan, J. (2019) Vertical farming: A summary of approaches to growing skywards, *The Journal of Horticultural Science and Biotechnology*, 94(3): 277–283, https://doi.org/10.1080/14620316.2019.1574214

Benke, K. & Tomkins, B. (2017) Future food-production systems: Vertical farming and controlled-environment agriculture, *Sustainability: Science, Practice and Policy*, 13(1): 13–26, https://doi.org/10.1080/15487733.2017.1394054

BP. (2023) *Energy Outlook 2023*, British Petroleum, London.

Brundtland, G. H. (1987) *Our Common Future: Report of the World Commission on Environment and Development*. United Nations, Geneva.

Budd, L. (2013) EUROPE 2020: A strategy in search of a regional policy rationale?, *Policy Studies*, 34(3): 274–290.

Carolan, M. (2022) It's about time: Temporal and spatial fixes find vertical farms and local food in the shadow of COVID-19, *The Journal of Peasant Studies*, 49(7): 1446–1465.

Chardigny, J. & Walrand, S. (2016) Plant protein for food: Opportunities and bottlenecks. *Oilseeds and Fats, Crops and Lipids*, 23(4): 6, https://doi.org/10.1051/ocl/2016019

Cohen-Blankshtain, G. & Rotem-Mindali, O. (2016) Key research themes on ICT and sustainable urban mobility, *International Journal of Sustainable Transportation*, 10(1): 9–17.

Daly, G. (2023) EU Cohesion in an Age of Environmental Breakdown: Rethinking the Territorial Agenda, in Medeiros E. (ed.) *Public Policies and Territorial Cohesion*. Springer, Cham, pp. 85–103.

EC. (1996) First Report on Economic and Social Cohesion, European Commission, Brussels.

EC. (2001) Second Report on Economic and Social Cohesion, European Commission, Brussels.

EC. (2004) Third Report on Economic and Social Cohesion, European Commission, Brussels.

EC. (2007) Fourth Report on Economic and Social Cohesion, European Commission, Brussels.

EC. (2010). Fifth Report on Economic, Social and Territorial Cohesion, European Commission, Brussels.

EC. (2014) Sixth Report on Economic, Social and Territorial Cohesion, European Commission, Brussels.

EC. (2017) Seventh Report on Economic, Social and Territorial Cohesion. My Region, My Europe, Our Future, European Commission, Brussels.

EC. (2019) The European Green Deal, European Commission, Brussels.

EC. (2020) Handbook of Sustainable Urban Development Strategies, Joint Research Centre (JRC), the European Commission's Science and Knowledge Service, Seville.

EC. (2022) Eight Report on Economic, Social and Territorial Cohesion. *Cohesion in Europe Towards 2050*, European Commission, Brussels.

FAO, IFAD, UNICEF, WFP and WHO. (2023) *The State of Food Security and Nutrition in the World 2023. Urbanization, Agrifood Systems Transformation and Healthy Diets Across the Rural–Urban Continuum*, Food and Agriculture Organization, Rome.

Fields, B. & Renne, J. (2021) *Adaptation Urbanism and Resilient Communities: Transforming Streets to Address Climate Change*, Routledge, New York.

Freeman, C. & Quigg, R. (2009) Commuting lives: Children's mobility and energy use, *Journal of Environmental Planning and Management*, 52(3): 393–412, https://doi.org/10.1080/09640560802703280

Guallart, V. (2010) *Self-Sufficient City: Envisioning the Habitat of the Future.* Actar, New York.

Hall, R. & Rosenstock, M. (1998) Agenda 2000 – The reform of EU cohesion policies, *European Planning Studies*, 6(6): 635–644.

Hartl, R, Harms, P. & Egermann, M. (2024) Towards transformation-oriented planning: What can sustainable urban mobility planning (SUMP) learn from transition management (TM)?, *Transport Reviews*, 44(1): 167–190, https://doi.org/10.1080/01441647.2023.2239497

Hasimuna, O., Maulu, S., Nawanzi, K., Lundu, B., Mphande, J., Phiri, C., Kikamba, E., Siankwilimba, E., Siavwapa, S. & Chibesa, M. (2023) Integrated agriculture-aquaculture as an alternative to improving small-scale fish production in Zambia, *Frontiers in Sustainable Food Systems,* 7 (2023): 1–13, https://doi.org/10.3389/fsufs.2023.1161121

Hess, D. & Gentry, H. (2019) 100% renewable energy policies in U.S. cities: Strategies, recommendations, and implementation challenges, *Sustainability: Science, Practice and Policy*, 15(1): 45–61, https://doi.org/10.1080/15487733.2019.1665841

Hodson, M. & Marvin, S. (2017) Intensifying or transforming sustainable cities? Fragmented logics of urban environmentalism, *Local Environment*, 22(1): 8–22, https://doi.org/10.1080/13549839.2017.1306498

Kehoe, P. (2023) Scaling up onsite water recycling systems in the US, Water Security, 20: 100153, https://doi.org/10.1016/j.wasec.2023.100153

Mantero, C. (2023) Sustainable, smart and safe mobility at the core of sustainable tourism in six European islands, *Transportation Research Procedia*, 72: 635–641, https://doi.org/10.1016/j.trpro.2023.11.449

Martin, M., Elnour, M. & Siñol, A. (2023) Environmental life cycle assessment of a large-scale commercial vertical farm, *Sustainable Production and Consumption*, 40: 182–193, https://doi.org/10.1016/j.spc.2023.06.020

May, T. & Marvin, S. (2017) The future of sustainable cities: Governance, policy and knowledge, *Local Environment*, 22(1): 1–7, https://doi.org/10.1080/13549839.2017.1394567

Medeiros, E. (2016) Territorial cohesion: An EU concept, *European Journal of Spatial Development*, 60, https://www.nordregio.org/publications/territorial-cohesion-an-eu-concept

Medeiros, E. (2017) Placing European territorial cooperation at the heart of ECP, *European Structural and Investment Funds Journal*, 5(3): 245–262.

Medeiros, E. (2019) Spatial planning, territorial development and territorial impact assessment. *Journal of Planning Literature*, 34(2): 171–182.

Medeiros, E. (2020a) Urban sustainability: A multi-dimensional policy evaluation framework proposal, *CIDADES, Comunidades e Territórios*, 40(Jun): 117–133.

Medeiros, E. (ed.). (2020b) *Territorial Impact Assessment. Advances in Spatial Science.* Springer, Cham.

Medeiros, E. (2022) Strategic-based regional development: Towards a theory of everything for regional development?, *European Journal of Spatial Development,* 19(5): 1–26.

Medeiros, E. (2023) *Reinforcing Territorial Cooperation and Addressing Challenges on European Integration,* European Commission, Brussels, https://ec.europa.eu/regional_policy/sources/policy/how/future-cohesion-policy/Expert_paper_Medeiros_230613.pdf

Medeiros, E. & Rauhut, D. (2020) Territorial cohesion cities: A policy recipe for achieving territorial cohesion?, *Regional Studies,* 54(1): 120–128.

Medeiros, E., Gonçalves, V. Castro, P. & Valente, B. (2022) How impactful are public policies on environmental sustainability? Debating the Portuguese case of PO SEUR 2014–2020, *Sustainability,* 14(13): 7917, https://doi.org/10.3390/su14137917

Medeiros, E. & Valente, B. (2023) Assessing impacts of public policies towards environmental sustainability in an EU region: North of Portugal, *European Planning Studies,* 32(2): 410–429, https://doi.org/10.1080/09654313.2023.2169068

Medeiros, E., Zaucha, J. & Ciołek, D. (2023a) Measuring territorial cohesion trends in Europe: A correlation with EU cohesion policy, *European Planning Studies,* 31(18): 1868–1884, https://doi.org/10.1080/09654313.2022.2143713

Medeiros, E., Scott, J., Ferreira, R., Boijmans, P., Verschelde, N., Guillermo-Ramírez, M., Gyula, O., Peyrony, J. & Soares, A. (2023b) European territorial cooperation towards territorial cohesion?, Regional Studies 58(8): 1518–1529, https://doi.org/10.1080/00343404.2023.2226698

Mouritse, P. (ed.). (2019) *Cities 100 Report,* C40 Cities Climate Leadership Group, London.

NG. (2022) National Geographic Concise Atlas of the World, 5th edition, National Geographic Partners, LLC, Washington.

Nitsch, J. (2018) The global potential of renewable energy sources, *Structural Engineering International,* 4(2): 72–75, https://doi.org/10.2749/101686694780650995

Orttung, R. (ed.). (2019) *Capital Cities and Urban Sustainability,* Routledge, London.

Popp, J., Váradi, L., Békefi, E., Péteri, A., Gyalog, G., Lakner, Z., & Oláh, J. (2018) Evolution of integrated open aquaculture systems in Hungary: Results from a case study. *Sustainability,* 10: 177, https://doi.org/10.3390/su10010177

Silva, A. (2023) Water supply and wastewater treatment and reuse in future cities: A systematic literature review, *Water,* 15(17): 3064, https://doi.org/10.3390/w15173064

Tortajada, C. & Ong, C. (2016) Reused water policies for potable use, *International Journal of Water Resources Development,* 32(4): 500–502, https://doi.org/10.1080/07900627.2016.1179177

Tyndall, S., Maloney, G., Cole, M., Hazell, N. & Augustin, M. (2022) Critical food and nutrition science challenges for plant-based meat alternative products, *Critical Reviews in Food Science and Nutrition,* 64(3), 638–653, https://doi.org/10.1080/10408398.2022.2107994

Ulpiani, G., Vetters, N., Shtjefni, D., Kakoulaki, G. & Taylor, N. (2023) Let's hear it from the cities: On the role of renewable energy in reaching climate neutrality in urban Europe, *Renewable and Sustainable Energy Reviews,* 183 (2023): 113444, https://doi.org/10.1016/j.rser.2023.113444

UN. (2016) *Transforming Our World: The 2030 Agenda for Sustainable Development,* United Nations, New York.

UN. (2020a) *World Cities Report, The Value of Sustainable Urban Development,* United Nations, New York.

UN. (2020b) *Human Development Report 2020. The Next Frontier. Human Development and the Anthropocene,* United Nations, New York.

UN. (2022) World Cities Report, United Nations, New York.

Urban Agenda. (2016) *Establishing the Urban Agenda for the EU 'Pact of Amsterdam', Agreed at the Informal Meeting of EU Ministers Responsible for Urban Matters on 30 May 2016,* Amsterdam.

Wester, J. & Broad, K. (2021) Direct potable water recycling in Texas: Case studies and policy implications, *Journal of Environmental Policy & Planning,* 23(1): 66–83, https://doi.org/10.1080/1523908X.2020.1798749

Williams, J. (2023) Circular cities: Planning for circular development in European cities, *European Planning Studies,* 31(1): 14–35, https://doi.org/10.1080/09654313.2022.2060707

Young, R. & Lieberknecht, K. (2019) From smart cities to wise cities: Ecological wisdom as a basis for sustainable urban development, *Journal of Environmental Planning and Management,* 62(10): 1675–1692, https://doi.org/10.1080/09640568.2018.1484343

Xiaolin, Y. & Kai, W. (2022) High-speed rail opening and green innovation – Evidence from China, *Frontiers in Environmental Science,* 10: 1–14. https://www.frontiersin.org/articles/10.3389/fenvs.2022.901879

2 Urban sustainable development via self-sufficiency planning approaches. A theoretical discussion

Marco Antonio Sánchez Trujillo and María Ángeles Huete García

2.1 Introduction: toward sustainable urban futures

In contemporary urban discourse, the pursuit of sustainability has emerged as an imperative response to the escalating challenges posed by rapid urbanization, environmental degradation, and social inequalities, embedded within a worldwide context defined by climate challenges. The pressing need for sustainable urban development necessitates comprehensive strategies that address these multifaceted challenges holistically, integrating environmental, economic, and social dimensions. At the heart of this multifaceted effort lies the concept of self-sufficiency planning, which advocates for the localization of resources and capabilities to enhance urban resilience and promote long-term viability. This chapter aims to delve deeply into the theoretical foundations, principles, and strategies of self-sufficiency planning, exploring its potential as a transformative approach to urban governance.

The seminal work of Meadows et al. (1972) underscored the finite nature of global resources, catalyzing discussions on sustainability and compelling the exploration of alternative development paradigms. Since then, scholars and practitioners have increasingly emphasized the paramount importance of transitioning toward self-sufficiency in urban contexts to effectively mitigate environmental degradation and foster sustainable development.

A fundamental aspect of the self-sufficiency approach to urban planning is the concept of limited growth in urban areas. This paradigm shift challenges the conventional wisdom of unlimited growth models, which often lead to resource depletion and exacerbation of environmental pressures. Instead, self-sufficiency planning advocates for controlled growth that carefully considers ecological and social boundaries. Such an approach necessitates the implementation of policies and practices that not only encourage urban densification but also seek to revitalize degraded areas and promote the development of sustainable infrastructure. This holistic perspective resonates deeply with the evolving urban lifestyle and the fundamental reevaluation of how societies meet their basic needs. For instance, Breheny (1992) delves into the intricate relationship between urban planning and transportation-related energy consumption, emphasizing the pivotal role of urban

DOI: 10.4324/9781003498216-4

densification and growth limitation in reducing cities' ecological footprint, thereby aligning closely with the principles of self-sufficiency planning.

It is crucial to understand that limiting urban growth does not equate to stifling development; rather, it involves redirecting development toward more sustainable and equitable trajectories. This paradigm shift emphasizes the quality of growth over sheer quantity, placing significant emphasis on enhancing citizens' quality of life and safeguarding the health of the urban environment. Moreover, it underscores the importance of efficiently utilizing local resources and reducing dependence on external resources, thereby bolstering the city's resilience in the face of external disruptions and economic crises. Beatley (1999) provides illuminating examples of sustainable urban development in European cities, emphasizing principles such as compactness, mixed land use, and sustainable transportation, all of which are pertinent to discussions of limited urban growth and self-sufficiency planning. Similarly, Jenks and Dempsey (2005) discuss a plethora of strategies and design principles aimed at fostering sustainable cities, including approaches to curtail urban growth while fostering self-sufficiency and resilience.

Furthermore, Newman and Kenworthy (1999) offer valuable insights into the interplay between urban form, transportation systems, and sustainability. Their research advocates for compact, mixed-use development and reduced reliance on automobiles, aligning seamlessly with the principles of limited urban growth and self-sufficiency planning.

Collectively, the scholarly works cited in this chapter provide robust theoretical frameworks, compelling case studies, and empirical evidence that substantiate the proposition that limited growth in urban areas, coupled with self-sufficiency planning, can pave the way for the emergence of more sustainable and resilient cities. However, to fully grasp the potential of self-sufficiency planning, it is imperative to explore additional dimensions such as its implications for social equity, cultural preservation, and innovative governance structures. By incorporating these nuanced aspects into the discourse, a richer understanding of self-sufficiency planning's potential and limitations can be attained, thereby enriching the ongoing dialogue on sustainable urban development.

The chapter follows a logical progression starting with an introduction that contextualizes the importance and urgency of addressing contemporary urban challenges through self-sufficiency planning. It then delves into an in-depth exploration of the urgency in navigating these complex urban challenges, highlighting the interconnectedness between rapid urbanization, climate change, and social disparities. This analysis sets the stage for the exploration of the concept of self-sufficiency planning as a paradigm shift in urban governance, emphasizing its fundamental dimensions centered around society, complexity, and landscape. Next, it delves into the principles and strategies of self-sufficiency planning, underscoring the significance of decentralization, diversification, and community engagement. Finally, it examines the broader implications of self-sufficiency planning, including its synergy with sustainability concepts, its role in managing the built environment and its alignment with global movements toward social and climate justice.

2.2 Understanding the urgency: navigating complex urban challenges

Urban areas are facing a multitude of interconnected challenges that demand immediate attention and innovative solutions. The landmark report by the Intergovernmental Panel on Climate Change (IPCC, 2018) underscores the existential threat posed by climate change, particularly its disproportionate impacts on urban populations. Moreover, studies such as the United Nations' World Urbanization Prospects (2019) highlight the unprecedented pace of urbanization, placing immense pressure on resources and infrastructure. Concurrently, social disparities within urban contexts have come to the forefront, necessitating action to address urban injustices and ensure equitable access to essential services irrespective of individual socioeconomic characteristics.

Addressing these multifaceted challenges requires transformative approaches that challenge conventional urban development paradigms. Within a world that is becoming increasingly urbanized, there is an urgent need to introduce alternative management frameworks tailored to the complexities of urban environments.

Embedded within this rapidly evolving urban landscape, urban ecology emerges as a vital framework for understanding and addressing contemporary challenges. By combining insights from natural and social sciences, urban ecology seeks to comprehend the dynamic interplay between human activities and the environment within urban boundaries and beyond (Grimm et al., 2008). This interdisciplinary approach is crucial as traditional governmental strategies have often overlooked the intricate relationship between cities and their surrounding ecosystems. Thus, viewing cities as heterogenous socioecological systems is essential for identifying both the root causes of urban challenges and potential solutions.

The structural impact of anthropogenic climate change on the built environment and urban development processes is evident in public policies aimed at mitigating risks associated with environmental hazards. However, beyond the economic implications of climate challenges, attention must be directed toward addressing the social inequalities and vulnerabilities exacerbated by these phenomena. Indeed, social inequality and vulnerability have emerged as critical dimensions that must be central to efforts aimed at enhancing urban resilience, moving beyond purely economic considerations.

The social dimension of urban climate challenges intersects with Henri Lefebvre's concept of the "right to the city" and the notion of urban citizenship. Lefebvre (1968) emphasized not only the economic and political aspects of urban life but also the social needs of urban dwellers. As urban populations burgeoned in the latter half of the 20th century, citizens' roles in shaping and transforming cities became increasingly significant, laying the groundwork for bottom-up initiatives and fostering a sense of community and belonging. In the context of contemporary urban climate challenges, the social inequalities inherent in how these challenges impact marginalized communities have further exacerbated disconnections from the urban environment and hindered access to essential resources and opportunities. Therefore, alongside economic and political considerations, it is imperative to recognize the social dimensions of urban climate challenges as a driving force behind the urgency to enact meaningful and inclusive solutions.

2.3 Exploring self-sufficiency planning: a paradigm shift in urban governance

Self-sufficiency planning represents a fundamental reimagining of urban governance, advocating for localized responses to global challenges. Inspired by the insights of Beatley (2012) and Holmgren (2002), this approach places resilience and adaptability at its core, equipping cities with the tools to navigate uncertainty and confront unforeseen events with agility. While the concept of self-sufficiency has only recently gained prominence in urban discourse, it has quickly emerged as a critical framework for addressing the complex interplay of climate challenges within local urban environments, as evidenced by the scholarly inquiries of Roggema (2017) and Ahmeti and Üstündağ (2022).

2.3.1 Society-based dimension

Central to self-sufficiency planning is the redefinition of the relationship between society, the research community, and governance structures. This dimension underscores the imperative of empowering local citizens within urban design processes, recognizing their invaluable insights and contributions. By embracing a diversity of knowledge and perspectives, including both specialized and everyday expertise, self-sufficiency planning seeks to democratize decision-making and foster a sense of ownership over urban development initiatives among all stakeholders.

2.3.2 Complexity-led dimension

Urban environments are inherently complex, comprising a myriad of interconnected systems and variables. Self-sufficiency planning acknowledges this complexity and advocates for a holistic approach to urban analysis and intervention. By prioritizing bottom-up assessments that capture the multifaceted nature of urban resilience, this dimension encourages cities to leverage the intricacies of their socioecological systems to enhance their adaptive capacity and fortify their resilience against future shocks and stresses.

2.3.3 Landscape-driven dimension

Self-sufficiency planning challenges conventional notions of urban development by foregrounding the natural landscape as a fundamental determinant of urban form and function. This dimension emphasizes the intrinsic value of the physical environment and its role in shaping sustainable urban futures. By reframing the urban landscape as the foundation upon which all design processes should be anchored, self-sufficiency planning promotes innovative solutions that harness the regenerative potential of natural systems to address pressing urban challenges.

These three dimensions provide the conceptual framework for six key design principles essential to the realization of urban sustainability (Roggema, 2017):

1 Closing cycles at the lowest technical scale. This principle underscores the importance of optimizing resource utilization and minimizing waste generation through small-scale interventions. By maximizing resource efficiency at the local level, cities can enhance their resilience and adaptability to future shocks and stresses.
2 Redundancy in design. Redundancy ensures that urban systems have the capacity to respond effectively to unexpected events by building in flexibility and adaptability. By incorporating redundancy into urban infrastructure and planning, cities can mitigate the impacts of climate change and other disruptions.
3 Anti-fragility of urban environments. This principle emphasizes the importance of designing urban responses that strengthen rather than weaken in the face of adversity. By fostering anti-fragile urban environments, cities can enhance their ability to respond rapidly and effectively to environmental challenges.
4 Urban citizens as design actors. Empowering local communities to actively participate in the design and implementation of urban interventions fosters a sense of ownership and responsibility for the built environment. By engaging citizens as co-creators of their urban futures, cities can tap into local knowledge and expertise to develop contextually appropriate and culturally sensitive solutions.
5 Landscape as the basis for urban growth. Recognizing the intrinsic connection between urban development and the natural landscape, this principle advocates for development that is rooted in local environmental conditions and ecosystems. By aligning urban growth with the natural landscape, cities can enhance biodiversity, mitigate climate change, and create more resilient and sustainable urban environments.
6 Rule-breaking design. Rule-breaking design encourages innovation and creativity in urban planning and design. By challenging conventional norms and embracing alternative approaches, cities can unlock new opportunities for sustainable development and address complex urban challenges in novel ways.

In conclusion, self-sufficiency planning represents a profound paradigm shift in urban governance, emphasizing the importance of localized solutions, community engagement, and interdisciplinary collaboration in achieving sustainable urban futures. While challenges remain in implementation, the diverse manifestations of self-sufficiency planning across different contexts offer valuable insights and lessons for cities seeking to enhance their resilience, adaptability, and sustainability. Through continued exploration and experimentation, self-sufficiency planning has the potential to revolutionize urban governance and create more inclusive, resilient, and sustainable cities for future generations. Case studies such as Transition Towns and the Eco-City Movement exemplify the diverse manifestations of self-sufficiency planning across different contexts (Hopkins, 2008; Register, 2006). These initiatives demonstrate the potential for communities to become more self-reliant by harnessing local resources and fostering collaborative decision-making processes, reinforcing the role and agency of the local population.

2.4 Synergies with sustainability concepts

Self-sufficiency planning intersects with various sustainability concepts, forging deep connections and fostering synergies that enrich urban development outcomes. The circular economy framework, advocated by influential figures such as Ellen MacArthur, places a strong emphasis on resource efficiency and waste minimization, which inherently align with the core objectives of self-sufficiency (Ellen MacArthur Foundation, 2013). Similarly, the principles of social equity and environmental justice converge seamlessly with self-sufficiency planning, ensuring that urban development is not only environmentally sustainable but also socially inclusive and equitable (Szerszynski et al., 2003). By integrating these foundational concepts into the frameworks of self-sufficiency planning, cities can propel themselves toward more resilient, inclusive, and environmentally friendly futures. Therefore, it is imperative for urban actors to grasp the profound implications of sustainability for current development paradigms and recognize that self-sufficiency planning cannot exist in isolation but must be integrated as a fundamental asset within ongoing innovative interventions, thereby enriching the urban discourse.

2.4.1 Expanding the Scope: managing the built environment

Self-sufficiency planning transcends the mere expansion of urban areas to meet tangible needs; it also entails the meticulous management of the existing built environment. Understanding this broader scope is paramount to comprehending the essence of self-sufficiency planning. It involves not only envisioning sustainable green infrastructure projects for new developments but also revitalizing and retrofitting existing urban spaces to achieve self-sufficiency across all layers of the city. To achieve such comprehensive goals, a fundamental reorganization of local production and consumption patterns is essential. Linked to the foundational concepts of self-sufficiency, circular economy, and resource efficiency, Shillington (2013) introduces the concept of urban metabolism and the associated rights, which are intricately intertwined with broader notions such as the right to the city and urban ecology. Urban metabolism delineates the intricate patterns of production and consumption within cities, shedding light on how these patterns are influenced by socioeconomic characteristics and urban contexts. Consequently, the right to urban metabolism seeks to address disparities between formal (high-income) and informal (low-income) urban areas, advocating for equitable resource management practices and initiatives aimed at waste reduction. However, as exemplified by Shillington (2013) in the case study of Managua (Nicaragua), it is often within low-income urban areas that innovative urban dynamics emerge out of necessity rather than innovation. This underscores the imperative for self-sufficiency planning to prioritize social justice and equity, emphasizing the importance of engaging local citizens regardless of their socioeconomic status.

2.4.2 Aligning with global movements: toward social and climate justice

By aligning multifaceted concepts within a unified urban discourse, cities can emerge as potent agents in advancing social and climate justice agendas on a global scale. Both self-sufficiency planning and environmental justice movements are deeply embedded within the broader struggle for justice, highlighting the interconnectedness of these approaches. Mohai et al. (2009) underscore the close relationship between environmental justice and social movements in the 2000s, signaling a collective push for broader social transformations and the democratization of urban development processes. This underscores the pivotal role of societal engagement in the complex management of urban environments. Consequently, marginalized voices that were historically overlooked have found a platform within the urban discourse, becoming indispensable stakeholders in the process of urban transformation.

In conclusion, the adoption of self-sufficiency planning principles is imperative in the face of the global climate crisis. However, it must be approached with foresight, acknowledging its intersectionality with traditional sustainability concepts and the need for diversified decision-making bodies. Only through a comprehensive, interconnected urban mindset that integrates diverse knowledge from all socioeconomic layers can cities truly harness the transformative potential of self-sufficiency planning and pave the way toward more resilient, inclusive, and sustainable urban futures.

2.5   Principles of and strategies toward self-sufficiency planning

Derived from synergies with sustainability concepts, the fundamental principles underpinning self-sufficiency planning encompass decentralization, diversification, and community engagement. These principles serve as the cornerstone of a paradigm shift in urban governance, prioritizing quality growth over sheer quantity in the development of new urban agendas.

Furthermore, it is imperative to delve into the intricate relationship between urban power dynamics and political agency to fully grasp the essence of self-sufficiency planning. Understanding how local agency extends beyond traditional political actors is crucial in addressing urgent challenges and fostering resilience within urban environments. An agency-centered perspective highlights the limitations of relying solely on political actors and underscores the need for a broader institutional framework that challenges systemic constraints (Davies and Msengana-Ndlela, 2015). This institutional framework not only drives the paradigm shift described but also revitalizes the focus on local agency.

Expanding on the notion of decentralization, it becomes evident that shifting decision-making processes away from centralized entities empowers local communities and enhances their capacity to respond effectively to local needs (Smit and Nasr, 1992). Decentralization is not merely about redistributing power but also about integrating new urban actors within governing bodies. Multidisciplinary approaches that incorporate formal and informal knowledge are essential for inclusive decision-making and urban design that truly reflect the diverse needs of communities.

Moreover, the concept of diversification emerges as a critical strategy for building urban resilience and reducing dependency on external resources. Diversifying energy sources, enhancing food sovereignty, and promoting alternative transportation modes are all integral components of a comprehensive self-sufficiency plan (Viljoen and Bohn, 2013). In an era marked by global uncertainties, such as geopolitical tensions and climate change, diversification mitigates the risks associated with over-reliance on external actors and resources.

Various strategies, ranging from green infrastructure development to participatory governance mechanisms, play a pivotal role in augmenting urban self-reliance and promoting sustainable resource management (Beatley and Manning, 1997; Ellen MacArthur Foundation, 2012). Green infrastructure, for instance, not only enhances ecological resilience but also provides multiple co-benefits, such as improved air quality and enhanced community well-being. Similarly, participatory governance mechanisms ensure that decision-making processes are inclusive and transparent, thereby fostering a sense of ownership and empowerment among local residents.

Community engagement lies at the heart of diversifying decision-making processes and ensuring that self-sufficiency planning initiatives truly reflect the needs and aspirations of local communities. Community and participatory planning approaches have demonstrated remarkable success, particularly within informal urban areas in the Global South. By actively involving residents in the planning and implementation of self-sufficiency strategies, cities can tap into local knowledge and expertise, thereby fostering a sense of ownership and collective responsibility.

In conclusion, self-sufficiency planning represents a transformative approach to urban governance, one that prioritizes resilience, inclusivity, and sustainability. By embracing principles of decentralization, diversification, and community engagement, cities can navigate the complexities of the modern urban landscape and emerge as resilient, self-reliant, and thriving communities.

2.6 Relationship between theoretical propositions and chapter content

In this last section, we aim to bridge the theoretical principles introduced in this chapter with the content of each chapter of the book. The purpose of such a comparison is to highlight how traditional and innovative urban discourses in the literature intertwine with the theory and case studies introduced in this book and the relevance of this work for academics, politicians, and local bodies that have become vital entities for the functioning of cities.

Within the EU ongoing context of socioeconomic and environmental regional cohesion, the role of self-sufficiency planning, through its landscape-driven dimension, is recognized as key in articulating territorial governance. In the first chapter, Medeiros exposes how environmental sustainability processes have been deployed over the past decades in the continent, and the need to focus on *ad hoc* territorial solutions to accomplish sustainable and carbon-neutral development. Hence, a paradigm shift in urban governance regarding the EU Cohesion Policy entails introducing autonomous local approaches that allow cities to govern their local territories embedded within wider sustainable urban development goals. This is what self-sufficiency planning portrays when implemented in urban areas by highlighting the importance of "the local" to attain development goals at higher sociopolitical levels.

In Chapter 3, Topaloglou introduces the concept of "just transition" via self-sufficiency as a way to attain urban justice and equal development. The theory developed in this chapter connects with the ongoing global discourse that cities ought to become key agents in attaining climate justice and social equity. Within the urban context, self-sufficiency is coupled with social movements and environmental justice as key concepts that target sustainability and self-management. This reinforces the assertion that self-sufficiency intersects with traditional concepts within long-lasting urban discourses which may ease the implementation of self-sufficiency principles in current urban environments.

Chapter 4 is dedicated to renewable energy production, consumption, and sustainable carbon-free urban development. Dahal emphasizes how, introducing smart solutions within cities to tackle climate challenges equally requires being aware of local limitations to deploy policy measures appropriately to accomplish set goals. This is especially important regarding the complexity of the urban environment in order to establish adequate solutions that intertwine the urgency of intervening, on the one hand, with the neutral-free goal, on the other. Consequently, in his chapter, Dahal exemplifies how urban climate urgency needs to be framed according to the city resources to develop sustainable solutions depending on the local capacity to act. In Chapter 5, Canelas follows a similar pathway when she introduces the role of the built environment and its developers, and the need to address their current role within urban development. This introduces a key issue in understanding the essence of self-sufficiency planning. Given that self-sufficiency transcends the expansion of urban areas, which is the aim of real estate and construction bodies, toward the management of the existing built environment, this paradigm shift reveals crucial for current urban development worldwide. Alongside this, Canelas chapter focuses on the importance of key actors in the transition to carbon neutrality, highlighting the role of landowners and real estate developers. In the analysis of London, the London Landed Estates are identified as prominent actors, known for their extensive ownership of urban land. This specific case demonstrates how these key actors are responding to the need for transition to carbon neutrality, emphasizing their commitments to net-zero emissions strategies. Additionally, the London analysis shows how these motivations influence the actions of the London Landed Estates, from improving energy efficiency to implementing renewable energy systems. Together, this chapter provides a concrete case that exemplifies the practical application of the theoretical concepts discussed throughout this chapter, demonstrating how key actors are addressing the transition to carbon neutrality in the urban real estate sector.

Chapter 6 provides a detailed insight into how the theoretical concepts presented in this chapter, highlighting the importance of integrated and sustainability-oriented urban planning to address mobility challenges in modern cities. The author addresses the issue of sustainable urban mobility from a practical and analytical perspective. The importance of addressing current mobility challenges in cities is highlighted, considering both environmental and socioeconomic impacts.

In line with the theoretical framework presented in this chapter, the need for a paradigm shift toward sustainable mobility is emphasized, and various practices and approaches to achieve this goal are explored. Gavanas focuses on concrete examples of strategic planning and implementation of sustainable urban mobility plans, such as the Sustainable Urban Mobility Plan (SUMP) and other plans implemented in metropolitan areas, cities, and specific neighborhoods. Innovative cases of emerging mobility services, such as shared mobility and Mobility as a Service (MaaS), as well as new modes of transportation like autonomous vehicles, are examined. The chapter also looks at specific cases of cities that have implemented innovative solutions in urban mobility, such as Copenhagen's Sustainable Urban Mobility Plan (Finger Plan), Curitiba's Bus Rapid Transit (BRT) system, and Barcelona's Superblocks. It highlights how these practices and approaches are contributing to the promotion of cleaner, smarter, and more sustainable mobility in cities, while addressing emerging challenges and opportunities in this field. The importance of integrating technologies and innovation into urban planning to effectively address mobility issues is emphasized.

Chapter 7 delves into the practical application of theoretical concepts introduced in this chapter, particularly emphasizing the importance of integrated and sustainable approaches to regional planning in addressing energy challenges. The theoretical framework presented initially underscores the imperative need for transitioning to sustainable energy systems to mitigate climate change impacts and ensure future societal well-being. This theoretical foundation sets the stage for the examination of electricity self-sufficiency in regional planning, as discussed in Chapter 7. By comparing the cases of São Paulo and Ceará, the chapter exemplifies how socio-technical perspectives are crucial in informing policy measures, aligning with the theoretical premise that human and social dimensions significantly influence technological and governance choices in energy policy. Moreover, the chapter's focus on renewable energy production, demand, and self-sufficiency underscores the practical manifestation of concepts such as sustainability, resilience, and local empowerment introduced in this chapter.

Finally, Chapter 8 underscores the importance of transitioning from a linear economic model to a circular model, where resources are reused, recycled, and redistributed. The theoretical foundation established earlier emphasizes the urgent need to rethink our economic approach in light of environmental degradation and resource scarcity. This sets the stage for the exploration of the circular economy as an alternative model that minimizes negative environmental impacts while promoting long-term sustainability. The chapter discusses innovative strategies and best practices for promoting the circular economy at the regional level, emphasizing the role of regional policies and governance in facilitating this transition. Moreover, it highlights the economic, social, and environmental benefits of implementing circular economy policies, such as self-sufficiency, resilience building, and environmentally sustainable regional planning, in line with the theoretical concepts introduced earlier. Ultimately, the chapter advocates for a paradigm shift in planning and development practices, urging regions to prioritize sustainability and circularity over the linear economy, whose limitations are now evident.

2.7 Conclusion

Self-sufficiency planning offers a promising pathway toward sustainable urban development in the face of escalating global challenges. By harnessing local resources, fostering community resilience, and integrating diverse sustainability principles, cities can mitigate vulnerabilities and thrive in an uncertain future. As urbanization continues to accelerate, embracing self-sufficiency planning becomes imperative for creating cities that are not only economically vibrant but also socially equitable and environmentally sustainable.

This chapter has revised why self-sufficiency planning needs to be regarded as an effective alternative intervention means that tackles the urgency in climate adaptation at the urban level. Even though innovations have been introduced at the urban level since the late 20th century, the key difference lies in the inclusion of local citizenry as an important, if not the main, actor within decision-making processes.

Self-sufficiency planning introduces a new paradigm shift within the urban scene wherein society, the complex urban milieu, and the physical location of urban areas all converge to create an alternative vision on the city and its capacity to become an independent entity that is able to cater for itself. To accomplish such a situation, a series of design principles have been developed as a result, which ought to be applied combined with one another to create an interrelated environment that is both sustainable and positive for urban dependency.

The interconnection of self-sufficiency principles with traditional concepts within the urban discourse is crucial for the understanding of self-sufficiency planning. Likewise, the intertwinement amongst urban concepts demonstrates how the urban future needs to take city history into account to discern flaws in the urban system and be able to solve them appropriately. Hence, the principles and strategies that sustain self-sufficiency planning revolve around decentralization, diversification, and engagement which all represent innovative approaches at the urban level.

Seeking for alternative frameworks and independence implies launching disruptive initiatives that question traditional approaches to the urban phenomenon. Case studies, particularly within cities of the Global South (see Sletto et al., 2010) and less developed neighborhoods in the Global North, have proved successful in showing how a real inclusion of local citizens as direct actors in decision-making processes reveals beneficial for the materialization of sustainable urban development.

These theoretical principles are evident in the content of the chapters that make up this publication, as shown in the last section of this chapter. Each chapter addresses key aspects of sustainable urban planning and its relationship with self-sufficiency, highlighting the importance of integrating innovative and traditional approaches to address contemporary urban challenges. From the need for territorial development policies adapted to self-sufficiency in the initial chapter to the focus on renewable energy and electrical self-sufficiency in later chapters, each contribution examines how self-sufficiency principles can inform and influence urban planning in different contexts.

All in all, current urban sustainable planning requires the introduction of self-sufficiency planning within the urban discourse to accomplish urban frameworks that sustain independence and urban autonomy which allow cities to design instruments ad hoc regarding climate challenge crisis and the need to introduce adequate responses. The future of cities requires greater societal equity that, undoubtedly, implies a consistent understanding of society as a valid and key actor within the entanglement of multifarious layers that we call city.

References

Ahmeti, S. and Üstündağ, K. (2022). Self-sufficient city as organizing principle for sustainable development: Making Bozcaada a self-sufficient and sustainable island. In M. D. Vujicic; A. Kasim; S. Kostopoulou; J. Chica Olmo; and M. Aslam (eds.), *Cultural Sustainable Tourism. Advances in Science, Technology & Innovation*. Springer.

Beatley, T. (1999). *Green Urbanism: Learning from European Cities*. Island Press.

Beatley, T. (2012). *Green Urbanism: Learning from European Cities*. Island Press.

Beatley, T., and Manning, K. (1997). *The Ecology of Place: Planning for Environment, Economy, and Community*. Island Press.

Breheny, M. (1992). The compact city and transport energy consumption. *Transactions of the Institute of British Geographers,* 17(1), 17–31.

Davies, J. S. and Msengana-Ndlela, L. G. (2015). Urban power and political agency: Reflections on a study of local economic development in Johannesburg and Leeds. *Cities,* 44, 131–138.

Ellen MacArthur Foundation. (2012). Towards the circular economy: Economic and business rationale for an accelerated transition, Ellen MacArthur Foundation, Cowes, Isle of Wight.

Ellen MacArthur Foundation. (2013). Towards the circular economy: Accelerating the scale-up across global supply chains, Ellen MacArthur Foundation, Cowes, Isle of Wight.

Grimm, N. B., Faeth, S. H., Golubiewski, N. E., Redman, C. L., Wu, J., Bai, X. and Briggs, J. M. (2008). Global change and the ecology of cities. *Science, New Series*, 319(5864), 756–760.

Holmgren, D. (2002). *Permaculture: Principles and Pathways beyond Sustainability*. Holmgren Design Services.

Hopkins, R. (2008). *The Transition Handbook: From Oil Dependency to Local Resilience*. Green Books.

IPCC. (2018). *Global Warming of 1.5°C.* Intergovernmental Panel on Climate Change.

Jenks, M. & Dempsey, N. (Eds.). (2005). *Future Forms and Design for Sustainable Cities*. Architectural Press.

Lefebvre, H. (1968). *Le Droit à la ville*. Paris.

Meadows, D. H., Meadows, D. L., Randers, J., and Behrens III, W. W. (1972). The Limits to Growth: A Report for the Club of Rome's Project on the Predicament of Mankind. Universe Books.

Mohai, P., Pellow, D. and Roberts, J. T. (2009). Environmental justice. *Annual Review of Environment and Resources*, 34, 405–430.

Newman, P. & Kenworthy, J. (1999). *Sustainability and Cities: Overcoming Automobile Dependence*. Island Press.

Register, R. (2006). *Ecocities: Building Cities in Balance with Nature*. New Society Publishers.

Roggema, R. (2017). The future of sustainable urbanism: Society-based, complexity-led, and landscape-driven. *Sustainability*, 9 (1442), 1–20.

Shillington, L. J. (2013). Right to food, right to the city: Household urban agriculture, and socionatural metabolism in Managua, Nicaragua. *Geoforum,* 44, 103–111.

Sletto, B., Muñoz, S., Strange, S. M., Donoso, R. E. and Thomen, M. (2010). El rincón de los olvidados: Participatory GIS, experiential learning and critical pedagogy in Santo Domingo, Dominican Republic. *Journal of Latin American Geography,* 9(3), 111–135.

Smit, J. & Nasr, J. (1992). Urban agriculture for sustainable cities: Using wastes and idle land and water bodies as resources. *Environment and Urbanization,* 4(2), 141–152.

Szerszynski, B., Urry, J. & Lafaye, C. (2003). Managing the coast: The coast of England and Wales. *Sociology,* 37(3), 555–572.

United Nations. (2019). *World Urbanization Prospects: The 2018 Revision.* United Nations Department of Economic and Social Affairs, Population Division.

Viljoen, A., & Bohn, K. (2013). *Second Nature Urban Agriculture: Designing Productive Cities.* Routledge.

3 Just Transition governance via self-sufficiency regional development

Lefteris Topaloglou

3.1 Introduction

The transition towards sustainable economic systems represents one of the most daunting yet essential challenges of our era, especially within the frameworks of environmental sustainability, social equity, and economic development (Adewumi et al., 2024). The concept of "Just Transition" has emerged as a pivotal framework that advocates a shift that not only minimizes environmental impacts but also equitably distributes the socio-economic benefits and burdens of such changes across all segments of society (Wang & Lo, 2021). This chapter delves into novel governance approaches that incorporate self-sufficiency principles into regional development strategies, proposing a pathway that supports both the ecological and community resilience necessary for a sustainable future.

As societies endeavour to move away from fossil fuel dependency, the importance of developing governance models that comprehensively address the needs of affected communities becomes paramount (Topaloglou & Ioannidis, 2022). This chapter suggests that including self-sufficiency, which refers to the ability of communities to independently fulfil their requirements for food, energy, and water at a local level, in regional development policies might effectively reduce the risks associated with this transition. Promoting self-sufficiency not only strengthens local resilience and autonomy but also supports the ideals of Just Transition by fostering social fairness and environmental care (Tolonen et al., 2023).

Nevertheless, the process of shifting towards a self-sufficient model is filled with difficulties, mostly concerning governance. The efficacy of self-sufficiency models primarily relies on their capacity to actively include local communities in the decision-making process, guaranteeing that the initiatives are inclusive and that they are customized to local needs and settings (Dall-Orsoletta et al., 2022). This contribution aims to dissect these governance frameworks, examining how they can facilitate a Just Transition that is both sustainable and inclusive. To this end, the following fundamental inquiries are addressed: What are the possible advantages of incorporating self-sufficiency into regional development strategies? How can these approaches guarantee that the shift towards sustainability is fair and leaves no one behind? By examining these questions, this chapter attempts to make a substantial contribution to the discussion on sustainable development and governance

DOI: 10.4324/9781003498216-5

by offering vital perspectives on how regions might effectively tackle the complex economic, environmental, and social concerns of the 21st century.

Following the Introduction, the second section examines the theoretical foundations of self-sufficiency and decentralization of government. The third section analyses the shift towards achieving renewable energy self-sufficiency. The fourth section discusses Just Transition governance with a focus on climate, energy, and environmental justice, while the fifth section analyses a variety of global case studies on self-sufficiency. The subsequent Discussion section addresses potential challenges, proposing strategic solutions and policy recommendations. The chapter concludes with the findings.

3.2   Self-sufficiency and decentralized governance

The last quarter-century has witnessed a significant shift towards decentralization, with the aim of enhancing democratic principles and the efficiency of public administration. This shift is grounded in the belief that decentralization increases transparency, strengthens government accountability, and generally enhances public satisfaction with governance processes (Shah, 2017). Anchored in the principle of "no taxation without representation", this movement supports local control over taxation and public expenditure, ensuring that these align more closely with the needs and preferences of local communities (Pantazatou, 2018). This decentralized approach postulates that errors at the local level are generally less detrimental and more manageable than those made at the national level, thus reducing overall risk to the state (Goel et al., 2017).

The increasing difficulties presented by climate change have further substantiated the need for decentralized government, especially in the context of shifting away from fossil fuels. As noted by major organizations like the Intergovernmental Panel on Climate Change and the United Nations Environment Programme, centralized approaches have often failed to effectively reduce CO_2 emissions (Dorsch & Flachsland, 2017; Imasiku et al., 2019). In contrast, decentralized governance enables the adoption of tailored energy policies that encourage innovation in renewable energy sectors and allow for rapid adjustments in policy and practice in response to environmental exigencies (Cowell et al., 2017). Moreover, decentralized methods are crucial for efficiently tackling the localized impacts of climate change, such as the raised frequency of extreme weather events, escalating sea levels, and alterations in agricultural output. Granting local communities the authority to undertake adaptive measures helps them to build resilience from a grassroots level, enabling more efficient reactions to climate-induced disturbances (Shi, 2021).

While decentralization offers numerous benefits, it also presents significant obstacles. The development of energy infrastructures, traditionally characterized by natural monopolies and large-scale investments, has historically favoured centralization (Burke & Stephens, 2018). However, the shift towards renewable energies, which are less capital intensive and more amenable to small-scale and distributed systems, supports a decentralized approach. This transition challenges traditional governance models, requiring a rethinking of roles and responsibilities across all government levels to this new paradigm. Decentralized governance also promotes a "local general interest" that may sometimes conflict with broader national priorities (Barone, 2018). This can result in uneven policy implementation and a potential disconnect between local actions and overarching national or global objectives, particularly concerning environmental sustainability and social equity (Broto & Westman, 2017).

Effective decentralized governance is not just about transferring powers but also involves capacity building at the local level. Local governments must possess the requisite expertise and resources to assume additional duties, particularly those pertaining to a shift in energy systems. This involves ongoing training, sufficient funding, and robust systems for monitoring and evaluation to ensure policies are effectively implemented and adjusted as needed (Topaloglou & Ioannidis, 2022). It is crucial for sustained decentralization that local governments possess the power to produce their own earnings and the capacity to carefully manage these funds (Shah, 2004). As regions and municipalities aim for self-sufficiency, particularly in energy production, local governance takes on an increasingly central role. Decentralized energy systems empower communities and decrease dependence on national grids, thereby fostering local economic growth by creating new markets and job opportunities in the energy industry (Heldeweg & Saintier, 2020).

Decentralization, which prioritizes climate, environment, and energy, offers a sustainable and aligned approach to attaining self-sufficiency and contributes to global climate mitigation objectives. Nevertheless, it necessitates meticulous execution, including suitable legal structures, financial backing, and actions to enhance capabilities. Decentralized governance can make a substantial contribution to sustainable development and climate change mitigation by fostering local sovereignty while also aligning with national and international goals. This approach fosters a more resilient and adaptive society.

3.3   Transition towards renewable energy self-sufficiency

The transition towards renewable energy self-sufficiency (RESS) necessitates a profound shift in how communities and regions generate, distribute, and consume energy (Young & Brans, 2017). This shift involves the incorporation of innovative technology along with the reassessment of cultural standards, financial frameworks, and mechanisms of authority to support the adoption of enduring energy methodologies. The transition to a system based predominantly on renewable energy is complex, involving numerous considerations that span social, ecological, economic, and technical domains (Gui & MacGill, 2018). Comprehending and executing RESS requires an interdisciplinary approach due to the intricate interplay of social, ecological, economic, and technical elements. The multifaceted nature of this transition involves integrating insights from diverse scientific disciplines to address the challenges of adopting new technologies, managing sustainable land use, and transforming political and decision-making processes at the local level (Söderholm, 2020). As regions strive for greater energy autonomy, they face the task of aligning their initiatives with the principles of a Just Transition. This requires guaranteeing that the transition to renewable energy is not only viable from technical and economic standpoints, but that it is also equitable and impartial from a social standpoint (Dou et al., 2023).

Communities and regions worldwide are increasingly adopting goals to transition their energy infrastructures to fully utilize renewable resources such as solar energy, wind energy, and bioenergy. This shift not only reflects a commitment to environmental sustainability but also aims to enhance local energy security and autonomy (Hassan et al., 2024). The concept of energy autonomy has been gaining traction, propelled by broader governance shifts towards localization and sustainability in public policies. The notion of energy autonomy emerged throughout the process of electrification and energy transformations in the early 20th century. These transformations aimed to lessen reliance on large-scale, centralized energy networks by focusing on disconnection and decentralization (Gonzalez-Garcia, 2023). More recently, the push for energy autonomy has been revitalized by the rise of renewable energy sources, which inherently support decentralized models of energy production and consumption (Boutaud, 2022).

Energy autonomy today, in addition to representing a physical state of self-sufficiency also encompasses legal and theoretical dimensions (Losada-Puente et al., 2023). Legally, it involves the delegation of energy management competencies from national to local governments, allowing for more localized control and adaptation of energy policies. Theoretically, it engages with concepts of self-determination and governance, challenging traditional centralized models of energy control and advocating a bottom-up approach in energy decision-making processes. The transition towards energy self-sufficiency is intricately connected to technological progress in renewable energy and enhancements in energy efficiency (Kapsalis et al., 2024). These advancements enable individuals, communities, and local governments to produce and manage their energy resources, which enhances local resilience and reduces external dependencies. This shift is not merely technical; it also involves a societal transformation where energy consumers become energy producers actively participating in the energy economy and decision-making (Lennon & Dunphy, 2023).

Implementing energy autonomy elicits several challenges. The involvement of a wide range of parties, including individuals and huge organizations, necessitates intricate coordination and integration of diverse interests and capacities. Furthermore, maintaining a delicate equilibrium between local autonomy and national energy policy is crucial, as local initiatives must conform to broader national and international goals, such as mitigating climate change and ensuring economic stability (Schnidrig et al., 2024). Energy self-sufficiency must be implemented through systems that not only generate an adequate amount of energy but also effectively control its distribution and utilization. This requires advanced management systems that are capable of managing the unpredictability of renewable

40 Lefteris Topaloglou

energy sources, integrating them into current energy grids, and ensuring that energy production aligns with demand patterns (Aziz et al., 2023).

3.4 Just Transition governance through the lens of climate, energy, and environmental justice

The notion of Just Transition has evolved from its inception within trade unions in the 1980s to a holistic framework that integrates climate, energy, and environmental justice in mitigating the challenges associated with shifting towards a society that is not dependent on carbon-based energy resources. In addition to emphasizing the shift from fossil fuels, this approach aims to ensure that this transition promotes greater social equity and environmental health, mitigating any adverse effects on vulnerable communities. This raises critical concerns about job loss and the potential for economic decline, which the Just Transition framework seeks to mitigate by promoting the creation of green jobs. However, this change also presents a conflict, often framed as 'jobs versus environment', creating a critical area of focus for policy-makers to carefully navigate (Sokołowski & Heffron, 2022).

Just Transition is a new framework of analysis that brings together climate, energy, and environmental (CEE) justice scholarships. A fair transition now represents an equitable process aimed at achieving a sustainable, post-carbon world where no community is left behind. The objective is to mitigate the social consequences associated with transitioning away from fossil fuels, including employment displacement in conventional energy industries, while simultaneously fostering new prospects in the green economy. This framework addresses global justice issues, including ethnicity, income, and gender disparities, with the recognition that the burdens and benefits of environmental changes are not distributed equally across or within societies (Menton et al., 2020). To this end, Just Transition is not limited to any single nation; it is a global imperative requiring international cooperation and solidarity. Thus, international policies and support mechanisms are essential to ensuring that these communities can transition without undue hardship.

Climate justice, under the framework of the Just Transition paradigm, seeks to address the long-lasting impacts of climate change and guarantee equitable treatment for all individuals, particularly those who are the least to blame for climate change but experience the greatest harm from its repercussions (Newell et al., 2021; Sultana, 2022). This dimension stresses the importance of global responsibility and the ethical obligation to reduce greenhouse gas emissions while simultaneously supporting vulnerable communities. It calls for international cooperation to ensure that the transition strategies implemented do not exacerbate climate vulnerability in these regions but rather enhance their resilience to climate impacts. It aims to protect those least responsible for climate change, which are often marginalized communities in developing countries, ensuring they receive support to cope with environmental changes (Tenzing, 2020). Climate Justice centres on ensuring fair and just treatment for all individuals and their entitlement to protection from the harmful consequences of climate change. This includes efforts to reduce greenhouse gas emissions and prevent climate impacts (Porter et al., 2020).

Environmental justice aims to mitigate the disproportionate impact of industrial pollution by advocating policies and practices that both remediate existing environmental damage and prevent future harm as part of the shift away from fossil fuels (Figueroa, 2022; Salcido, 2021;). Environmental justice literature has predominantly focused explicitly on the restorative angle (Forsyth et al., 2021). In environmental justice literature, the concept of Just Transition has primarily focused on examining the successes and failures of using solely "green" (environmental concerns) and "brown" (employment and public health issues) frameworks to rally opposition against energy infrastructure projects (Méndez, 2020). The historical tension between preserving jobs and protecting the environment has often led to divisions between community groups and labour movements. Recognizing the Just Transition framework as a pivotal approach merges concerns for both the environment and job security, offering a potential solution to unify these divided interests (Wilgosh et al., 2022).

Energy justice has recently become a prominent interdisciplinary research theme, aiming to integrate principles of justice into various aspects of energy policy, production, consumption, activism, security, and the broader political economy, as well as within the contexts of the energy trilemma and climate change (Lacey-Barnacle et al., 2020; Jenkins et al., 2021; Yenneti, 2021). The energy justice aspect of Just Transition ensures that the shift to renewable energy sources is equitable and inclusive, addressing immediate and tangible issues related to energy production and consumption (Garvey et al., 2017). This includes ensuring equitable access to energy, particularly renewable sources, as well as addressing the distribution of energy benefits and burdens, including the affordability, accessibility, and sustainability of energy. Energy justice also involves engaging communities in the energy decision-making process, ensuring that the transition does not just replace one form of inequity with another. Therefore, energy transition should be human-centred and fair to future generations (Sovacool et al., 2017).

3.5 Linking CEE justice with the principles of distributional, recognition, and procedural justice

Connecting climate, environmental, and energy justice with the principles of distributional, recognition, and procedural justice in the context of self-sufficiency creates a comprehensive framework for a sustainable and equitable transition. Every component has a vital function in guaranteeing that the transition towards self-reliance not only tackles environmental and climate issues but also fosters justice and equality across diverse populations.

3.5.1 *Climate justice and Just Transition principles*

Distributional justice: Ensuring equitable distribution of both the benefits and burdens of climate mitigation efforts is essential. To foster self-sufficiency, legislation should facilitate fair and equal access to renewable energy technologies and resources, without unjustly disadvantaging any one group. For instance, subsidies or financial incentives for solar panels and wind turbines should be accessible to all socio-economic groups to prevent exacerbating existing inequalities (Caney, 2018).

Recognition justice: Climate justice emphasizes acknowledging the unique vulnerabilities and contributions of different communities, particularly indigenous peoples and marginalized groups who are often most affected by climate change. In striving for self-sufficiency, it is crucial to integrate local knowledge and practices that may contribute to sustainable living and climate resilience, recognizing and valuing these contributions in policy development and implementation (Schlosberg & Collins, 2014).

Procedural justice: It is crucial to engage communities in the decision-making processes that impact local climate circumstances. This means creating platforms for genuine engagement and ensuring that policies related to self-sufficiency and climate resilience are transparent and that they promote accountability (Holland, 2017).

3.5.2   *Environmental justice and Just Transition principles*

Distributional justice: Environmental justice seeks to prevent situations where environmental burdens are placed disproportionately upon disadvantaged communities. In the context of self-sufficiency, this involves careful planning to ensure that the infrastructure for renewable energy does not adversely impact underprivileged areas. Conversely, it should aim to enhance environmental quality in all communities, thereby improving overall health and well-being (Martin et al., 2020).

Recognition justice: Recognizing the cultural significance of land and natural resources is vital. Policies must uphold and safeguard regions of cultural, historical, and ecological significance, guaranteeing that endeavours towards environmental autonomy do not result in cultural displacement or deterioration (Massarella et al., 2020).

Procedural justice: It is imperative that all stakeholder groups, especially marginalized and indigenous populations, participate in environmental planning and policy-making. This ensures that endeavours to attain environmental self-sufficiency are meticulously designed and implemented, taking into account the distinct demands and conditions of the local region (Obaji, 2020).

3.5.3   *Energy justice and Just Transition principles*

Distributional justice: In achieving energy self-sufficiency, it is essential to ensure that new energy systems are accessible to all and not just to economically privileged groups. This includes affordable access to energy-efficient appliances and renewable energy sources as well as retrofitting services to lower energy costs and enhance sustainability across diverse communities (Myerson, 2024).

Just Transition governance 43

Recognition justice: Energy justice requires recognizing different energy needs and consumption patterns across various communities. This includes understanding how energy policies affect different socioeconomic groups and ensuring that the shift towards energy self-sufficiency does not perpetuate energy poverty or exclusion (Van Bommel & Höffken, 2021).

Procedural justice: Facilitating community involvement in energy planning and policy-making is critical. Incorporating a diverse array of community perspectives into the decision-making procedures concerning energy generation, distribution, and usage makes it feasible to customize energy systems to suit the particular requirements and capacities of local communities. Consequently, this encourages the implementation of more efficient and enduring energy solutions (Suboticki et al., 2023).

Incorporating these concepts of justice into the process of becoming self-reliant in the climatic, environmental, and energy sectors guarantees a well-rounded approach that tackles the technical elements of sustainability while also advocating fairness and safeguarding vulnerable communities. This holistic approach not only makes the transition more just but also more robust, increasing its likelihood of being supported by a broad cross-section of society.

3.6   Case studies on self-sufficiency in the energy sector

This section explores specific case studies across the globe, where local actors are leading the transition towards renewable energy, aiming for self-sufficiency by utilizing wind, solar, and bioenergy resources. Exploring regional transitions toward renewable energy through case studies provides insights into the practical challenges and successes of these initiatives. The effectiveness of these programs frequently arises from favourable policy frameworks, strong community involvement, and innovative collaborations between the public and commercial sectors. In most cases, local municipalities have been at the forefront of the transition towards renewable energy. Decentralizing energy supply systems has allowed these regions to retain a greater share of economic benefits locally, boosting regional economies and encouraging local innovation in energy technologies.

1 *The Ancien Régime village, France:* The historical evolution of energy self-sufficiency, as illustrated by the use of biomass in the Ancien Régime village or the early adoption of hydroelectric power, provides valuable lessons on the potential and limits of local self-sufficiency. These historical examples highlight that the level of self-sufficiency can fluctuate significantly with changes in technology and energy sources. Moreover, these examples emphasize the significance of contemporary systems possessing adaptability and resilience in order to efficiently adapt to changing energy landscapes. https://www.euronews.com/green/2023/02/03/this-french-village-enjoys-no-bills-after-building-wind-turbines-and-solar-panels

2 *The city of Amiens, France:* The city of Amiens' initiative to become an energy self-sufficient city by 2050 showcases a comprehensive and ambitious

approach to integrating renewable energy into urban planning. The creation of Energaia, a cluster dedicated to energy autonomy, exemplifies how collaboration between various stakeholders can drive substantial progress towards energy goals. The cluster method not only enables the sharing of resources and expertise but also guarantees that the projects are closely connected with the city's economic and social goals. https://www.nordfranceinvest.com/news/amiens-set-to-become-european-energy-storage-capital/

3 *Orkney Islands, Scotland:* The Orkney Islands have become a significant test site for renewable energy technologies, particularly wind and marine power. The archipelago generates more electricity than it needs from renewable sources, primarily wind turbines. Surplus energy is then used to produce hydrogen fuel, which powers ferries and other forms of transportation. This project not only supports local energy needs but also contributes to the broader goals of energy independence and emission reduction. https://www.orkney.com/life/energy/renewables

4 *Sonnen Community, Germany:* In the small village of Wildpoldsried, Sonnen GmbH has implemented a revolutionary concept where homes are equipped with solar panels and battery storage systems, creating a decentralized grid of energy producers and consumers. This community model allows for the sharing of surplus energy among residents, effectively reducing reliance on traditional power grids and fostering local energy autonomy. The approach highlights the potential for smart technology and community cooperation in achieving energy self-sufficiency. https://sonnengroup.com/sonnencommunity/

5 *Güssing, Austria:* Güssing, once a poor town near the Hungarian border, transformed its economy through renewable energy. By developing a biomass district heating system and later diversifying into other forms of renewable energy, Güssing became energy self-sufficient and stopped importing fossil fuels. The town now hosts numerous research facilities dedicated to sustainable energy technologies and has spurred significant economic growth through this green initiative. https://www.gussingrenewable.com/

6 *Samsø Island, Denmark:* Samsø Island is another exemplary case of a community transforming itself into a renewable energy hub. Through community engagement and strategic investments, the island now produces all of its electricity from wind turbines and has a significant portion of its heating supplied by solar power and biomass energy. Samsø has become a carbon-negative region by producing more renewable energy than it consumes, exporting the surplus. The success can be attributed mostly to the extensive involvement of the community and the implementation of a collaborative framework for energy management, wherein inhabitants have a vested interest in the renewable energy initiatives. https://www.visitsamsoe.dk/en/inspiration/energy-academy/

7 *Kodiak Island, Alaska, USA:* Kodiak Island has achieved nearly 100% renewable energy generation by harnessing wind and hydroelectric power. The region's approach includes the operation of large wind turbines and a

hydroelectric dam, supplemented by batteries for energy storage. This energy strategy has stabilized local electricity costs and reduced the environmental impact of diesel generators, previously a significant energy source for the island. https://www.ktoo.org/2017/09/15/kodiak-almost-100-percent-renewable -power-took-sci-fi-tech-get/

8 *Tokelau, New Zealand:* Tokelau became the first territory in the world to meet 100% of its electricity needs from solar power. By installing solar panels on every household and backing up power with battery storage, Tokelau eliminated its dependence on imported diesel fuel for electricity generation. This transition was crucial for the island group, reducing both its carbon footprint and its vulnerability to volatile fuel prices. https://www.tokelau.org.nz/Solar+ Project.html

9 *El Hierro, Canary Islands, Spain:* El Hierro, the smallest of the Canary Islands, aims to become the first island in the world to be entirely energy self-sufficient through renewables. The key component of El Hierro's energy system is the Gorona del Viento hydro-wind plant, which combines a wind farm with a hydroelectric pump storage system. The wind turbines generate electricity, and when production exceeds demand, the excess energy is used to pump water into a reservoir on a mountain. This setup covers around 60% of the island's energy needs, with the goal of reaching 100%. https://www. endesa.com/en/projects/all-projects/energy-transition/renewable-energies/ el-hierro-renewable-sustainability

10 *Jühnde, Germany:* Jühnde is a pioneering bioenergy village in Germany that produces all of its heating and electricity from organic waste and wood chips. The community employs a biogas plant that converts agricultural waste from nearby farms, and the surplus heat produced from generating electricity is utilized to warm homes via a local district heating network. This approach not only provides energy self-sufficiency but also significantly reduces the village's carbon footprint and enhances local agricultural practices. https:// www.100-percent.org/juehnde-germany/

11 *King Island, Tasmania, Australia:* King Island, near the coast of Tasmania, is notable for its Hybrid Renewable Energy System, which integrates wind, solar, and diesel generation with energy storage technologies. The system's objective is to diminish the island's dependence on costly and ecologically harmful diesel fuel. King Island often achieves periods of 100% renewable energy, and the project serves as a model for remote communities worldwide. https://www.hydro. com.au/clean-energy/hybrid-energy-solutions/success-stories/king-island

12 Tocco, Italy: The small Italian town of Tocco has invested in a combination of solar, wind, and biomass energy solutions to achieve energy independence. With government incentives, Tocco installed photovoltaic panels on residential and public buildings and developed a biomass facility that uses agricultural waste. These efforts not only meet the energy needs of the local government but also allow it to produce excess electricity for commercial transactions with the power network, leading to economic benefits for the community. http://

vneec.gov.vn/tin-tuc/energy-database/t9809/the-entire-town-of-tocco-italy-powered-by-green-energy.html

13 Feldheim, Germany: Feldheim is a unique example of a village that has achieved complete energy independence and is the first to be entirely self-sufficient in both electricity and heat in Germany. The village owns its energy grid and sources its power from wind, solar, and biogas plants. Residents of Feldheim enjoy significantly lower energy costs, and the model has attracted international attention as a leading example of sustainable development. https://www.euronews.com/2022/09/30/energy-the-self-sufficient-german-town-that-gives-back-to-the-grid

3.6.1 Climate justice and Just Transition principles

3.6.1.1 Distributional Justice

- *Orkney Islands, Scotland:* Uses surplus wind and marine energy to support local needs and broader energy independence, distributing the benefits of renewable energy locally and reducing emissions.
- *El Hierro, Canary Islands, Spain:* Focuses on 100% renewable energy through a hydro-wind plant, aiming to balance energy production and consumption sustainably across the community.

3.6.1.2 Recognition Justice

- *Samsø Island, Denmark:* Recognizes community inputs in renewable energy projects, enabling them to become stakeholders in energy transformation and management.
- *Kodiak Island, Alaska, USA:* Tailors energy solutions to local conditions, using wind and hydro power adapted to local geographic and climatic conditions.

3.6.1.3 Procedural Justice

- *Tokelau, New Zealand:* Engaged the entire community in the shift to solar power, ensuring community involvement in planning and implementation to meet their energy needs fully from solar power.

3.6.2 Environmental justice and Just Transition principles

3.6.2.1 Distributional Justice

- *Güssing, Austria:* Transformed from a poor town to a prosperous community by developing local renewable energy resources, significantly reducing environmental impact, and fostering economic growth.
- *Jühnde, Germany:* Utilizes local agricultural waste for energy, turning a potential environmental burden into a community resource.

3.6.2.2   Recognition Justice

- *Tocco, Italy:* Developed a multifaceted approach using wind, solar, and biomass resources, recognizing the diverse potential of local renewable resources to meet energy needs.

3.6.2.3   Procedural justice

- *Feldheim, Germany:* Achieved complete energy independence by involving the community in the ownership and operation of local energy resources, fostering a collaborative approach to energy management.

3.6.3   Energy justice and Just Transition principles

3.6.3.1   Distributional justice

- *Sonnen Community, Germany:* Promotes local energy production and consumption, allowing residents to share surplus energy, which reduces reliance on external energy sources and enhances local energy autonomy.
- *King Island, Tasmania, Australia:* Integrates various renewable technologies to reduce reliance on diesel, distributing energy production capabilities across the community.

3.6.3.2   Recognition justice

- *The city of Amiens, France:* The Energaia project aims to multiply renewable energy production by recognizing the city's capacity for and commitment to sustainability, aligning it with economic and social objectives.

3.6.3.3   Procedural Justice

- *The Ancien Régime village, France:* Historical lessons from biomass use and hydroelectric power highlight the need for adaptable energy systems that involve community insights and adaptations to changing technological landscapes.

By examining and classifying these case studies through the lenses of different types of justice, we see that sustainability is not just about environmental and energy outcomes but also about how these outcomes are achieved – ensuring fairness, equity, and inclusivity in both benefits and responsibilities. These case studies collectively underline the importance of integrating justice into sustainability initiatives. Each community's approach to incorporating various forms of justice not only enhances the effectiveness of environmental and energy projects but also ensures greater community support and resilience. Each example provides unique insights into how different regions can leverage their local resources and socio-economic structures to create sustainable and resilient energy systems. In addition

48 *Lefteris Topaloglou*

to supporting local energy objectives, these projects also contribute to global endeavours in addressing climate change and fostering sustainable development.

3.7   Discussion

Attaining self-sufficiency through renewable energy requires more than simply adopting technology; it requires a profound shift in humans' comprehension of and involvement with energy systems. Regions can reduce their reliance on fossil fuels and centralized energy systems by directing resources towards local energy production infrastructure, encompassing solar panels, wind turbines, and bioenergy facilities. This transition not only helps mitigate environmental impacts but also stimulates local economies by creating jobs and fostering new industries in renewable energy sectors.

Incorporating self-sufficiency principles into regional development strategies for a Just Transition governance model can yield several benefits. Firstly, it can help regions respond effectively to crises during challenging times, acting as a buffer to provide resilience to local communities and farms. Moreover, embracing self-sufficiency principles can preserve traditional livelihood strategies and promote food sovereignty, which is essential for sustainable local systems. By intertwining self-sufficiency with regional development policies, regions can enhance their ability to navigate transitions away from industries like coal or oil and gas towards more sustainable practices, ensuring economic stability and community well-being in the face of change.

Added value in a social-ecological renewable energy (RE) self-sufficiency scenario is organized in partnership. Hence, it is beneficial for all stakeholders to engage in the endeavour over a prolonged duration. In the spirit of a good partnership, the involved actors exchange ideas, reveal their own interests, synchronize their activities, and fairly distribute the costs and benefits across the value chain. Similar and contrasting viewpoints are communicated and made transparent. The cooperating businesses wish to stay independent in the long-term, which means that they have to be economically profitable. Fair competition takes place between the various value chains, thus promoting an economical supply of energy at regional market prices. The actors participating in the value chain are also cognizant of their obligation to the community.

An important argument for self-sufficiency with renewable energies is that a large part of the added value is generated locally, thereby benefitting the region. However, important information about the added value is often missing. Which value is being alluded to? Which individuals or groups have achieved success and which ones have experienced failure or disadvantage? How can monetary values be quantified? In addition, data for determining the monetary added value are not readily available. Sensitive company data or private information about actors is often difficult to access. Moreover, attaining self-sufficiency in renewable energy requires that different actors work together in value chains in order to guarantee the local RE supply. This cooperation can lead to conflicts when differing interests and values exist and activities are not well coordinated.

Achieving RE self-sufficiency and ensuring justice involves addressing a multitude of interconnected drivers and parameters across social, economic, technical,

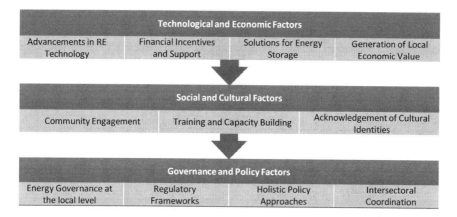

Figure 3.1 Critical drivers and parameters that enhance renewable energy self-sufficiency and justice.

Source: Own Elaboration.

and ecological domains. Figure 3.1 shows some critical drivers and parameters that can enhance both renewable energy self-sufficiency and ensure justice.

3.7.1   Technological and economic factors

Advances in solar, wind, biomass, and hydroelectric technologies are fundamental to increasing the capacity and efficiency of renewable energy systems. This improves the practicality of attaining self-sufficiency by increasing the cost-efficiency of renewable sources. Government subsidies, tax incentives, and grants can effectively stimulate investment and facilitate expansion in the renewable energy sector. Financial support helps overcome the initial high capital costs associated with renewable energy installations, making these projects more accessible and economically viable. The establishment of reliable and continuous energy provision is pivotal to achieving self-sufficiency. Encouraging local production and consumption of energy fosters economic resilience. By focusing on local job creation and skill development, regions can retain more economic benefits, supporting a more equitable distribution of resources.

3.7.2   Social and cultural factors

Active involvement of local communities in planning and decision-making processes ensures that the energy projects are aligned with local needs and values, promoting procedural justice. Through the dissemination of knowledge about the benefits of renewable energy and the provision of training to community members in managing and maintaining energy systems, local individuals are empowered, hence fostering long-term sustainability. Recognizing and integrating cultural values and practices in the development of energy projects ensures that these initiatives are respectful and inclusive of local traditions and lifestyles, which enhances recognition justice.

3.7.3 Governance and policy factors

Local control over energy policies and projects can lead to more responsive and tailored approaches to energy management, which is critical for both self-sufficiency and procedural justice. Strong legal frameworks that support renewable energy adoption and ensure fair practices are essential to promoting renewable energy and protecting community interests. Policies that consider and integrate energy, environmental, and social goals can help manage the trade-offs between these areas, ensuring a Just Transition that is equitable and sustainable. Coordination between different sectors (energy, environment, economy) and levels of government (local, regional, national) is necessary to effectively aligning goals and pool resources, thereby enhancing the overall impact and justice of energy transitions.

Enhancing renewable energy self-sufficiency while ensuring justice requires that policy recommendations focus on creating supportive frameworks that address both technological and social dimensions. These policies should prioritize the advancement of renewable energy, ensuring equal and fair access to energy resources and the fair distribution of the benefits of the transition. Figure 3.2 demonstrates some tailored policy recommendations.

Figure 3.2 Policy recommendations that can enhance renewable energy self-sufficiency and justice.

Source: Own Elaboration.

The policy recommendations outlined provide a comprehensive approach to fostering renewable energy self-sufficiency that aligns with broader economic, social, and environmental goals. Implementing financial incentives and subsidies such as tax credits, grants, and subsidies for both residential and commercial renewable energy installations can help to reduce the financial barriers to entry. Offer attractive and affordable financing alternatives for renewable energy initiatives to encourage investments, encompassing both small-scale and large-scale endeavours. Establish clear mandatory regulatory support for renewable energy targets for utilities to ensure a steady increase in the share of renewables in the energy mix. Enact feed-in tariffs to provide long-term contracts and pricing assurances to renewable energy producers, making projects more financially viable. Promoting decentralization and local empowerment can support the development of community-owned renewable energy projects, which in turn keep economic benefits within local areas and increase local acceptance and participation. Empower local governments by delegating authority and providing the necessary resources to plan and implement local energy solutions.

Investing in comprehensive education and capacity building raises public awareness about the benefits of renewable energy and training individuals in renewable energy management and maintenance. Facilitate knowledge exchange and skills development by establishing collaborations among governments, educational institutions, and industry. Deploying innovative technology and research reduces costs and improves efficiency and reliability. Support pilot projects and test beds for new technologies to assess their feasibility and effectiveness before implementing them on a wide scale. Enhancing grid infrastructure and integration handles a higher proportion of renewable energy sources and ensures a reliable, uninterrupted power supply. Deploy intelligent grid technologies to optimize energy efficiency and facilitate seamless integration of decentralized energy resources. Developing policies that ensure equitable access for vulnerable communities helps address energy poverty explicitly through targeted programs that help low-income households access clean energy technologies.

Creating guidelines for sustainable land use and environmental policies can minimize ecological disruption and honour land rights, particularly in indigenous and rural areas. Perform environmental impact evaluations to guarantee that renewable energy projects do not have negative effects on nearby ecosystems or communities. Fostering public participation and transparency in energy planning and policy-making allows community input and feedback on renewable energy projects. Ensure transparency in how energy projects are chosen, developed, and managed to build trust and support among local communities. Encouraging cross-sectoral coordination between the energy sector and other critical sectors can create integrated solutions that maximize social and environmental benefits. Align renewable energy policies with broader economic and industrial policies to ensure coherent and supportive frameworks.

3.8   Conclusions

The investigation into novel governance models that facilitate a Just Transition by integrating self-sufficiency into regional development strategies has underscored the profound potential for enhancing social equity, environmental stewardship, and economic resilience. This chapter has illustrated that self-sufficiency does not merely pertain to achieving autonomy in energy production but also involves comprehensive community empowerment and sustainable resource management.

Efficient governance models rely on actively engaging local populations in decision-making processes. This participation guarantees that transitions are comprehensive and at the same time customized to address local needs and conditions, hence increasing the probability of effective implementation and acceptance of sustainable practices. To attain self-sufficiency in renewable energy systems, it is essential to adopt a comprehensive approach that considers the social, ecological, economic, and technical aspects. This method facilitates a thorough understanding of the intricate difficulties and opportunities that result from the implementation of new technologies and the alteration of energy systems.

Various global case studies have demonstrated successful implementations of self-sufficiency principles, revealing that localized energy solutions can significantly enhance community resilience and reduce dependence on unsustainable energy sources. These instances offer insightful lessons regarding the possibilities and constraints of local self-sufficiency. The research has identified various obstacles to implementing Just Transition governance models, such as technological constraints, budgetary limitations, and socio-political impediments. Strategic solutions and policy proposals are suggested to overcome these challenges, with an emphasis on the necessity of providing supportive frameworks that facilitate fair access to resources and encourage sustainable growth.

This research emphasizes the significance of establishing policy conditions that encourage the shift towards self-sufficiency. Policies need to be flexible to adapt to local contexts and robust enough to guide and sustain long-term transitions. This contribution attempted to enhance the discussion on sustainable development and governance by providing vital insights into the efficient management of the intricate interplay of economic, environmental, and social issues in the present time. By fostering local autonomy while ensuring alignment with broader global objectives, the proposed governance models hold the promise of advancing a more resilient, adaptive, and equitable transition.

Acknowledgement

This research has been carried out within the framework of the National Recovery and Resilience Plan Greece 2.0, funded by the European Union – Next Generation EU (Project Number H.F.R.I.: 16592).

References

Adewumi, A., Olu-lawal, K. A., Okoli, C. E., Usman, F. O., & Usiagu, G. S. (2024). Sustainable energy solutions and climate change: A policy review of emerging trends and global responses. *World Journal of Advanced Research and Reviews,* 21(2), 408–420.

Aziz, S., Ahmed, I., Khan, K., & Khalid, M. (2023). Emerging trends and approaches for designing net-zero low-carbon integrated energy networks: A review of current practices. *Arabian Journal for Science and Engineering,* 49(2024), 6163–6185.

Barone, S. (2018). Building a narrative on environmental policy success. Reflections from a watershed management experience. *Critical Policy Studies,* 12(2), 135–148.

Boutaud, B. (2022). *Energy Autonomy: From the Notion to the Concepts.* John Wiley & Sons.

Burke, M. J., & Stephens, J. C. (2018). Political power and renewable energy futures: A critical review. *Energy Research & Social science,* 35, 78–93.

Caney, S. (2018). *Distributive Justice and Climate Change.* Oxford University Press, New York.

Castán Broto, V., & Westman, L. (2017). Just sustainabilities and local action: Evidence from 400 flagship initiatives. *Local Environment,* 22(5), 635–650.

Cowell, R., Ellis, G., Sherry-Brennan, F., Strachan, P. A., & Toke, D. (2017). Energy transitions, sub-national government and regime flexibility: How has devolution in the United Kingdom affected renewable energy development?. *Energy Research & Social Science, 23, 169–181.*

Dall-Orsoletta, A., Cunha, J., Araujo, M., & Ferreira, P. (2022). A systematic review of social innovation and community energy transitions. *Energy Research & Social Science,* 88, 102625.

Dorsch, M. J., & Flachsland, C. (2017). A polycentric approach to global climate governance. *Global Environmental Politics,* 17(2), 45–64.

Dou, Y., Zagaria, C., O'Connor, L., Thuiller, W., & Verburg, P. H. (2023). Using the nature futures framework as a lens for developing plural land use scenarios for Europe for 2050. *Global Environmental Change,* 83, 102766.

Figueroa, R. M. (2022). Environmental justice. In *The Routledge Companion to Environmental Ethics* (pp. 767–782). Routledge.

Forsyth, M., Cleland, D., Tepper, F., Hollingworth, D., Soares, M., Nairn, A., & Wilkinson, C. (2021). A future agenda for environmental restorative justice?. *International Journal of Restorative Justice,* 4(1), 2589–0891.

Garvey, A., Norman, J. B., Büchs, M., & Barrett, J. (2022). A "spatially just" transition? A critical review of regional equity in decarbonisation pathways. *Energy Research & Social Science,* 88, 102630.

Goel, R. K., Mazhar, U., Nelson, M. A., & Ram, R. (2017). Different forms of decentralization and their impact on government performance: Micro-level evidence from 113 countries. *Economic Modelling,* 62, 171–183.

González-García, A., Díaz-Pastor, S. J., & Moreno-Romero, A. (2023). A comprehensive approach to the governance of universal access to sustainable energy. *Sustainability,* 15(22), 15813.

Gui, E. M., & MacGill, I. (2018). Typology of future clean energy communities: An exploratory structure, opportunities, and challenges. *Energy Research & Social Science,* 35, 94–107.

Hassan, Q., Nassar, A. K., Al-Jiboory, A. K., Viktor, P., Telba, A. A., Awwad, E. M.,... & Barakat, M. (2024). Mapping Europe renewable energy landscape: Insights into solar, wind, hydro, and green hydrogen production. *Technology in Society,* 77, 102535.

Heldeweg, M. A., & Saintier, S. (2020). Renewable energy communities as 'socio-legal institutions': A normative frame for energy decentralization?. *Renewable and Sustainable Energy Reviews,* 119, 109518.

Holland, B. (2017). Procedural justice in local climate adaptation: Political capabilities and transformational change. *Environmental Politics,* 26(3), 391–412.

Imasiku, K., Thomas, V., & Ntagwirumugara, E. (2019). Unraveling green information technology systems as a global greenhouse gas emission game-changer. *Administrative Sciences,* 9(2), 43.

Jenkins, K. E., Sovacool, B. K., Mouter, N., Hacking, N., Burns, M. K., & McCauley, D. (2021). The methodologies, geographies, and technologies of energy justice: a systematic and comprehensive review. *Environmental Research Letters*, 16(4), 043009.

Kapsalis, V., Maduta, C., Skandalos, N., Bhuvad, S. S., D'Agostino, D., Yang, R. J.,... & Karamanis, D. (2024). Bottom-up energy transition through rooftop PV upscaling: remaining issues and emerging upgrades towards NZEBs at different climatic conditions. *Renewable and Sustainable Energy Transition, 5*, 100083.

Lacey-Barnacle, M., Robison, R., & Foulds, C. (2020). Energy justice in the developing world: A review of theoretical frameworks, key research themes and policy implications. *Energy for Sustainable Development, 55*, 122–138.

Lennon, B., & Dunphy, N. P.(2023). Energy and citizenship in a time of transition and socio-technical change. In *The Palgrave Handbook of Global Social Change* (pp. 1–15). Springer International Publishing.

Losada-Puente, L., Blanco, J. A., Dumitru, A., Sebos, I., Tsakanikas, A., Liosi, I.,... & Rodríguez, F. (2023). Cross-case analysis of the energy communities in Spain, Italy, and Greece: progress, barriers, and the road ahead. *Sustainability*, 15(18), 14016.

Martin, A., Armijos, M. T., Coolsaet, B., Dawson, N., AS Edwards, G., Few, R.,... & White, C. S. (2020). Environmental justice and transformations to sustainability. *Environment: Science and Policy for Sustainable Development*, 62(6), 19–30.

Massarella, K., Sallu, S. M., & Ensor, J. E. (2020). Reproducing injustice: Why recognition matters in conservation project evaluation. *Global Environmental Change, 65*, 102181.

Méndez, M. (2020). *Climate Change from the Streets: How Conflict and Collaboration Strengthen the Environmental Justice Movement.* Yale University Press.

Menton, M., Larrea, C., Latorre, S., Martinez-Alier, J., Peck, M., Temper, L., & Walter, M. (2020). Environmental justice and the SDGs: From synergies to gaps and contradictions. *Sustainability Science, 15*, 1621–1636.

Myerson, A. (2024). *How Much is Enough?: Redistributive Power for a Just Energy Transition* (Master's thesis), Utrecht University, Utrecht.

Newell, P., Srivastava, S., Naess, L. O., Torres Contreras, G. A., & Price, R. (2021). Toward transformative climate justice: An emerging research agenda. *Wiley Interdisciplinary Reviews: Climate Change*, 12(6), e733.

Obaji, S. (2020). *Evaluating environmental justice in Nigeria: Procedural justice in the environmental impact assessment process,* Doctoral dissertation, University of Birmingham.

Pantazatou, K. (2018). 'No taxation without representation' or 'No representation without taxation'? In search of democratic legitimacy for taxation in the post-crisis EU. *KritV, CritQ, RCrit,* 101(3), 236–263.

Porter, L., Rickards, L., Verlie, B., Bosomworth, K., Moloney, S., Lay, B.,... & Pellow, D. (2020). Climate justice in a climate changed world. *Planning Theory & Practice,* 21(2), 293–321.

Salcido, R. E. (2021). Retooling environmental justice. *UCLA Journal of Environmental and Policy*, 39, 1.

Schlosberg, D., & Collins, L. B. (2014). From environmental to climate justice: Climate change and the discourse of environmental justice. *Wiley Interdisciplinary Reviews: Climate Change*, 5(3), 359–374.

Schnidrig, J., Chuat, A., Terrier, C., Maréchal, F., & Margni, M. (2024). Power to the people: On the role of districts in decentralized energy systems. *Energies,* 17(7), 1718.

Shah, A. (2004). *Fiscal Decentralization in Developing and Transition Economies: Progress, Problems, and the Promise* (Vol. 3282). World Bank Publications.

Shah, A. (2017). Fostering fiscally responsive and accountable governance: Lessons from decentralization. In *Evaluation and Development* (pp. 81–107). Routledge.

Shi, L., & Moser, S. (2021). Transformative climate adaptation in the United States: Trends and prospects. *Science,* 372(6549), eabc8054.

Söderholm, P. (2020). The green economy transition: The challenges of technological change for sustainability. *Sustainable Earth*, 3(1), 6.

Sokołowski, M. M., & Heffron, R. J. (2022). Defining and conceptualising energy policy failure: The when, where, why, and how. *Energy Policy,* 161, 112745.

Sovacool, B. K., Burke, M., Baker, L., Kotikalapudi, C. K., & Wlokas, H. (2017). New frontiers and conceptual frameworks for energy justice. *Energy Policy*, 105, 677–691.

Suboticki, I., Heidenreich, S., Ryghaug, M., & Skjølsvold, T. M. (2023). Fostering justice through engagement: A literature review of public engagement in energy transitions. *Energy Research & Social Science*, 99, 103053.

Sultana, F. (2022). Critical climate justice. *The Geographical Journal*, 188(1), 118–124.

Tenzing, J. D. (2020). Integrating social protection and climate change adaptation: A review. *Wiley Interdisciplinary Reviews: Climate Change,* 11(2), e626.

Tolonen, E., Shakeel, S. R., & Juntunen, J. K. (2023). Promoting Just Transition or enhancing inequalities? Reflection on different energy community business models in terms of energy justice. In *Trading in Local Energy Markets and Energy Communities: Concepts, Structures and Technologies* (pp. 151–180). Springer International Publishing.

Topaloglou, L., & Ioannidis, L. (2022). From transition management towards Just Transition and place-based governance. The case of Western Macedonia in Greece. *Journal of Entrepreneurship, Management, and Innovation*, 18(3): 37–74. https://doi.org/10.7341/20221832

Van Bommel, N., & Höffken, J. I. (2021). Energy justice within, between and beyond European community energy initiatives: A review. *Energy Research & Social Science*, 79, 102157.

Wang, X., & Lo, K. (2021). Just Transition: A conceptual review. *Energy Research & Social Science*, 82, 102291.

Wilgosh, B., Sorman, A. H., & Barcena, I. (2022). When two movements collide: Learning from labour and environmental struggles for future Just Transitions. *Futures*, 137, 102903.

Yenneti, K. (2021). The trilemma of energy justice. In *Environment and Sustainable Development* (pp. 50–64). Routledge.

Young, J., & Brans, M. (2017). Analysis of factors affecting a shift in a local energy system towards 100% renewable energy community. *Journal of Cleaner Production*, 169, 117–124.

Part II

Urban planning for self-sufficient cities

4 Intra-city renewable energy production

Karna Dahal

4.1 Introduction

Cities are the economic backbone of a nation and much of the global economic activities occur in the cities. The global cities population has been steadily increasing over the past few decades. According to the United Nations (UN), the world's cities population is projected to continue growing, reaching 68% of the global population by 2050, up from 56% in 2021 (UN-Habitat, 2022). This indicates a substantial ongoing urbanization trend globally. The increase in population and economic activities drives an increase in energy consumption and thus energy-intensive emissions are high at the city level. According to the Intergovernmental Panel on Climate Change (IPCC), global cities contribute 71%–76% of total energy-related carbon dioxide (CO_2) emissions (IRENA, 2020c). This suggests that cities are the high-impact areas for reducing carbon emissions and deciding whether the current climate battle is won or lost (REN21, 2021). It is crucial to understand the present energy transition landscape along with social, regulatory, and economic aspects of energy production, supply, and consumption to contribute to carbon neutrality at city level (Dahal et al., 2018).

Cities are both energy producers and consumers, as their governments, populations, and commercial and industrial organizations account for over three-quarters of total global energy use (REN21, 2021). These are also essential authorities for accelerating the deployment of renewable energy resources in local levels. Therefore, the role of cities for reducing global carbon emissions and transforming cities' energy systems is vital. Cities' well-defined climate and energy policies can greatly affect the reduction of carbon emissions produced within their territories (Dahal et al., 2018). The decisions taken today to build low-carbon or carbon-neutral energy systems for cities will determine not only the self-sufficiency of cities but also the sustainability of our society as a whole in the future.

The city governments are becoming increasingly aware of the potential contribution of renewable energy to the creation of equitable, liveable, and ecologically sustainable communities (REN21, 2021). Numerous cities around the world have taken actions to boost the uptake of renewable energy in various sectors in their territories. These cities have installed, purchased, and contracted for renewable energy to meet the needs of their own buildings and fleets of vehicles. They have

DOI: 10.4324/9781003498216-7

60 *Karna Dahal*

also supported community energy initiatives and set renewable energy goals and policies to promote the production and use of renewable energy locally (REN21, 2021). However, the ability of cities to scale up renewables is largely determined by the availability of renewable energy resources, financial possessions, market dynamics, the extent of their economic reliance on fossil fuels, and decarbonization and carbon-neutral goals and policies enacted by national governments (Dahal et al., 2018; REN21, 2021). In addition, global-level policies such as EU energy policies (e.g., RePower), United Nation Sustainable Development Goals (e.g., Goal 7.2) also impact on their renewable energy goal settings and policy formation (IRENA, 2020c).

4.2   Energy infrastructures of cities

City areas generally possess more advanced energy infrastructures compared to remote regions. Similar to conventional energy supply systems, energy systems in cities operate by utilizing distribution networks and energy management systems to deliver a diverse range of services to fulfil the energy demands of consumers (IRENA, 2020c). The cities' energy systems possess distinctive characteristics due to several factors, including the high levels of economic and social activity, continuous innovations in technologies and business strategies, and the visible environmental effects within city areas. The infrastructures of the cities behave as sociotechnical interface that are directly linked to its own residents. For instance, emerging technologies such as rooftop solar PV systems with battery storage, net metering, smart energy management, highly efficient appliances, Internet of Things (IoTs), artificial intelligence fuelled by big data, and blockchain technology that change the relationship between the producers and consumers of energy systems (IRENA, 2019a, 2020c). For that reason, consumer behaviour holds greater significance beyond merely the functioning of the energy system itself.

The increasing decentralization of electricity generation facilitated by renewable energy sources and digital innovations is fundamentally altering the interplay between the physical energy infrastructure, conventionally managed by utilities, and energy end-users (IRENA, 2020c). In addition, the emergence of new technological solutions and operational practices together with innovative business models and regulatory frameworks for distribution grids has effectively connected the city and national-level energy systems on both technical and institutional fronts (IEA, 2023; IRENA, 2020c). Using sector coupling technologies such as heat pumps, smart charging for electric cars, and different energy storage systems has made it much easier to add renewable energy sources (e.g., solar panels and wind turbines) to the power grid (IRENA, 2019a, 2020c). In the field of heat provision, the shift to renewable energy sources has been slower compared to the power sector. Nevertheless, there have been limited but notable instances of substitution such as the deployment of solar thermal collectors and ground-source geothermal energy instead of conventional natural gas-based heating methods (IRENA, 2020c; Lund & Toth, 2020).

Intra-city renewable energy production 61

In cities, people generally use energy provided by companies through a centralized system but with prosumers, who both use and produce energy, as with solar energy production in building, it will change energy management and regulatory obligations (Brown et al., 2020). This can also challenge how energy companies work and require new infrastructure and rules for everyone to be treated fairly in the future (Brown et al., 2020). In addition, the emergence of a virtual power plant, which collects several distributed energy resources into a single entity to engage and trade in power or service markets, can also change user practices and market niches (IRENA, 2019a).

City energy infrastructures are inherently interconnected with the national energy grid, and it is economically impractical for cities to operate autonomously from this larger system. Nevertheless, cities possess significant authority in energy governance, particularly in the context of addressing global climate challenges and realizing local environmental improvements and societal well-being enhancements. Over the past decades, an increasing number of cities have become autonomous in their energy systems, notably by advocating for increased adoption of renewable energy sources (IRENA, 2020c). This is a key pre-condition for attaining intra-city self-sufficiency in energy consumption.

4.3   The role of cities' renewables in global energy transition

Due to the widespread adoption of renewable energy sources, the global energy landscape is undergoing a profound transformative shift. This shift is fuelled by substantial cost reductions in renewable energy technologies such as solar photovoltaic (PV) and onshore wind power, which have become increasingly competitive with traditional energy sources in recent years (IEA, 2023). Solar PV costs have witnessed a remarkable (~80%) decrease over the past decade and similar trends are observed in battery storage technologies. The costs for both are expected to undergo a further (~60%) reduction in the coming years (IRENA, 2020b). These cost dynamics play a pivotal role in making renewable energy more competitive with conventional fuels and thus fostering its increased adoption in cities' energy systems. In addition, other factors for this transition include the digitalization of the power sector, the rise of decentralized energy resources, and the electrification of various sectors currently reliant on fossil fuels (IRENA, 2020c). Innovation in decentralized power generation technologies further propels this change, facilitating the scalability of renewable-based decentralization (Brown et al., 2020; IRENA, 2020c).

Cities, being major energy consumers and contributors to carbon emissions, play a crucial role in global energy transition (Dahal et al., 2018). The emergence of innovative renewable energy technologies enables the development of decentralized energy systems within city areas, offering effective solutions for self-sufficiency for energy and long-term sustainability of cities. The integration of renewable energy at the local level not only reduces carbon footprints but also generates significant economic benefits for cities (IRENA, 2020c). This transition offers cities a powerful tool to curb their energy-related CO_2 emissions from

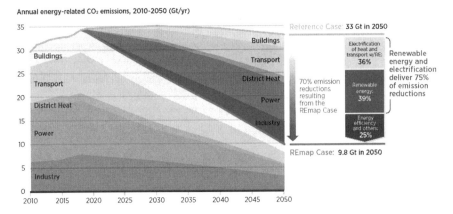

Figure 4.1 Global reduction of energy-related carbon emissions until 2050: Current plans vs. energy transformation.

buildings, transportation, and industrial sectors. Furthermore, embracing local renewable energy development holds the promise of boosting cities' GDP and employment rates, marking a significant economic opportunity alongside environmental benefit (IEA, 2023). It is projected to elevate global GDP by 2.4% in 2050 and create 42 million jobs worldwide in the renewables sector, reshaping cities' energy and fostering sustainable growth (IRENA, 2020c).

Despite several progresses made, the contribution of renewable energy to cities' energy needs remains relatively small. However, by focusing on deeper integration and electrification, renewable energy shows potential in drastically reducing carbon emissions and transitioning to carbon neutrality (Figure 4.1). Achieving a sustainable city future requires a comprehensive approach to strategic deployment of renewable energy. Recognizing the potential for renewables to achieve substantial cuts in energy-related emissions across all sectors is crucial for realizing ambitious climate goals of the cities. Despite renewables currently constituting only 20% of cities' energy use, there's vast potential for deeper integration, particularly in sectors such as buildings, transportation, and industry (IRENA, 2020c). By leveraging locally available renewable sources and integrating them into small-scale decentralized power systems, cities can accelerate their transition towards sustainable, low-carbon city environments. This can also play a key role in global efforts to limit temperature rise.

4.4 Renewable energy technologies used in cities

Various renewable energy technologies are harnessed to meet the energy demands of city dwellers while reducing carbon emissions and mitigating climate impact. The sources of renewable energy typically used or produced within the city administrative boundary are wind, solar thermal, solar photovoltaic, geothermal heat

Intra-city renewable energy production 63

pumps, ocean energy (e.g., tide, and wave energy), hydropower, biomass, landfill gas, sewage treatment plant gas, and biogas (IRENA, 2020c). Notably, solar thermal and solar photovoltaic technologies currently dominate the renewable energy landscape within cities, reflecting their widespread adoption and effectiveness in meeting cities' energy needs (Ulpiani et al., 2023). As cities continue to prioritize sustainability and resilience, these renewable energy technologies play a pivotal role in shaping the future of cities' energy systems and meeting their carbon-neutral and climate goals.

4.4.1 Solar photovoltaics (PVs)

The city landscape offers a plethora of opportunities for harnessing solar energy, predominantly through photovoltaic (PV) systems integrated within buildings and their surroundings. The increase of solar PV technology in cities has been remarkable. The global installed capacity of solar PV technology has skyrocketed from 23 GW in 2009 to an incredible amount of 1.2 TW by 2022 (IEA PVPS, 2023). Within city areas, solar PV systems are installed on rooftops and building façades, offering a decentralized approach to energy generation. These systems are smaller in scale compared to ground-mounted installations. They are often installed closer to energy demand centres, which reduces transmission losses and improves system resilience (IRENA, 2019a). Despite such benefits, challenges persist, particularly concerning land constraints and integration issues in cities. Yet, innovative solutions such as aggregated PV plants coupled with battery storage are emerging to address such challenges and optimize solar energy utilization in cities (Lü et al., 2023).

4.4.2 Building-integrated PV (BIPV)

Building-integrated PV (BIPV) represents a promising frontier in solar energy production in cities, which connects lines between infrastructure and renewable energy generation. BIPV encompasses various products, including façade-integrated systems and roof-integrated solutions such as solar shingles and tiles. These innovations not only generate electricity but also contribute to the structural integrity of buildings, offering aesthetic appeal and ease of installation (Shi & Zhu, 2023). While BIPV holds immense potential for city environments, challenges related to cost and technological maturity persist. Despite a significant decline in costs over the years, BIPV remains more expensive than conventional PV systems which alerts the need for further research and market incentives for widespread adoption (Shi & Zhu, 2023).

4.4.3 Solar thermal technologies

Solar thermal energy is a promising solution for meeting the heating and cooling demands of city areas. While concentrated solar power (CSP) technologies excel in large-scale electricity generation, their applicability within city environment is restricted due to the lack of extensive land areas and optimal solar irradiance (Tripanagnostopoulos et al., 2021). However, non-concentrated solar thermal systems offer a practical alternative, particularly for supplying heat to city buildings and industrial processes. These systems, including flat plate collectors, evacuated tube collectors, and low concentrating collectors efficiently convert solar radiation into heat, achieving up to 80% efficiency (Omeiza et al., 2023). Installed on rooftops, façades, or other building exteriors, solar thermal collectors not only provide renewable heat but also contribute to building insulation and reduce heating and cooling demands (Omeiza et al., 2023).

Solar thermal technologies are applied remarkably in solar water heating systems and district heating network. They can offer substantial energy savings for residential and commercial buildings (Laveet et al., 2022). Currently, China is leading the market in installed capacity of solar water heating systems which is proving instrumental in reducing reliance on fossil fuels and curbing greenhouse gas emissions (Laveet et al., 2022). Furthermore, the integration of solar thermal collectors into district heating systems represents a pivotal advancement in city's energy infrastructure. By leveraging solar district heating, cities can achieve stable, emission-free heat supply, while simultaneously reducing dependence on finite resources and mitigating climate change (Reda et al., 2021). As the demand for sustainable heating and cooling solutions continues to grow, solar thermal energy stands poised to play a central role in shaping the energy landscape of the cities (IRENA, 2020c).

4.4.4   PV-thermal (PV-T) hybrid systems

Innovations in PV-thermal (PV-T) hybrid systems not only combine solar electricity and heat generation but also provide improved energy conversion efficiencies. Such hybrid systems help maximizing solar energy utilization in city environments. These advancements also optimize land utilization while facilitating sustainable energy production. These hybrid systems leverage advanced technologies such as air heaters, nanoparticles, and transparent insulating fronts to optimize both electrical and thermal output (Bae et al., 2024). PV-T systems are still in the early stages of development and are facing challenges related to high investment costs and knowledge gaps (Herrando & Ramos, 2022). As solar manufacturing grows and technology advances, PV-T hybrids emerge as a promising solution for local renewable energy production within cities, aiding the transition to carbon neutrality and fostering sustainable city development.

4.4.5   Bioenergy and waste-to-energy technologies

Bioenergy and waste-to-energy (WtE) technologies represent a multifaceted solution for cities to manage waste sustainably and generate energy. The utilization of local biomass feedstocks, such as municipal solid waste, industrial and wastewater sludge, and urban agricultural and forestry waste, offers cities a viable means to address both environmental and logistical challenges (Panepinto et al., 2017; Varjani et al., 2022). Cities' bioenergy initiatives not only leverage a reliable renewable energy supply but also aid waste management endeavours to reduce waste volume and promote the principles of a circular economy (Varjani et al., 2022). In addition, cities' bioenergy reduces greenhouse gas emissions and contribute to the climate change mitigation.

Key WtE conversion technologies used in cities are direct combustion plants, anaerobic digestion, and gasification which offer unique pathways for converting biomass into energy (Alao et al., 2022). Combustion of waste biomass directly creates steam which is often used with combined heat and power (CHP) systems to make energy use more efficient (Alao et al., 2022). Advanced combustion technologies and flue gas cleaning measures help mitigate emissions, although challenges remain in addressing fine dust emissions and managing by-products such as fly ash and incinerator bottom ash (Alao et al., 2022). In addition, small-scale combustion plants such as stoves and boilers using wood and pellets are also promising technologies for space heating in many cities in cold climatic regions, such as Nordic countries. They also help promote the decentralization of energy systems in cities.

Anaerobic digestion stands as another prominent WtE technology, widely utilized in municipal wastewater treatment plants and food-processing facilities. Through bacterial digestion processes, biodegradable waste is converted into biogas, primarily composed of methane, which can be used for electricity generation, heating, or vehicle fuel (Alao et al., 2022). Large-scale urban biogas production, alongside emerging small-scale biodigester systems, highlights the flexibility of anaerobic digestion in addressing cities' organic waste challenges (Alao et al., 2022). Currently, Austria, France, Germany, and the Netherlands are leading in the adoption of anaerobic digestion technologies, demonstrating its potential for sustainable energy production in cities (Davis, 2014).

At present, cities are increasingly scaling up biogas production to decarbonize different sectors, such as transport and industry, by utilizing biomass as an alternative to fossil fuels (Ulpiani et al., 2023). However, the implementation of bioenergy technologies in cities is not without its limitations. Ensuring a sustainable supply of feedstock poses challenges due to uncertainties in waste management systems and limited collection distances for agricultural and forestry residues (Varjani et al., 2022). To address these issues, close collaboration between the energy and waste management sectors along with advances in biomass conversion technology and public awareness campaigns are essential to realizing the full potential of bioenergy in cities. Technologies such as on-site densification of biomass feedstock into wood pellets and briquettes offer promising solutions to improve logistics and enhance the quality of feedstock for combustion (IRENA, 2020d). With the adoption of innovative solutions and supportive policies, cities can harness the power of bioenergy to create cleaner, more resilient city environments. In addition, circular economy models, such as using energy and gas produced from waste management plants to power waste collection vehicles, are central to maximizing the efficiency and sustainability of bioenergy systems in cities (Alao et al., 2022).

66 Karna Dahal

4.4.6 Wind energy technologies

Wind energy is one of the key renewable resources to generate energy in cities. Wind energy has made significant advances in recent years, but its integration into city environments remains limited due to various barriers. These barriers include the size and efficiency of conventional wind turbines, which struggle to capture low wind speeds and turbulent flows of wind in cities. In addition, concerns such as visual and noise disturbance further hinder the widespread adoption of wind energy in cities (Stathopoulos et al., 2018).

Wind turbine applications for cities typically fall into three categories: stand-alone, retrofitted on existing buildings, and architecturally integrated into buildings (Stathopoulos et al., 2018). These turbines can be either horizontal-axis or vertical-axis, with each type having its advantages and limitations. Horizontal-axis turbines, although less effective in cities architectures due to turbulence and noise, offer high efficiency and scalability (Gil García et al., 2022). On the other hand, vertical-axis turbines as a novel technology show promise for city applications by harnessing turbulent and multidirectional winds. While vertical-axis turbines may be less efficient, they offer simpler design, lower maintenance, and better suitability for rooftop installations (Stathopoulos et al., 2018).

Wind energy expansion planning in cities must consider various factors, including spatial planning, legal barriers, and public acceptance. Some prudent strategies such as citizen energy cooperatives and private investment involvement can enhance local ownership and support for wind energy projects in cities (Ulpiani et al., 2023). In addition, upgrading existing wind power plants and integrating renewable energy infrastructure into city features such as roads can maximize the potential for clean energy generation while revitalizing abandoned areas and promoting sustainability. These interventions not only contribute to renewable energy generation but also address local needs and constraints such as geographical features and public acceptance. By addressing technical limitations, leveraging innovative designs, and considering local needs and opportunities, cities can harness the potential of wind power to transition towards sustainable and resilient energy systems.

4.4.7 Direct geothermal energy technologies

Geothermal energy offers a promising solution to meet the heating needs of cities, e.g., for space heating, cooling, and hot water systems, in a sustainable and cost-effective manner. Cities can obtain such a renewable and reliable energy source by capturing heat trapped beneath the ground, which typically ranges in depth from ten metres to hundreds of metres (IRENA, 2020c). Temperatures in this depth ranges from around $10°C$ to $150°C$ for geothermal energy production which are particularly ideal for meeting the direct thermal heating demands of cities (Bayer et al., 2019).

The deployment of direct geothermal energy systems in cities has been steadily increasing, with the adoption increasing number of geothermal heat pumps that are

Intra-city renewable energy production   67

primarily used for space heating applications (Lund & Toth, 2020). Geothermal heat pump systems use either open-loop or closed-loop ground systems, with vertical and horizontal configurations for the closed-loop option. While geothermal borehole drilling is often necessary, horizontal systems can minimize costs but require more land area for trenching, posing challenges in city conditions (IRENA, 2020b). In addition, hybrid systems that combine geothermal heating and cooling with thermal energy storage technologies further enhance the efficiency and economic viability of geothermal energy systems in cities (Bayer et al., 2019).

One of the key applications of geothermal energy in cities is its integration into district heating systems. By replacing fossil fuel heat sources with geothermal alternatives, cities can achieve renewable and baseload heating solutions that are economically viable (IRENA, 2020c). This approach also reduces carbon emissions and contributes to the profitability and sustainability of cities' heating infrastructure.

While deploying geothermal energy systems in new city developments is relatively straightforward, retrofitting existing structures presents challenges. Yet, innovative solutions have enabled the feasibility of integrating geothermal energy into established city areas. For instance, a significant number of geothermal technologies have been installed in existing buildings in Switzerland (Lund & Toth, 2020). These initiatives underscore the feasibility and potential of incorporating geothermal energy systems into pre-existing city landscapes. With ongoing technological advancements and increasing global deployment, geothermal energy is poised to play a significant role in decarbonizing cities' heating systems and advancing towards a more sustainable energy future.

4.4.8   *Urban and coastal hydro power*

Urban and coastal hydropower offer promising opportunities for cities to achieve their renewable energy goals. By leveraging local water resources and innovative technologies, cities can harness the vast potential of hydropower to meet their energy needs while promoting sustainability and resilience. In recent years, cities worldwide have been actively exploring the potential of urban and coastal hydropower as a key component of their renewable energy strategies. Feasibility studies and small-scale projects are underway to harness the power of water resources within city boundaries (Boroomandnia et al., 2022). Some cities have reached almost 100% renewable electricity mainly from hydropower (Ulpiani et al., 2023).

One notable approach involves integrating small hydroelectric turbines into existing water systems within cities. By harnessing the flow of rivers, streams, and municipal water infrastructure, these turbines can generate sustainable electricity to power city areas (Ulpiani et al., 2023). Coastal cities are also exploring the untapped potential of ocean energy such as wave and tidal energy as a valuable renewable resource. Through research and development and scalable interventions, some cities such as Mutriku (Spain), San Francisco, (USA), Portland (USA), Brest (France), Lisbon (Portugal), Perth (Australia), and Orkney Islands (Scotland) are beginning to exploit ocean to generate energy (IEA-OES, 2023).

68 *Karna Dahal*

However, realizing this potential requires investments in research and development to enhance existing technologies and identify optimal production areas.

4.4.9 *Hydrogen and carbon capture and storage (CCS) technologies*

In recent years, cities have been increasingly exploring the potential of innovative technologies such as hydrogen and carbon capture and storage (CCS) for green energy transition. Green hydrogen produced through electrolysis using renewable electricity is gaining momentum as an alternative source of heat and electricity and alternative fuels for decarbonizing transportation and industrial sectors, including ports. Cities are promoting a circular economy through green hydrogen production, utilizing by-products such as heat and oxygen to enhance sustainability (Ulpiani et al., 2023). Solar-powered hydrogen electrolysers are being integrated into city districts to cover energy needs for buildings and micro-mobility (e.g. electric vehicles and charging stations) (UN-Habitat, 2022). This demonstrates the ongoing technological shift towards decentralized hydrogen production in cities.

Cities are also exploring upcycling production processes for green hydrogen production, such as extracting hydrogen from cities' waste streams, particularly from mechanical biological treatment plants (Ulpiani et al., 2023). Fuel cells running on a blend of hydrogen and natural gas are being deployed, providing zero-emission electricity and heating to critical infrastructure such as airports (Ruf et al., 2018). These technological advancements are not only reducing carbon emissions but also contributing to operational stability, energy security, and citizens' health while promoting circular economy in energy production.

On the other hand, CCS holds promise in capturing carbon emissions from industrial processes and power generation, contributing to overall emission reduction goals. CCS technologies are still relatively less explored in city environments (CNCA, 2020). Only a few cities have begun integrating CCS with biomass and waste incineration facilities as part of their energy transition strategies (Ulpiani et al., 2023). Some cities are also exploring avenues to integrate CCS with wastewater treatment to further enhance environmental sustainability and circular economy (CNCA, 2020).

As cities continue to invest in innovative technologies related to hydrogen and CCS, partnerships between public and private sectors, along with research institutions, will be crucial for driving technological advancements and overcoming implementation challenges. By leveraging these technologies, cities can accelerate their transition towards renewable energy sources, reduce carbon emissions, achieve their climate neutral targets, and create more sustainable and resilient urban environments.

4.4.10 *District thermal energy networks*

District thermal energy networks play a crucial role in providing sustainable heating and cooling solutions for city areas. At the moment, majority of district heating systems have relied heavily on fossil fuels for energy production from CHP

Intra-city renewable energy production 69

plants which supply the majority of the heat to these networks (Helin et al., 2018). However, with the increasing focus on renewable energy, there has been a significant shift towards integrating renewable heat sources into district heating systems. Modern thermal grid technology now enables the utilization of lower-temperature heat sources, including solar thermal and geothermal energy, along with electric heat pumps (Helin et al., 2018).

The incorporation of renewable energy sources such as surplus renewable electricity, electric boilers, industrial waste heat, and heat pumps offers viable alternatives for heat generation in district heating systems (Helin et al., 2018). By integrating these technologies, significant reductions in fuel consumption can be achieved, leading to improved energy efficiency and economic performance (Helin et al., 2018). In addition, WtE and waste heat from CHP or industrial processes are being explored as part of efforts to decarbonize cities' energy systems (Helin et al., 2018).

District heating systems have advanced significantly in recent years but district cooling systems remain less prevalent due to technological obstacles and adverse economies of scale. Yet, the growing demand for cooling brings about opportunities for the expansion of renewable-driven district cooling systems (Al-Nini et al., 2023). Utilization of free cooling sources such as rivers, lakes, and ambient air, along with solar thermal-driven absorption chillers, can provide sustainable cooling solutions for city areas (Al-Nini et al., 2023).

Thermal energy storage (TES) systems play a crucial role in enhancing the efficiency and flexibility of district heating and cooling networks. TES systems enable better alignment between supply and demand by decoupling heat or cold generation from consumption. In addition, they facilitate the integration of renewable energy sources and off-peak electricity (IRENA, 2020a). Innovative designs, such as ectogrid™, aim to further improve energy efficiency by utilizing wasted thermal energy and integrating heat pumps to optimize temperature levels within the network (IRENA, 2020c).

4.5   Global cities' actions on the deployment of renewable energy resources

Global cities are increasingly taking action to deploy renewable energy resources as part of their efforts to mitigate climate change and energy transition to carbon neutrality (Dahal et al., 2018). This shift towards renewables is driven by the recognition of the environmental and economic benefits they offer, including reduced greenhouse gas emissions, improved air quality, and enhanced energy security. The cities in developed nations (e.g., cities in Europe and North America) have been proactive in setting renewable energy targets while cities in developing nations (e.g., cities in Asia and Africa) are lagging behind despite their immense potential of renewable energy resources (IRENA, 2020c).

However, cities globally are ramping up efforts to deploy renewable energy resources within their boundaries. A growing number of cities are embracing solar energy, utilizing rooftops and vacant lots for solar installations to generate clean electricity (Ulpiani et al., 2023). Cities are increasingly looking into urban and offshore wind farms to utilize wind power. Moreover, geothermal heat pumps and biomass facilities are being implemented to provide heating, cooling, and electricity (Ulpiani et al., 2023).

While solar energy use in cities is rising, there's still enormous untapped potential. Surprisingly, many cities with excellent solar potential lack the political commitment to scale up renewable energy, as seen in the case of cities with high solar potential but no set targets (IRENA, 2020c). In Asia, countries such as China, Japan, India, the Philippines, and Thailand are leading in solar power plant deployment in and near cities. However, regions such as Africa, despite abundant solar resources, have minimal representation in solar power plants due to low urbanization rates and inadequate infrastructure (IRENA, 2020c).

Wind energy is another renewable resource gaining traction in global cities. Urban and offshore wind farms are being developed to harness the power of wind, providing clean electricity to city populations (IRENA, 2020c). While wind energy projects face challenges such as land availability and public acceptance, technological advancements and supportive policies are driving their growth in cities worldwide. Therefore, wind energy potential remains largely untapped in many cities, even in regions where wind resources are favourable (IRENA, 2020c).

Hydropower, waste-to-energy, and bioenergy also play crucial roles in achieving city-level renewable energy targets (Dahal et al., 2018). Despite challenges such as waste management issues and limited infrastructure, waste-to-energy facilities are widespread in all regions globally. However, there's still significant potential for growth, especially in developing countries (IRENA, 2020c). In developed countries, especially in Nordic countries, small-scale combustion technologies such as pellet and wood stoves and boilers, saunas and inserts are also widespread throughout the city buildings. Geothermal energy is also a promising energy for cities, but it faces regulatory and technical challenges, limiting its role in city renewable energy targets (Ulpiani et al., 2023). Nonetheless, direct use of geothermal energy presents a more accessible option, offering heating and cooling solutions in cities with substantial global potential (Lund & Toth, 2020).

Despite the progress in deploying renewable energy resources, cities face various challenges, including policy barriers, financing constraints, and limited technical expertise (Dahal et al., 2018). The integration of renewable energy technologies into city infrastructure requires careful planning and coordination among stakeholders. The initiatives such as renewable energy targets, supportive policies, greater communication among governments, and international collaborations are helping cities overcome these challenges and accelerate the energy transition to carbon neutrality and achieve a low-carbon and sustainable future.

4.6   Future of renewable energy in cities

The above-mentioned studies and cities' initiatives have shown evidence that the future of renewable energy production is poised to witness significant growth. Cities around the world are increasingly embracing renewable energy sources (RES) technologies, with a focus on local heat/cold storage, demand response, and the deployment of various RES sources and technologies. With this trend, nearly double the number of cities is expected to engage in RES interventions in the near future (Ulpiani et al., 2023).

Currently, solar energy, including both photovoltaic (PV) and solar thermal technologies, remains the most popular choice among cities, comprising the largest share of RES deployment (Ulpiani et al., 2023). The expansion of RES generation will be needed from other sources than solar such as wind, geothermal, and biomass. Wind and ambient energy (energy from heat pump) are expected to experience significant boosts in adoption due to the number of cities planning to exploit these resources (Ulpiani et al., 2023). In addition, there is a growing interest in geothermal energy, as many cities around the world are planning to harness its potential (Lund & Toth, 2020). Furthermore, there is a notable uptick in energy production from waste and wastewater, as the cities are increasingly emphasizing sustainable waste management practices (Alao et al., 2022; Ulpiani et al., 2023).

In the case of biomass, a significant number of cities already incorporate sustainable biomass into their RES mix, and many cities are also aiming to develop biomass power plants and district heating and cooling (DH/C) systems that integrate biomass energy in the future (Ulpiani et al., 2023). Retrofitting and upscaling of existing infrastructure to adopt renewable energy technologies are also key priorities for many cities. In addition, several cities also have focus on increasing the efficiency of co-generation systems and expanding biomass-based DH/C networks (Al-Nini et al., 2023).

Similarly, the transportation sector is also undergoing a transformation towards renewable energy adoption, with a shift towards battery electric vehicles (BEVs) and battery/hydrogen-fuel-cell hybrid vehicles (Ruf et al., 2018). These technologies are expected to dominate various modes of transportation, including light-duty ground vehicles, trains, ferries, and short-haul aircraft in the near future. In addition, efforts are underway to develop electric and hydrogen-fuel-cell-powered aircraft and ships, with the aim of achieving all-electric short-haul flights by the early 2030s and transitioning to hydrogen fuel cell-electric hybrids for long-haul flights by 2035–2040 (Dahal et al., 2021; Ruf et al., 2018).

In the context of electricity generation, there are plans to deploy an energy mix of wind, solar, hydropower, tidal, and wave technologies into the cities' energy systems focusing on utility-scale and rooftop PV, onshore and offshore wind turbines, and hydropower plants. In addition, national and city governments have implemented various interventions to enhance energy efficiency, promote renewable energy communities, and address energy poverty through the installation of solar PV in low-income households (Dahal et al., 2018; Ulpiani et al., 2023). The key measures that global cities are adopting to boost the deployment of the renewable energy sources include:

- *Use of Renewable Energy in Buildings:* The future of renewable energy in cities' buildings is promising as cities are increasingly adopting sustainable practices to reduce carbon footprints and enhance energy efficiency in their boundaries. Key measures include fuel shift to renewables and the adoption of efficient heating systems such as solar-powered heat pumps in the buildings (REN21, 2021). The use of solar PV, solar collectors, vertical wind turbines, and heat pumps are increasingly used by many cities and others have planned to adopt these technologies in their own office buildings and city dwellers private buildings (Ulpiani et al., 2023). Cities are also exploring innovative solutions to improve building energy efficiency and integrate renewable energy generation. Strategies include updates of building codes, subsidies for renewable installations, and energy performance contracting. In addition, cities are pushing for nearly zero energy buildings and smart districts, using rooftop solar panels and other renewables to meet their sustainable energy goals (Backe & Kvellheim, 2020).

- *Renewable Energy for city Districts:* Cities are focusing on district-level interventions to leverage enhanced energy sharing, trading, and storage. The rehabilitation and revitalization of city spaces towards energy savings and renewable energy generation are key priorities. Strategies include the creation of net-zero or positive energy districts, energy communities, micro-district heating systems powered by renewable sources, and smart districts (Backe & Kvellheim, 2020; Dahal et al., 2018). For instance, the city of Helsinki has created smart district in Kalasatama which includes smart heating, cooling and electricity grids incorporation with various renewable energy plants (e.g., solar plants), smart metering, EV charging stations, and new storage solutions for electricity (Dahal & Niemelä, 2016). Many cities are envisioning a significant boost in local renewable energy production at the district or neighbourhood scale. Additional plans of the cities include maximizing rooftop solar potential, creating 'Solar Neighbourhoods cities' 'zero emission neighbourhood' to include residents and businesses that can benefit from the integration of renewable energy in the neighbourhood city buildings, and establishing circular bioenergy communities in peri-urban and rural areas (Backe & Kvellheim, 2020; REN21, 2021).
- *Renewable Energy in Public Lighting:* Cities are focusing on maximizing renewable energy capacity in public lighting systems, particularly through the installation of autonomous LED lighting fixtures powered by solar collectors. Strategies also include the integration of solar-powered lighting with electric vehicle charging infrastructure to promote sustainable mobility (REN21, 2021).
- *Smart Energy Management:* Cities are adopting smart energy management solutions to optimize public lighting systems and enhance energy efficiency. Measures include the deployment of virtual power plants (VPPs) to power street lighting and the integration of energy storage systems to balance supply and demand (Ulpiani et al., 2023).
- *Integrated Solutions:* Cities are pursuing integrated solutions, a holistic approach to energy transition, that simultaneously target buildings, public lighting, district heating, transportation, and energy generation. Strategies include deep building renovations, renewable energy integration, and the deployment of energy storage systems to enhance flexibility and optimize energy use (Ulpiani et al., 2023). Integrated solutions aim to address energy poverty by reducing maintenance and energy costs through smart building retrofits and the creation of

micro-district heating systems (Ulpiani et al., 2023). These initiatives promote social inclusion and environmental sustainability.

- *Development and Deployment of Smart Grids:* Cities are investing in the development and deployment of smart grids to enhance grid resilience and facilitate the integration of renewable energy sources. Smart grid technologies enable real-time monitoring, demand response, and energy storage optimization, thereby improving overall system efficiency (IRENA, 2020c).
- *Technological Innovations:* Technological innovations such as thermal energy storage systems enhance the efficiency and flexibility of district heating and cooling networks. By decoupling heat or cold generation from consumption, thermal energy storage systems enable better alignment between energy supply and demand of cities especially in cold climate regions and facilitate the integration of renewable energy sources (IRENA, 2020c).
- *Other Types of Energy Usages:* Cities are also exploring innovative applications of renewable energy in various sectors, including maritime shipping, waste management, and industrial processes. Strategies include the integration of renewable energy systems in port operations, thalasso-thermal loops also called marine thermal energy for heat recovery from the sea, and renewable energy-powered industrial facilities (Ulpiani et al., 2023).

While cities are making significant strides in renewable energy deployment, several challenges and opportunities remain. Key challenges include policy barriers, limited room for manoeuvre in renewable energy projects, and the need for buy-in from other levels of government. The future of renewable energy generation in cities relies on a holistic approach that integrates renewable energy solutions into buildings, districts, and public infrastructure. By embracing innovative technologies, implementing supportive policies, and fostering community engagement and collaboration with the private sector, and scaling up renewable energy production at the local level, cities can accelerate the transition towards a sustainable energy future while addressing pressing environmental challenges.

4.7   Conclusion

Cities play a pivotal role in the local and global energy landscape and contribute significantly to energy consumption and carbon emissions. Cities' responsibility to reduce carbon emissions becomes increasingly critical as urbanization continues. Renewable energy technologies offer promising solutions for cities to curb emissions and energy transition towards carbon neutrality. New and continual advancements in these technologies are encouraging since decreasing costs for solar and wind power are making them competitive with fossil fuel-based energy solutions. Despite progress, the contribution of renewable energy to city energy consumption is currently limited.

The growing use of some of the renewable energy technologies such as solar photovoltaics, solar thermal, wind, geothermal, hydro, and bioenergy reflects the increasing commitment of cities to prioritize sustainability, resilience, and cleaner future. From rooftop solar panels to integrated wind turbines and district heating networks powered by geothermal heat pumps, cities are embracing innovative approaches to energy transition towards renewable energy resources. Furthermore, the integration of thermal energy storage systems and district heating and cooling networks represents a pivotal advancement in enhancing energy efficiency and flexibility. Thermal energy storage enables better alignment between energy supply and demand, separates energy generation from consumption, and facilitates the integration of renewable energy resources. The innovation and designs of smart energy networks optimize efficiency of energy systems by using wasted thermal energy and heat pumps to regulate temperature. As cities continue to invest in district heating and cooling infrastructure and explore opportunities for renewable-driven systems, thermal energy storage will also play a crucial role in maximizing the effectiveness of these networks.

Cities' endeavours to enhance their capacity for RES are dependent on the level of emissions and their evolution over time, along with the financial resources and regulatory capacities available to the cities. Yet, renewable energy adoption in cities is progressing well and the transportation sector is shifting towards battery electric and hydrogen-fuel-cell vehicles. Many cities have adopted stringent climate and energy policies encompassing a wide range of interventions, including updates to building codes, the creation of smart districts, and the development of renewable energy-powered public lighting systems. Integrated solutions are being pursued to address energy poverty and enhance grid resilience through the deployment of smart grids and technological innovations such as thermal energy storage systems. Cities are also investing in renewable energy infrastructure and exploring more and more on emerging technologies such as hydrogen and carbon capture and storage. These efforts not only contribute to carbon neutrality and energy transition but also foster economic growth, enhance energy security, and improve the quality of life for city dwellers.

Several challenges persist, however, to implement technologies and policies. The new innovations for technological advancements and cooperation between public and private sectors will be crucial. Hence, cities should maximize the use of locally available sources, encourage distributed energy generation and local energy resource integration into cities' infrastructure, and become independent, avoiding importing renewables. The implementation of innovative renewable energy technologies, adoption of a holistic approach on policies, and investment in energy storage solutions are required to accelerate the cities' transition towards sustainable city development. In addition, there will also be a need for increasing awareness to prevent climate change, reduce reliance on fossil fuels, and ensure the overall sustainable future of cities and their residents.

References

Alao, M. A., Popoola, O. M., & Ayodele, T. R. (2022). Waste-to-energy nexus: An overview of technologies and implementation for sustainable development. *Cleaner Energy Systems*, 3, 100034. https://doi.org/10.1016/j.cles.2022.100034

Al-Nini, A., Ya, H., Almahbashi, N., & Hussin, H. (2023). A review on green cooling: Exploring the benefits of sustainable energy-powered district cooling with thermal energy storage. *Sustainability,* 15, 5433. https://doi.org/10.3390/su15065433

Backe, S., & Kvellheim, A. K. (2020). *Zero Emission Neighbourhoods: Drivers and Barriers Towards Future Development,* Norwegian University of Science and Technology and SINTEF, Trondheim.

Bae, S., Chae, H., Lyu, N., & Nam, Y. (2024). Development of photovoltaic-thermal using attachable solar collector based on on-site construction. *Applied Thermal Engineering,* 238, 121971. https://doi.org/10.1016/j.applthermaleng.2023.121971

Bayer, P., Attard, G., Blum, P., & Menberg, K. (2019). The geothermal potential of cities. *Renewable and Sustainable Energy Reviews,* 106, 17–30. https://doi.org/10.1016/j.rser.2019.02.019

Boroomandnia, A., Rismanchi, B., & Wu, W. (2022). A review of micro hydro systems in urban areas: Opportunities and challenges. *Renewable and Sustainable Energy Reviews,* 169, 112866. https://doi.org/10.1016/j.rser.2022.112866

Brown, D., Hall, S., & Davis, M. E. (2020). What is prosumerism for? Exploring the normative dimensions of decentralised energy transitions. *Energy Research & Social Science,* 66, 101475. https://doi.org/10.1016/j.erss.2020.101475

CNCA. (2020). *Cities Aim at Zero Emissions. How Carbon Capture, Storage and Utilisation Can Help Cities Go Carbon Neutral.* https://carbonneutralcities.org/

Dahal, K., Brynolf, S., Xisto, C., Hansson, J., Grahn, M., Grönstedt, T., & Lehtveer, M. (2021). Techno-economic review of alternative fuels and propulsion systems for the aviation sector. *Renewable and Sustainable Energy Reviews,* 151, 111564. https://doi.org/10.1016/j.rser.2021.111564

Dahal, K., Juhola, S., & Niemelä, J. (2018). The role of renewable energy policies for carbon neutrality in Helsinki Metropolitan area. *Sustainable Cities and Society,* 40, 222–232. https://doi.org/10.1016/j.scs.2018.04.015

Dahal, K., & Niemelä, J. (2016). Initiatives towards carbon neutrality in the Helsinki metropolitan area. *Climate,* 4(3), 36. https://doi.org/10.3390/cli4030036

Davis, R. C. (2014). *Anaerobic Digestion – Pathways for Using Waste as Energy in Urban Settings,* The University of British Columbia, Vancouver.

Gil García, I. C., García-Cascales, M. S., & Molina-Garcia, Á. (2022). Urban wind: An alternative for sustainable cities. *Energies,* 15, 4759. https://doi.org/10.3390/en15134759

Helin, K., Zakeri, B., & Syri, S. (2018). Is district heating combined heat and power at risk in the nordic area?—An electricity market perspective. *Energies,* 11, 1256. https://doi.org/10.3390/en11051256

Herrando, M., & Ramos, A. (2022). Photovoltaic-thermal (PV-T) systems for combined cooling, heating and power in buildings: A review. *Energies,* 15(19), 3021. https://doi.org/10.3390/en15093021

IEA. (2023). *World Energy Outlook 2023,* International Energy Agency, Paris.

IEA-OES. (2023). *Annual Report: An Overview of Ocean Energy Activities in 2022,* International Energy Agency, Ocean Energy Systems Paris.

IEA PVPS. (2023). *Snapshot of Global PV Markets, The IEA Photovoltaic Power Systems Programme,* IEA PVPS, Rheine.

IRENA. (2019a). *Innovation Landscape for a Renewable-Powered Future: Solutions to Integrate Variable Renewables,* International Renewable Energy Agency, Abu Dhabi.

IRENA. (2019b). *Global Energy Transformation: A Roadmap to 2050,* International Renewable Energy Agency, Abu Dhabi.

IRENA. (2020a). *Innovation Outlook: Thermal Energy Storage*, International Renewable Energy Agency, Abu Dhabi.

IRENA. (2020b). *Renewable Power Generation Costs in 2019*, International Renewable Energy Agency, Abu Dhabi.

IRENA. (2020c). *Rise of Renewables in Cities: Energy Solutions for the Urban Future*, International Renewable Energy Agency, International Renewable Energy Agency, Abu Dhabi.

Laveet, K., Junaid, A., Mamdouh El Haj, A., & M., H. (2022). Prospects and challenges of solar thermal for process heating: A comprehensive review. *Energies, 15*(22), 8501. https://doi.org/10.3390/en15228501

Lü, X., Lu, T., Karrinne, S., Mäkiranta, A., & Clements-Croome, D. (2023). Renewable energy resources and multi-energy hybrid systems for urban buildings in nordic climate. *Energy and Buildings, 282*, 112789. https://doi.org/10.1016/j.enbuild.2023.112789

Lund, J., & Toth, A. (2020). Direct utilization of geothermal energy 2020 worldwide review. *Geothermics, 90*, 101915. https://doi.org/10.1016/j.geothermics.2020.101915

Omeiza, L. A., Abid, M., Dhanasekaran, A., Subramanian, Y., Raj, V., Kozak, K., Mamudu, U., & Azad, A. K. (2023). Application of solar thermal collectors for energy consumption in public buildings – An updated technical review. *Journal of Engineering Research*, 1–17. https://doi.org/10.1016/j.jer.2023.09.011. https://www.sciencedirect.com/science/article/pii/S2307187723002158

Panepinto, D., Zanetti, M., Gitelman, L., Kozhevnikov, M., Magaril, E., & Magaril, R. (2017). Energy from biomass for sustainable cities. *IOP Conference Series: Earth and Environmental Science, 72*, 012021. https://doi.org/10.1088/1755-1315/72/1/012021

Reda, F., Ruggiero, S., Auvinen, K., & Temmes, A. (2021). Towards low-carbon district heating: Investigating the socio-technical challenges of the urban energy transition. *Smart Energy, 4*, 100054. https://doi.org/10.1016/j.segy.2021.100054

REN21. (2021). *Renewables 2021 Global Status Report. REN21* Renewables Now, Paris.

Ruf, Y., Lange, S., Pfister, J., & Droege, C. (2018). *Fuel Cells and Hydrogen for Green Energy in European Cities and Regions*, Roland Berger GmbH, Munich.

Shi, S., & Zhu, N. (2023). Challenges and optimization of building-integrated photovoltaics (bipv) windows: A review. *Sustainability, 15*(22), 15876. https://doi.org/10.3390/su152215876

Stathopoulos, T., Alrawashdeh, H., Al-Quraan, A., Blocken, B., Dilimulati, A., Paraschivoiu, M., & Pilay, P. (2018). Urban wind energy: Some views on potential and challenges. *Journal of Wind Engineering and Industrial Aerodynamics, 179*, 146–157. https://doi.org/10.1016/j.jweia.2018.05.018

Tripanagnostopoulos, Y., Huang, G., Wang, K., & Markides, C. (2021). Photovoltaic/thermal solar collectors. *Reference Module in Earth Systems and Environmental Sciences, 3*, 294–345. https://doi.org/10.1016/B978-0-12-819727-1.00051-0

Ulpiani, G., Vetters, N., Shtjefni, D., Kakoulaki, G., & Taylor, N. (2023a). Let's hear it from the cities: On the role of renewable energy in reaching climate neutrality in urban Europe. *Renewable and Sustainable Energy Reviews, 183*, 113444. https://doi.org/10.1016/j.rser.2023.113444

UN-Habitat. (2022). *Envisioning Future Cities: World Cities Report 2022*, United Nations, Habitat, Nairobi.

Varjani, S., Shahbeik, H., Popat, K., Patel, Z., Vyas, S., Shah, A., Barceló, D., Sonne, C., Lam, S. S., Aghbashlo, M., & Tabatabaei, M. (2022). Sustainable management of municipal solid waste through waste-to-energy technologies. *Bioresource Technology, 355*, 127247. https://doi.org/10.1016/j.biortech.2022.127247

5 Urban stewardship and net zero

The case of the London Landed Estates

Patricia Canelas

5.1 Introduction

The pressing need to transition to a carbon-neutral urban environment has recently gained considerable prominence. The urgency of this transition has been underscored in the latest Intergovernmental Panel on Climate Change (IPCC) report (2023), emphasising the necessity for global human-induced carbon dioxide emissions to achieve net zero by 2050. Various terms related to greenhouse gas emissions are used depending on the stage of products, buildings, and infrastructure (World GBC, 2019). The concepts of carbon neutrality and net zero are central to this discussion and mean reducing human-caused carbon emissions to zero or close to zero and removing the remaining emissions through carbon removal processes until zero carbon is reached.

Discussions and practices towards net zero have been consolidating since the 2015 Paris Agreement at the COP21 summit, where 194 countries signed a pledge to keep global heating below 1.5°C. This is critical in mitigating long-lasting or irreversible changes to the earth's ecosystems and atmosphere (IPCC, 2023). The property sector, responsible for nearly 40% of carbon dioxide emissions, is under escalating pressure from diverse legislative endeavours that mandate action within the industry to decarbonise the building sector by 2050 (McKinsey, 2023). However, progress has been slow, and many questions must be resolved before reaching a clear and consistent consensus on what net zero implies for the property industry (BBP, 2022).

Governments have 'carrot' and 'stick' policies to work with to achieve carbon neutrality. Carrot policies award certain more efficient energy behaviours or technologies through fiscal benefits or grants. Typical examples include incentives to install solar heating and energy and more efficient windows or envelope insulation. Stick policies can be described as financially penalising or forbidding specific actions. These may include higher taxes for certain less efficient products, prohibiting certain materials, or raising minimum energy standards (Weatherall et al., 2018). Carrot and stick policies individually and together shape markets by enabling specific markets to grow and others to shrink.

Alongside governmental action, initiatives from the civil and private sectors are exploring avenues for net zero buildings and ways of living. This includes

DOI: 10.4324/9781003498216-8

communities living in eco-villages (Fischer, 2017) and the not-so-new wave of smart cities, including Masdar City in Abu-Dhabi (Gunel, 2019) and others such as the proposed neighbourhood in Toronto's Lake Sore by Sidewalk, a Google-affiliated company (O'Kane, 2022). This denotes a range of interested stakeholders and different approaches to the transition towards net zero.

The property industry has played an active role in advancing sustainability by developing metrics, guidance, best practices, standards, and certifications. This engagement is essential given the sector's wide-ranging impact on its entire value chain. However, concerns about greenwashing have surfaced as corporations face growing scrutiny regarding their roles and the societal impact they claim to have (Foerester & Spencer, 2023; Gözlügöl & Ringe, 2022; Newell, 2008). This chapter delves into the property industry's progression toward carbon-neutral urban settings by scrutinising the actors involved, their motivations and their capacity to act. Through this investigation, the chapter aims to contribute to the ongoing debate on the complexities and dynamics shaping the real estate industry's efforts towards carbon neutrality and sustainability.

This chapter adopts a qualitative case-study approach to explore how stewardship informs and may help us understand the private sector's role in achieving net zero and advancing self-sufficiency. Specifically, it focuses on the London Landed Estates, representing some of the oldest and largest landowners and property developers. The chapter explores how stewardship influences the property industry's transition to net zero portfolios alongside long-term investment outlooks, disclosure requirements, and reputational concerns. This chapter is structured as follows: it first explores the connections between net zero and the property industry and then introduces an urban stewardship framework drawing from environmental and corporate governance literature. Subsequent sections include a methods overview, a discussion on the property industry's engagement with net zero through stewardship theory leans, and a concluding reflection on urban stewardship's broader implications and potential.

5.2   Net zero in the real estate industry

Low-carbon, carbon-neutral, and net zero are often used when discussing ways to reduce, eliminate, and offset greenhouse gases (GHG) in cities, neighbourhoods, buildings, and building processes. The term 'carbon' is colloquially used as shorthand for the full range of GHG, and gases' global warming potential is usually quantified in units of carbon dioxide equivalence (Co_2e) (World GBC, 2019). Cities with low carbon emissions typically feature dense development, along with the availability of non-motorised transportation options and public transit, to reduce the demand for motorised travel. Additionally, these cities often employ energy-efficient building designs, promote the use of vehicles with high fuel economy, utilise waste-to-energy technologies, and encourage behaviour changes that foster conservation (Seto et al., 2021). This is a rapidly developing field in terms of technology and regulation, which represents a challenge for the real estate industry, often locked in traditional ways of working (Muldoon-Smith and Greenhalgh, 2019).

Buildings are responsible for 40% of energy-related carbon emissions globally (OECD, 2022), making it a priority to retrofit the existing stock. It is worth noting that of the buildings expected to exist in 2050, 80% have already been constructed (McKinsey, 2023: (10). In the European Union alone, 75% of the current stock is not energy efficient (EU, 2021). Building retrofits can be broadly defined as:

'Energy efficiency improvements to building fabric (insulation or improved windows); installation or upgrades to deliver more efficient, lower carbon and renewable energy heating systems; energy efficiency upgrades to other fixed energy-using systems in the building (lighting, ventilation, and elevators); installation of renewable electricity generation (principally solar photovoltaics); and installation of smart metering or other building energy management system' (Weatherall et al., 2018: 1642).

Addressing energy inefficiency in existing buildings through comprehensive retrofits is crucial for mitigating carbon emissions and achieving sustainability goals, highlighting the urgent need for widespread adoption of retrofit strategies.

As a society, we should have a good understanding of what is necessary to upgrade our buildings. According to a UNEP (2022) report, as of 2021, 74 green building certification schemes existed globally – some of the most famous being BREEAM and LEEDS – with buildings certified under these systems present in at least 184 countries. However, limitations with green building certifications include limited accounting for whole life cycle analysis (Nugent et al., 2022) and whole value chain (McKinsey, 2023). Moreover, many green building certificates focus primarily on operational emissions – emissions related to running the buildings and infrastructure – with not enough consideration given to embodied emissions – the emissions involved in producing and transporting building materials (UNEP, 2022). The same applies to energy-efficient building regulations, where little consideration is often given to the link between energy performance improvements and embodied energy (Crawford et al., 2016).

According to McKinsey (2023), two-thirds of the emissions produced by the built environment are due to operational emissions, while the remaining one-third is due to embodied emissions. The report highlights several cost-effective and marginally more expensive ways to reduce both types of emissions. Some key abatement levers for operational emissions include improving the efficiency of space heating and cooling, water heating, cooking, appliances, and lighting. Ways to reduce embodied emissions include optimising design through standardisation, substituting materials with low-carbon alternatives, improving on-site practices such as using clean energy sources, and decarbonising the entire supply chain (McKinsey, 2023).

Regarding reporting, the GHG Protocol provides a guide for corporate accounting and reporting of GHG. Updated in 2022 and amply used by the real estate industry, it was first published in 2001 by the World Resources Institute (WRI) and the World Business Council for Sustainable Development (WBCSD). With significant uptake, it introduced the idea of 'Scopes' (Scopes 1, 2, and 3) to differentiate different types of emissions. Scope 1 emissions are the direct emissions controlled by the organisation. These are typically the easier-to-control emissions;

examples include the organisation's mobility fleet, electricity and heating systems. Scope 2 emissions are indirect emissions that result from the business consumption of energy. Scope 3 emissions are typically considered the hardest to control as they relate to the whole value chain of a company (WRI and WBCSD, 2021).

In terms of building regulation, following the 2010 European Union (EU) Energy Performance for Buildings Directive, which all 28 EU countries signed, energy standards for rental residential and commercial properties have become more stringent, requiring member states to implement measures to improve the energy efficiency of new and existing buildings (EU, 2010). In the UK, the Minimum Energy Efficiency Standard (MEES) introduced in 2015 and gradually made more strict means that landlords must ensure that their properties meet a minimum energy performance rating, typically demonstrated by an Energy Performance Certificate (EPC) that rates buildings from A to G where A stands for the best performing (French, 2020).

The complexity of the net zero pathway is evident as it navigates the intersection of mandatory and optional standards and regulations. This context involves a mix of increasingly stringent standards imposed at the international, national, and local levels, alongside standards defined and voluntarily adopted by organisations and civil society. Until recently, carbon transitions have been seen either as the result of governmental action or an altruistic choice and less of a business necessity (Muldoon-Smith and Greenhalgh, 2019). To gain a deeper understanding of self-imposed pathways towards sustainability with a focus on net zero, the exploration of stewardship theory offers valuable insights.

5.3   The rising field of stewardship

The emerging societal commitment to environmental stewardship, as articulated by the Environmental Protection Agency (EPA) in 2005, emphasises a shared responsibility for environmental quality among all individuals whose actions impact the environment. This commitment extends beyond regulatory frameworks, advocating for a proactive approach to environmental care. The EPA highlights the potential of environmental stewardship in addressing complex environmental challenges and fostering collaborations among diverse stakeholders. Stewardship theory has been found relevant in urban studies, particularly within environmental management (Fernandes, 2020). This is in the context of growing recognition of the interconnectedness between human activities and environmental well-being, prompting a shift towards collective responsibility and sustainable practices.

Environmental stewardship entails a spectrum of activities ranging from conservation to restoration and the sustainable utilisation and management of natural resources. It encompasses many actions, such as establishing protected areas, habitat restoration projects, reforesting efforts, sustainable harvesting practices, pollution reduction measures, community gardening initiatives, and adopting eco-friendly products (Bennet et al., 2018). Environmental stewardship scale and scope can range from global to local and rural to urban (Benett et al., 2018). Environmental stewardship can focus on non-urban places, while urban stewardship initiatives focus on urban areas.

Environmental stewardship may also take different names when used to refer to these different scales. At a more macro level, the concept of ecosystem stewardship emerges to express the idea 'that society's use of resources must be compatible with the capacity of ecosystems to provide services, which, in turn, is constrained by the life-support system of the planet' (Chapin et al., 2009: 6). The term local stewardship or environmental stewardship tend to be used to refer to communities that act as stewards in promoting sustainability in their local ecosystems (Fisher et al., 2012). There are differences in who the key stakeholders are depending on the scale and scope of different environmental stewardship projects.

Focusing on how different groups steward, Fisher et al. (2012) suggest that environmental stewardship can involve 'a combination of larger public agencies operating at the citywide, regional and state-scales along with civil society groups, which are both large formal non-profit organisations and informal community groups, operating in ecological regions, across cities, and in specific neighbourhoods' (2012: 31). The authors note that organisation characteristics of the groups matter in the sort of activities they engage with. They note that accompanying the well-identified environmental stewardship strategies of 'lobbying, letter writing, media campaigns, protests, boycotts, sit-ins' (2012: 28), tactics can also incorporate 'elements of civic education, self-help, and community capacity-building to contribute to the environmental restoration and sustainability of local communities through participation in collaborative, locally based resource management' (2012: 28). They also noted that groups that do not simply rely on voluntaries and have a more robust governance structure tend to embrace more complex projects such as green buildings.

Focusing on organisational stewardship, the International Corporate Governance Network (ICGN) provides an international framework for investors through its Global Stewardship Principles. Their 2020 edition defines stewardship as 'preserving and enhancing long-term value as part of a responsible investment approach. This includes the consideration of wider ethical, environmental, and social factors as core components of fiduciary duty' (ICGN, 2020: 4). This perspective aligns with Dallas and Lubrano (2023: 54), who emphasise that 'the case for stewardship and sustainability is a matter of both ethics and economics'. While some investors embrace this broader role, others may struggle to see beyond their economic fiduciary obligation. Insights from this literature emphasise the importance of boards, with a focus on the individuals who serve on them, as highlighted in the work of Oxford economist Renee Adams ('Boards, and the Directors Who Sit on Them', cited in Dallas and Lubrano, 2023).

Identified limits of the concept of stewardship include that stewardship assumes that individuals have agency or capacity, yet many people do not have it (Rodgers, 2009). By focusing on an owner-steward relationship, we might overcome some issues with agency or capacity, but not all. Owners may have the right to steward their property but not the resources. This could include time or money. They might have the will and the possibility but not the power. Therefore, more than the steward-owner pair is needed to help explain why some individual stewards are involved or what good stewardship might be (Bennett et al., 2018). Moreover, the owner-steward may lead to the instrumentalisation of the concept of stewardship. The steward possession reasoning narrows the definition of stewards into a functionalist one: to capture the greater benefit from one's property.

Additionally, Bennett et al. (2018), noting the absence of an integrative framework within stewardship theory, propose one that hinges on three elements – actors, motivations, and capacity. This includes the following definition of stewardship: 'the actions taken by individuals, groups or networks of actors, with various motivations and levels of capacity, to protect, care for or responsibly use the environment in pursuit of environmental and/or social outcomes in diverse social-ecological contexts' (2018: 599).

On actors, Bennett et al. (2018) note that they can be individual, collective, multi-stakeholder, and possibly hybrid associations. The authors argue that understanding who stewards are helps to understand why they steward. Acknowledging that the literature on stewardship motivations is vast, they propose two categories: intrinsic and extrinsic. Intrinsic motivations include 'underlying ethics, morals, values and beliefs … [and] the need for belonging' (2018: 602); this may also include 'a sense of responsibility for a piece of land or resource' (2018: 602). Extrinsic motivations 'are associated with the expected achievement of separable outcomes, such as social reinforcements or economic benefits that are external to the self', which include 'externally provided rewards or sanctions which can be economic, social, physical or legal' (2018: 602). In terms of capacity they propose six categories: 'social capital (i.e., relationships, trust, networks), cultural capital (e.g., connections to place, traditions, knowledge, and practices), financial capital (e.g., income, credit, debt), physical capital (i.e., infrastructure and technology), human capital (e.g., education, skills, and demographics), and institutional capital (e.g., empowerment, agency, and options)' (Bennett et al. 2018: 601). However, the omission of explicit references to property ownership in this framework should be noted, as this current chapter demonstrates that it is a critical part of motivation and capacity.

The following section outlines the methodology used in this exploration, which involves applying a stewardship framework to assess the net zero pathways of the London Landed Estates.

5.4   Methods

This chapter uses qualitative case study methods to explore how stewardship can enhance our understanding of the real estate industry's voluntary efforts toward achieving carbon neutrality. It specifically focuses on the London Landed Estates (LLEs) case study for several reasons. Firstly, the LLEs represent one of England's oldest and most significant forms of land ownership, offering valuable insights into the importance of scale and long-term investment outlooks in transitioning to net zero real estate.

Secondly, concentrated land ownership is becoming more common in other regions and countries. This trend includes universities operating as property developers and investors, exemplified by the Begbroke estate led by Oxford University Development. Therefore, the theoretical framework and findings from this study can inform similar and emerging cases across different geographies.

Lastly, access to data is another critical consideration. These estates implement sustainability initiatives and prioritise strategy visibility through extensive reporting on estate management strategies. Most LLEs have published their net zero strategies, providing valuable research material. Using stewardship theory as a lens, this chapter examines the relationship between land ownership, environmental outcomes, and the urban development and investment processes. It analyses two cases: the traditional Cadogan estate and the 'newer' Shaftesbury Capital estate.

5.5   The London Landed Estates

5.5.1   Background

The LLEs are a group of landowners and property developers representing some of the oldest forms of land ownership, development, and management in England and beyond. This group of landlords dominates significant portions of central London (NLA, 2013). These landowners have mixed-use portfolios, and they control the destinies of Central London, much like they did, some of them, centuries ago (Olsen, 1964). Some of these estates, primarily the traditional ones, have been in the hands of the same aristocratic families for centuries. Examples of old estates include the Grosvenor's and the Cadogan estates. Others have been recently assembled by real estate property companies or investment vehicles. These 'newer' estates have been put together through so-called patient capital, which involves acquiring individual, standing property in the same area or neighbourhood. Examples of these newer estates include Shaftesbury Capital and Land Securities. Despite their distinct origins, both old and newer estates significantly shape London's present and future.

Historically, instead of developing their land, the landowners of LLEs used to sell their leasehold interest to leaseholders for development (Olsen, 1964). These leaseholds would usually last for 99 years, and at the end of the lease, the property would revert to the freeholders. The freeholders would thus be interested in the quality of the buildings being constructed on their estates. Referred to as 'villages', these Estates were developed as self-contained and self-sufficient entities (Jenkins, 1975; Olsen, 1964). They included green spaces, residential and commercial spaces, accommodating, to a certain extent, different income levels, divided across the front and back streets, and lower and higher floors. Being a locus of concentrated wealth and an expression of hereditary benefit, these places continue to attract controversy. If some see them as resilient (Davis, 2018), others enquire about how their knowledge sources and investment logics continue to shape the destinies of London (Canelas and Raco, 2021).

Today, both old and newer estates are professionally managed as real estate businesses. These estates typically consist of mixed-use portfolios that include ground-level and upper-level units. Combined, they comprise significant parts of city-centre London neighbourhoods (NLA, 2013). Due to their concentrated

84 *Patricia Canelas*

property ownership and long-term investment outlooks, the estates are managed with a curatorial approach to both private and public spaces. This approach includes managing public spaces, such as providing additional cleaning and security beyond what the state provides. It also involves curating public spaces through events and activities like busking. The motivations behind this approach are economic, such as increasing the attractiveness of the estates' neighbourhoods. However, the extreme long-term timescales of estate ownership also justify activities contributing to the estates' reputational value. This might include supporting local charities and community initiatives and investing in uses that are not financially self-sustaining, such as concert halls or art exhibition venues (Canelas, 2019; Canelas and Raco, 2021).

5.5.2   *A pathway to net zero*

5.5.2.1   *Shaftesbury Capital*

Shaftesbury Capital is a Real Estate Investment Trust (REIT) that resulted from the 2021 merger of Shaftesbury and Capital and Counties (Capco). Their net zero strategy, launched in 2021, followed their 2020s announced commitment to establishing an Environmental, Sustainability, and Community (ESC) committee and strategy (Capco, 2021: 58). The Shaftesbury Capital 'Net Zero Carbon Pathway' (2023) outlines the strategy leading to their 2030 net zero carbon target, along with their intermediate goals. As a recently merged company, its net zero baseline combines Shaftesbury and Capco's carbon baselines, accounting for approximately 77,000 tCO_2e (Shaftesbury Capital, 2023).

Regarding Shaftesbury and Capital's motivations to pursue and publish their net zero pathway, factors are both extrinsic and intrinsic. Regarding extrinsic factors, carbon reporting and energy efficient regulations have played a critical role. According to Capco's annual report, 'following the Government's 2019 announcement that the Scope of mandatory carbon reporting was to be extended, we have expanded our disclosure' (Capco, 2020: 45). In addition to reporting disclosure, there is the motivation of minimising their portfolio's risk exposure to more demanding regulations, including the Minimum Energy Efficiency Standard (MEES). These extrinsic motivations have faced some internal resistance, as the company feared having their assets carbon-stranded due to 'increased operating costs to meet reporting and target metrics and compliance [and] increased capital costs of retrofitting' (Capco, 2021: 30). On the other hand, when framing their net zero motivation through intrinsic factors, they claim that 'we will continue to focus on responsible stewardship, implementing our ESC [Environmental Social, Community] strategy, and working to achieve our Net Zero Carbon target by 2030' (Capco, 2021: 14). Their motivations thus appear to be multifaceted, encompassing both extrinsic and intrinsic drivers.

Shaftesbury Capital's 2023 combined carbon footprint reduction is 15% against their 77,000 tCO_2e baseline, which they claim exceeds the 13% requirement for a 1.5-degree pathway as set by the Science-Based Targets initiative (SBTi) (Shaftesbury Capital, 2023: 6). Their carbon reduction strategy involves an energy hierarchy defined as 'first dealing with retrofits, second with energy sources, and third with onsite energy production' (Shaftesbury Capital, 2023: 8). Regarding retrofits, as of November 2023, 78% of Shaftesbury Capital's portfolio by Estimated Rental Value was rated EPC C or better, representing a 10% improvement from 2022 (Shaftesbury Capital, 2023). Strategies related to energy sources and production include gas removal and trialling energy generation technologies such as photovoltaic (PV) roof tiles. In terms of scope, their baseline analysis shows that Scope 3 emissions are responsible for 96.6% of the total emissions, while Scope 1 and Scope 2 emissions account for only 1.1% and 2.3%, respectively (Shaftesbury Capital, 2023).

Regarding data gathering and disclosure, they note the need to adjust estimation methodologies, prioritise the use of actual emissions data when possible, and incorporate third-party verification of carbon emissions and offsets. Prioritising using actual emissions data involves continuing the rollout of smart meters. It also includes expanding signing 'green leases' – 'a standard form lease with additional clauses included which provide for the management and improvement of the environmental (and social) performance of a building by both owner and occupier(s)' (BBP, online: no page number). In terms of third-party verification, Shaftesbury was part of the original working group of The Better Buildings Partnership (BBP) Net Zero Carbon Pathway, alongside other significant players in the industry, such as the Great Portland Estate and the Crown Estate (see BBP, 2022: 18).

After their merger, Shaftesbury Capital aligned with the BBP framework, though not being signatories. They refer to several additional frameworks, including Building Research Establishment Environmental Assessment (BREEAM), the Climate Risk Real Estate Monitor (CRREM) for individual asset pathways, and the Greenhouse Gas (GHG) Protocol for emission calculation guidelines. Other standards they note they follow include the UK Net Zero Carbon Building Standard and the Oxford Principles for carbon offsetting projects. They are also seeking re-validation through the Science-Based Targets initiative (SBTi), for which they need one complete year of combined data (Shaftesbury Capital, 2023).

For their 2030 target, they estimate a 46% reduction to their baseline with the remaining 36,000 tCO_2e to be offset (mainly Scope 3 embodied but also operational carbon) (Shaftesbury Capital, 2023: 8). Although their offsetting strategy is still under development, they expect to follow industry best practices by offsetting only what they consider to be 'unavoidable residual emissions' (Shaftesbury Capital, 2023: 8). However, they acknowledge issues with offsetting, as many offsetting approaches are not delivering the results they claimed they would have.

5.5.2.2 Cadogan estate

As signatories of the Better Building Partnership Climate Change Commitment, Cadogan committed to achieving net zero emissions by 2030. This commitment includes annually disclosing their progress towards the goal and setting intermediate goals (see the complete list of responsibilities in BBP, 2022: 3). Cadogan's 'Net Zero Pathway' outlines how they plan to achieve their carbon reduction targets. Launched in 2021, this pathway is part of their broader sustainability strategy,

86   *Patricia Canelas*

including investments in green infrastructure and well-being initiatives referred to as 'Chelsea 2030' (see Cadogan, 2021a, 2021b).

In terms of their motivations, they are both extrinsic and intrinsic. A key extrinsic motivation for investing towards net zero includes staying ahead of regulation, notably the impending 2028 Minimum Energy Efficiency Standards (MEES), which require a minimum EPC rating of B for commercial buildings and a minimum of C for residential buildings (Cadogan, 2021a: 14). They highlight intrinsic motivations when stating that their approach is 'consistent with our values over a long time' and emphasise the importance of having a broader purpose beyond delivering returns to shareholders (Cadogan, 2023: 6). Additionally, they note that they 'recognise our role as one in which we can support industry-wide innovation and act as a catalyst for change' (Cadogan, 2023: 66). This suggests that Cadogan's shift explicitly from the 'single bottom line' reflects a set of complex, extrinsic and intrinsic motivations.

According to their latest annual report, Cadogan reduced their emissions by 10% from their 2019 baseline of approximately 36,000 tCO_2e to around 32,000 tCO_2e by December 2022. They are committed to achieving net zero by 2030, which they plan to accomplish by further reducing their carbon footprint and offsetting the remainder. They aim to achieve a 53% reduction by 2030, which would leave around 16,500 tCO_2e to offset (Cadogan, 2023: 66). However, their 2019 baseline was 'rebaselined', from about 95,000 tCO_2e to 36,000 tCO_2e for the same year of 2019, with this over 60% decrease accomplished merely by altering accounting procedures. Although 'rebaselining' is considered a common procedure for many firms, this significant decrease in emissions raises concerns about the standardisation of reporting standards (Drunford, 2023).

Cadogan has allocated £90 million to its decarbonisation programme, which includes several tasks organised by emission scope. Their stated focus is on what they consider to be the areas with more significant impact. According to Cadogan's carbon baseline, 88% of all emissions fall within Scope 3, with the remaining 7% in Scope 2 and about 5% in Scope 1. Scope 3 is where most emissions occur, and occupier consumption comprises 62% of their impact, while 20% comes from their supply chain. However, Cadogan notes challenges with estimation methodologies for Scope 3 emissions, (see Appendix C in Cadogan, 2023, for more detail).

Having limited to no control over the energy use of the commercial and residential property, the way forward in dealing with this largest share of emissions is value change engagement. Cadogan has engaged with over 100 companies within their supply chain, including sole traders, contractors, and planning consultants, through a collaborative approach and training programs (Cadogan, 2023). As a result, Cadogan now has actual information from supplier emissions from 26% of their supply chain spend. Cadogan has identified occupier operations as a critical risk in their transition towards a net zero portfolio, especially if high-end fashion retailers and other luxury goods do not adopt more robust ESG strategies. Cadogan notes that the lack of regulation in the fashion industry is not helpful (Cadogan, 2023: 47).

5.6 Discussion

5.6.1 The actors

The London Landed Estates, self-defined as placemakers and stewards of place, emphasise a commitment to fostering and preserving the character and quality of the areas under their control (Canelas, 2019; Canelas and Raco, 2021). Their considerable land holdings and long-term investment outlooks grant them substantial influence over the development and direction of the neighbourhoods they own and curate.

The historical and contemporary links between ownership and the power to shape the destinies of places are as evident today as in the past. As Olsen (1964) argued, the Landed Estates in England historically operated almost as political entities, exerting control over every aspect of their estates, behaving almost as a political body, ruling every aspect of their estates over which the state chose not to intervene. This continues to resonate today, highlighting the enduring impact of land ownership in shaping urban landscapes and communities (Canelas, 2019). This forces us to consider the links between stewardship and ownership. When applied to ownership, stewardship suggests more than mere possession or control – it implies a commitment to ethical and sustainable management practices. Exploring the links between stewardship and ownership prompts critical reflection on the ethical dimensions of property rights and their associated obligations.

In line with the literature on the London Landed Estates, both Shaftesbury Capital and Cadogan aim to position themselves as industry leaders in a net zero pathway (see Drundford, 2023 for Grosvenor and Howard de Walden). By implementing and demonstrating innovative approaches to achieving net zero objectives, these estates seek to be seen to influence and inspire change across the construction sector. This responsibility extends not only to fellow estate owners and other property developers, investors, and managers but also to the broader construction industry. This has, however, proved challenging so far.

5.6.2 Their motivations

After signing the pledge to reduce their emissions, these property industry players can position themselves on the right side of history, enhancing their reputational value by demonstrating a commitment to advancing global net zero goals in alignment with the latest scientific recommendations for carbon reduction. However, their reputational value is also at risk once they commit to standards that exceed legal requirements. All in all, there seems to be a business case, what the industry has referred to as '...false compromises between climate action and bottom line protection' (SBTi, 2023: 6). This underscores the delicate balance between the net zero ambitions and business imperatives within the real estate sector.

88 *Patricia Canelas*

Climate change and energy-efficient building legislation are key extrinsic factors behind these estates signing and implementing their net zero pledges. The concept of stranded assets is critical in this regard – assets and portfolios that may see their value decrease due to functional or legal reasons. Neglecting energy retrofits could eventually lead to assets being stranded by legislation and becoming unrentable (French, 2020; Muldoon-Smith and Greenhalgh, 2019). This underscores the importance of regulation and the state's role in setting the direction of travel. While the LLEs may exceed regulatory requirements, the mere existence of regulation is an extrinsic motivation that aligns with their other motivations.

In addition to reputational value and climate regulation, reporting requirements motivate these estates to embrace the net zero pathway. Their net zero reports and other publicly available corporate materials highlight adherence to several standard-setting and reporting frameworks, consistent with investigations into the practices of Grovesnor, Howard de Walden, and the Cadogan estate as suggested by Durnford (2023). As emphasised in an industry report, 'there is a strong desire for market transparency and integrity concerning the verification and certification of net zero carbon buildings and portfolios' (BBP, 2022: 8). This underscores the estates' commitment not only to pursuing net zero pathways but also to adhering to guidelines and certifications to demonstrate their dedication to sustainable practices and market transparency.

5.6.3   *Their capacity (or lack of)*

Using the capacity framework proposed by Bennett et al. (2018), it is evident that both estates possess significant capacities, such as financial capital and human capital. They have allocated substantial financial resources to support their net zero strategies. Additionally, they exhibit significant human capital, which refers to the individual and group attributes that enable stewardship. This is evidenced by the committees and boards created to define and deliver their net zero pathways. They also acknowledge that they must continue working beyond their 2030 deadline. Therefore, they will have to maintain both the financial and the human capital in the medium and long term.

Both financial and institutional capital are required to incorporate the broad range of external standards and certification frameworks for validating their pathway. Institutional capacity is particularly critical here, encompassing laws, policies, and formal and informal organisations that shape the external validation process. With robust institutional support, the estates are in a stronger position to learn from standards and demonstrate their pathway through established and accepted methodologies, albeit with room for improvement.

Through these capacities, the LLEs demonstrate their ability to address Scopes 1 and 2 emissions, but they also highlight the limits of their capacity. Consistent with previous research, both estates have shown limited capacity to address Scope 3 emissions, similar to the Grosvenor and Howard de Walden estates (see, e.g., Durnford, 2023). This is particularly concerning given that Scope 3 emissions account for more than 90% of their carbon footprint. Assuming the estates continue reducing Scope 1 and 2 emissions leading up to the 2030 net zero target, the relative importance of Scope 3 emissions in their overall carbon footprint will increase. While addressing Scope 1 and 2 emissions is crucial, Scope 3 emissions are critical in achieving significant progress toward net zero goals. The LLEs demonstrate substantial limitations with this and claim state support to legislate other industries.

Both estates rely heavily on and expect to continue to rely on offsetting. However, offsetting is problematic, as they acknowledged. Results have been discouraging, and currently, there is distrust over some of the largest offsetting schemes and companies behind them (Axelsson et al., 2024). Therefore, offsetting is not an ideal solution the estates can rely on without exposing themselves to greenwashing criticism. These are, moreover, very significant percentages of their emission, about 50% of the baseline emissions (Shaftesbury 56% and Cadogan 47%). Therefore, both estates work with tenants and their supply chains. The LLEs can address issues over which they have direct power, namely the Scope 1 and 2 direct emissions, but they have less influence over matters related to their value chain. Their limited capacity to influence their value chain may mean that achieving their net zero targets without over-relying on offsetting will remain challenging until the industry moves towards net zero. The estates are not alone in grappling with Scope 3 emissions challenges. According to a survey by SBTi of companies that had not submitted a net zero target, 21% cited the challenge of understanding and managing Scope 3 emissions (Bryan and Pooler, 2024). This highlights the broader industry need for innovative solutions and collaborative efforts to address Scope 3 emissions and advance towards comprehensive net zero strategies.

5.7   Conclusions

This paper used the environmental stewardship framework proposed by Bennett et al. (2018) to investigate the motivations and capacity of long-term land and property owners in their net zero trajectories. It aims to explore how to better understand the motivations and capacity of some property industry actors in their trajectory towards net zero. The framework enabled exploring LLEs' net zero strategies based on published sources through the lens of stewardship theory and exploring the relationship between land ownership and environmental outcomes via the urban development and investment process.

The findings indicate that motivations driving sustainable practices are both intrinsic and extrinsic. LLEs are in a favourable position to prioritise net zero goals, including exceeding the required standards. Their extensive property portfolios in some of the most expensive parts of London, coupled with long-term investment outlooks, provide them with the necessary resources and capacity to develop and reach out to technical experts to develop and implement their net zero strategies.

Regarding extrinsic motivations, regulatory rewards and sanctions, such as mandatory reporting systems and Minimum Energy Efficient Standards, including EPC ratings, play a crucial role. The need for disclosure is an extrinsic incentive to perform well, with the potential for damaging reputational value if the estates are not perceived as doing the right thing. External sources assess the Estates, which helps to avoid criticism of greenwashing of 'just lip service'. The current rise of the doing well while doing good industry further supports this opportunity for the Estates.

When considering these urban stewards' practices in transitioning towards net zero, it is crucial to recognise that this transition co-occurs on multiple fronts. One aspect involves material interventions in the built environment, such as improving building energy efficiency and implementing renewable energy systems. However, the discursive level of intervention is equally significant. Strategies play a crucial role in shaping the discourse around net zero. These documents articulate goals, priorities, and approaches for achieving net zero targets, influencing decision-making processes, including procurement practices and guiding action at various levels of their value chains.

Moreover, the critical distinction that emerges based on emission scopes is essential for understanding the true impact of net zero initiatives within real estate companies. While Scope 1 emissions, which include direct emissions from owned or controlled sources like buildings and vehicles, may be on target to reach net zero, it is essential to recognise that this is only one part of the equation. The value chain emissions, encompassing Scope 2 (indirect emissions from purchased electricity, heat, or steam) and Scope 3 (indirect emissions from sources not owned or controlled by the company, such as supply chains and tenant activities), present a more significant challenge. These emissions comprise a substantial part of a company's carbon footprint, and addressing them requires cooperation and coordination across multiple stakeholders.

While the LLEs may be making progress in reducing their Scope 1 emissions through material interventions in the built environment, such as energy-efficient retrofits, low carbon new build and renewable energy installations, their value chain emissions remain a concern. Material interventions are crucial for achieving net zero emissions within a company's direct operations, but equally, attention to the discursive level is important for addressing value chain emissions. Strategies, procurement regulations, and green leases can influence stakeholders throughout the value chain to prioritise sustainability and adopt practices that contribute to the overall goal of transitioning towards a net zero future.

To conclude, expanding the urban stewardship agenda involves delving deeper into the identities of those identified and/or who self-identify as stewards of urban spaces. By examining their motivations, practices, and the outcomes of their actions, we can gain valuable insights into how to advance this agenda further. This exploration allows us to understand the diverse range of individuals and groups who are seen or claim to be responsible for caring for and enhancing urban environments. It enables us to uncover the underlying values, beliefs, and goals that drive these stewards and the strategies and approaches they employ to fulfil their roles. Through a comprehensive understanding of these factors, we can identify opportunities to support and empower urban stewards, amplify their impact, and foster greater collaboration and collective action towards the sustainable management and improvement of urban spaces.

References

Axelsson, K., Wagner, A., Johnstone, I., Allen, M., Caldecott, B., Eyre, N., Fankhauser, S., Hale, T., Hepburn, C., Hickey, C., Khosla, R., Lezak, S., Mitchell-Larson, E., Malhi, Y., Seddon, N., Smith, A. and Smith, S.M. (2024) *Oxford Principles for Net Zero Aligned Carbon Offsetting* (revised 2024). Oxford: Smith School of Enterprise and the Environment, University of Oxford.

BBP. (2022) Better Buildings Partnership: Net Zero Carbon Pathway Framework. Supporting Signatories of the BBP Climate Commitment. Version 2, June, 2022.

BBP. (2024) Better Buildings Partnership. Available here: Green Leases toolkit. https://www.betterbuildingspartnership.co.uk/green-lease-toolkit/about-green-leases. [Accessed 3 May 2024].

Bennett, N. J., Whitty, T. S., Finkbeiner, E., Pittman, J., Bassett, H., Gelcich, S. and Allison, E. H. (2018) Environmental stewardship: A conceptual review and analytical framework. *Environmental Management,* 61, 597–614. https://doi.org/10.1007/s00267-017-0993-2.

Bryan, K., and Pooler, M. (2024) Companies take step back from making climate target promises. *Climate Change: Financial Times,* 15, 2024. Online. Available here: https://www.ft.com/content/3ebc5b56-a8f0-4fcd-99dd-9023d7a20013. [Accessed 17 April 2024].

Cadogan. (2021a). Net Zero Pathway. Available here: https://issuu.com/cadoganlondon/docs/3005_net_zero_pathway_22_v5_sps?fr=sNzRlZDE1NjgwODE/. [Accessed 17 April 2024].

Cadogan. (2021b) Chelsea 2030. Available here: https://issuu.com/cadoganlondon/docs/cadogan_chelsea2030_v06?fr=sOGE5MzE1NjgwODE. [Accessed 17 April 2024].

Cadogan. (2023) Cadogan Annual Report 2022. 7 Jun 2023. Available here: https://issuu.com/cadoganlondon/docs/2970_cadogan_annual_report_2022_digital_aw2_sps [Accessed 17 April 2024].

Cadogan. (2020) Capital & Counties Property PLC. Annual Report & Accounts 2019. Available here: https://www.shaftesburycapital.com/en/investors/results-reports-presentations.category1.year2020.html. [Accessed 19 April 2024].

Cadogan. (2021) Capital & Counties Property PLC. Annual Report & Accounts 2020. Available here: https://www.shaftesburycapital.com/en/investors/results-reports-presentations.category1.year2020.html. [Accessed 19 April 2024].

Canelas, P. (2019) Place-making and the London estates: Land ownership and the built environment. *Journal of Urban Design,* 24(2): 232–248. https://doi.org/10.1080/13574809.2018.1433531

Canelas, P. and Raco, M. (2021) The work that place does: The London Landed Estates and a curatorial approach to estate management. *European Urban and Regional Studies,* 28(3): 263–281. https://doi.org/10.1177/0969776421999764

Crawford, R., Bartak, E.L., Stephan, A. and Jensen, C. (2016) Evaluating the life cycle energy benefits of energy efficiency regulations for building. *Renewable and Sustainable Energy Reviews,* 63 (September): 435–451, https://doi.org/10.1016/j.rser.2016.05.061.

Dallas, G. and Lubrano, M. (2023) *Governance, Stewardship and Sustainability.* London: Routledge.

Davis, J. (2018) The resilience of a London great estate: Urban development, adaptive capacity and the politics of stewardship. *Journal of Urbanism,* 11(1): 103–127. https://doi.org/10.1080/17549175.2017.1360378.

Durnford, M. (2023) Contemporary challenges for historic bodies: An assessment of the net zero strategies of London's Landed Estates. Unpublished MSc Dissertation, MSc in Sustainable Urban Development, University of Oxford.

EPA. (2005) *Everyday Choices: Opportunities for Environmental Stewardship.* US Environmental Protection Agency's Innovation Action Council Report, Washington, D.C:

EU. (2010) Energy and Performance of Buildings Directive. Available here: https://eur-lex.europa.eu/LexUriServ/LexUriServ.do?uri=OJ:L:2010:153:0013:0035:en:PDF. [Accessed 29 April, 2024].

EU. (2021) Energy and Performance of Buildings Directive. Available here: https://eur-lex.europa.eu/legal-content/EN/TXT/PDF/?uri=CELEX:02010L0031-20210101. [Accessed 29 April, 2024].

Fernandes, E. (ed.). (2020). *The Challenge of Environmental Management in Urban Areas: Lessons from Africa and Latin America.* Routledge Revivals, London.

Fischer, F. (2017) *Climate Crisis and the Democratic Prospect: Participatory Governance.* Oxford: Oxford Press University.

Fisher, D., Campbell, L. K. and Svendsen, E.S. (2012) The organisational structure of urban environmental stewardship. *Environmental Politics,* 21(1): 26–48, https://doi.org/10.1080/09644016.2011.643367

Foerester, A. and Spencer, M. (2023) Corporate net zero pledges: A triumph of private climate regulation or more greenwash? *Griffith Law Review,* 32 (1):110142, https://doi.org/10.2139/ssrn.4360634

French, N. (2020) Property valuation in the UK: Climate change targets and the value of UK investment properties – A change in sea level. *Journal of Property Investment & Finance,* 38 (5): 471–482, https://doi.org/10.1108/JPIF-04–2020–0043.

Gözlügöl, A. and Ringe, W. (2022) Private companies: The missing link on the path to net zero (March 22, 2022). forthcoming in the *Journal of Corporate Law Studies* (2023), European Corporate Governance Institute – Law Working Paper No. 635/2022, SAFE Working Paper No. 342, LawFin Working Paper No. 38, https://doi.org/10.2139/ssrn.4065115

Gunel, G. (2019) *Spaceship in the Desert: Energy, Climate Change, and Urban Design in Abu Dhabi.* Duke University Press, Durham.

ICGN. (2020) *Global Stewardship Principles.* International Corporate Governance Network. Available here: https://www.icgn.org/sites/default/files/2021-06/ICGN%20Global%20Stewardship%20Principles%202020_1.pdf. [Accessed 29 April 2024].

IPCC. (2023) *Climate Change 2023. Synthesis Report for Policymakers.* Intergovernmental Panel on Climate Change. Available here: https://www.ipcc.ch/report/ar6/syr/downloads/report/IPCC_AR6_SYR_SPM.pdf. [Accessed 19 April 2024].

Jenkins, S. (1975) *Landlords to London: The Story of a Capital and Its Growth.* London: Constable.

McKinsey. (2023) Building Value by Decarbonizing the Built Environment. Available here: https://www.mckinsey.com/industries/engineering-construction-and-building-materials/our-insights/building-value-by-decarbonizing-the-built-environment. [Accessed 29 April 2024].

Muldoon-Smith, K. and Greenhalgh, P. (2019) Suspect foundations: Developing an understanding of climate-related stranded assets in the global real estate sector. *Energy Research and Social Science,* 54: 60–67, https://doi.org/W10.1016/j.erss.2019.03.013.

Newell, P. (2008) Civil society, corporate accountability and the politics of climate change. *Global Environmental Politics,* 8 (3): 122–153, https://doi.org/10.1162/glep.2008.8.3.122.

NLA. (2013) *Great Estates: How London's Landowners Shape the City.* London: New London Architecture.

Nugent, A., Montano-Owen, C., Pallares, L., Richardson, S. and Rowland, M. (2022) *EU Policy Whole Life Carbon Roadmap.* London: World Green Building Council. Available at: https://viewer.ipaper.io/worldgbc/eu-roadmap/?page=1. [Accessed 19 April 2024].

OECD. (2022) *Decarbonising Buildings in Cities and Regions.* OECD. Available here: https://www.oecd.org/publications/decarbonising-buildings-in-cities-and-regions-a48ce566-en.htm. [Accessed 29 April 2024].

O'Kane, J. (2022) *Sideways: The City Google Couldn't Buy.* Penguin: Random House Canada.

Olsen, D. J. (1964) *Town Planning in London: The Eighteenth & Nineteenth Centuries.* New Haven, CT: Yale University Press.

Rodgers, C. (2009) Nature's place? Property rights, property rules and environmental stewardship. *Cambridge Law Journal,* 68(3): 550–574. https://doi.org./10.1017/S00081 97309990146.

SBTi. (2023) SBTi Monitoring Report 2022: Looking Back at 2022 and Moving Forward to 2023 and Beyond. Available here: https://sciencebasedtargets.org/resources/files/SBTiMonitoringReport2022.pdf. [Accessed 29 April 2024].

Seto, K., Churkina, G., Hsu, A., Keller, M., Newman, P. W.G., Qin, B., and Ramaswami, A. (2021) From low- to net zero carbon cities: The next global agenda. *Annual Review Environmental Resources,* 46: 377–415, https://doi.org/10.1146/annurev-environ-050120–113117.

Shaftesbury Capital. (2023) Shaftesbury Capital. Net Zero Carbon Pathway. Available here: https://www.shaftesburycapital.com/en/responsibility/environment/net-zero-carbon-pathway.html#:~:text=We%20recognise%20the%20need%20to,1%20%26%202%20emissions%20by%202025. [Accessed 19 April 2024].

Shrubsole, G. (2019) *Who Owns England? How We Lost Our Green & Pleasant Land & How to Take it Back.* London: William Collins.

UNEP. (2022) *Global Status Report for Buildings and Construction.* United Nations Environment Programme. Available here: https://www.unep.org/resources/publication/2022-global-status-report-buildings-and-construction. [Accessed 19 April 2024].

Weatherall, D., McCarthy, F. and Bright, S. (2018) Property law as a barrier to energy upgrades in multi-owned properties: Insights from a study of England and Scotland. *Energy Efficiency,* 11: 1641–1655, https://doi.org/10.1007/s12053-017-9540-5

World GBC. (2019) *Bringing Embodied Carbon Upfront.* World Green Building Council. Available here: https://worldgbc.org/advancing-net zero/embodied-carbon/. [Accessed 30 April 2024].

WRI and WBCDS. (2021) *The Greenhouse Gas (GHG) Protocol. A Corporate Accounting and Reporting Standard* (revised edition). World Resources Institute and World Business Council for Sustainable Development. Available here: https://ghgprotocol.org/sites/default/files/standards/ghg-protocol-revised.pdf. [Accessed 19 April 2024].

6 Intra-city clean smart and sustainable mobility

Nikos Gavanas

6.1 Introduction

Nowadays, cities account for more than 56% of the global population, a share that is expected to exceed 68% by 2050 (UN Habitat, 2022). The number of people of 65 years old or more is expected to double over the period 2021–2050, reaching 1.6 billion in 2050 (United Nations, 2023). Apart from ageing, society is currently faced with growing income inequalities (World Inequality Lab, 2021) worsened by economic, health and climate crises. These vulnerable social groups, as well as people with mobility impairments and other disabilities, require an accessible, inclusive, and resilient urban transport system (United Nations, 2022).

Over 70% of global CO_2 emissions are generated by cities (Alves et al., 2023). With approximately 95% of its energy needs covered by fossil fuels, the transport sector is responsible for approximately 25% of Green House Gas (GHG) emissions (United Nations, 2021). An average increase of 1.7% in transport emissions was observed in the period 1990–2022, which is equal to the increase in industry and higher than any other sector (IEA, 2023). Urban mobility is responsible for a high share of these transport emissions. In the European Union (EU), for example, it is responsible for approximately 23% of all transport GHG emissions (European Commission, 2023), as well as for 7 million premature deaths and 600,000 road traffic fatalities per year (United Nations Economic Commission for Europe, 2020). At the same time, cities are important drivers of the economy, accounting for more than 80% of the global GDP (The World Bank, 2023). Seamless transportation is an essential component for their economic growth.

According to the above, urban development is strongly connected with the city's transport system. One way to explain this interaction is through the lens of land-use organisation (Wegener & Fürst, 1999). Depending on the spatial distribution of land uses, different activities take place in different locations. To overcome the distance between these locations, transport infrastructure and services are needed. However, the development of transport infrastructure and services not only allows to access the location of a specific activity but changes the overall accessibility conditions. As a result, it affects location decisions of households, businesses, public facilities etc. and influences land-use distribution.

DOI: 10.4324/9781003498216-9

Newman and Kenworthy (1996) propose a typology of the relationship between urban development and the development of the transport system. According to this approach, the "walking city", which was the typical form of cities before public transport, was a compact, relatively small city of mixed land use and high density (10,000–20,000 residents/km^2). The implementation of fixed route public transport networks, mainly tramways and urban trains, in the 19th century contributed to the radial expansion of cities along corridors expanding from the city centre. Sub-centres of mixed land use developed around rail stations. The average population density dropped to 5,000–10,000 residents/km^2, with variations in the urban area. In the 1950s, road transport and, more specifically, private cars offered flexible "door-to-door" mobility. Road connections developed to vertically connect the existing rail corridors and then, to expand the limits of the wider urban area.

The car-oriented lifestyle was, and still is, a main driver of urban sprawl (Glaeser & Kahn, 2004). The increase in car traffic is also the cause of congestion's vicious cycle (Figure 6.1). Congestion can be described as an imbalance between the supply of transport infrastructure and travel demand (Morris, 1977). Under congestion, the available transport infrastructure fails to effectively service the mobility needs, resulting into delays and a lower level of service. Each year, drivers in the EU spend from 20 to 75 hours (depending on the country) in congestion (European Commission, Directorate-General for Mobility and Transport, 2018). The obvious response to the problem of congestion, which derives from insufficient transport infrastructure, is the development of new infrastructure to increase

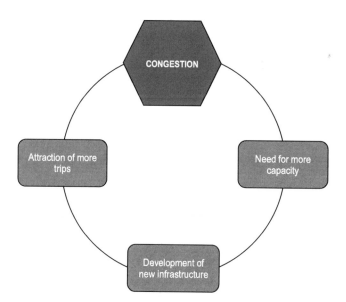

Figure 6.1 The vicious cycle of congestion.
Source: Own elaboration.

96   Nikos Gavanas

the network's capacity. The increase in capacity improves the mobility conditions, attracting new trips and eventually leading to more congestion. This vicious cycle does not only affect the road users but also the whole city and the environment. Time losses, dense flows and stop-and-go traffic conditions have a wider impact on the economy, public health, social welfare, energy consumption and emissions. Congested transport networks affect the continuity of the urban landscape and the connectivity of the city's regions. Moreover, transport infrastructure, and especially roads and parking areas, occupy a significant share of the available land in cities (Rodrigue, 2024). The above impacts are called external impacts (or externalities) of transport and comprise impacts on society which derive from, but are not taken into account, by transport users (Maibach et al., 2008; Verhoef, 1994).

It can be argued from the above that a self-sufficient city is a city whose transport system can effectively address the constantly changing mobility needs of all, as well as the effects on socio-economic development and the environment. Planning for the city's transport system should incorporate all these elements into sustainable and smart mobility solutions.

In this framework, the current chapter aims to enhance the understanding of planning approaches for self-sufficient cities with a focus on urban mobility, by presenting concrete examples from international experience and current practice. Addressing smart mobility, new technologies and disruptive innovation in transport, the chapter also discusses the potential of new mobility services (NMS) to support the transition towards sustainable and smart urban mobility. The rest of this chapter is structured as follows: Sections 6.2 and 6.3 refer respectively to the definition, dimensions and priorities of sustainable and smart urban mobility, and their relevance with the United Nation's (UN) Sustainable Development Goals (SDGs) (United Nations, 2015). Next, well-known examples are analysed from the viewpoint of urban mobility, i.e., (i) The Sustainable Urban Mobility Plan (SUMP) approach, as an example of strategic planning for urban mobility; (ii) The Finger Plan of Copenhagen, Denmark; (iii) The Bus Rapid Transit (BRT) system of Curitiba, Brazil; and (iv) The Supeblocks of Barcelona, Spain, as examples of city plans motivated by urban mobility solutions. Section 6.5 discusses the opportunities and challenges of NMS, in specific: shared mobility; mobility as a service (MaaS); and autonomous vehicles (AVs), for sustainable urban mobility. Based on the above, the final section deals with the identification of the main components of an effective planning approach for clean, smart and sustainable urban mobility.

6.2   The concepts of sustainable and smart mobility

There is no generally accepted definition of sustainable mobility. All attempts to describe sustainable mobility adopt the sustainable development dimensions: Environment, society, and economy (United Nations, 1987). One of the definitions of sustainable transport is the following:

> The provision of services and infrastructure for the mobility of people and goods—advancing economic and social development to benefit today's and

Intra-city clean smart and sustainable mobility 97

future generations—in a manner that is safe, affordable, accessible, efficient, and resilient, while minimising carbon and other emissions and environmental impact.

(United Nations, 2016)

Smart mobility is considered part of the smart city concept, which can be described as the digitalisation of urban infrastructure and services for increasing efficiency, inclusiveness and sustainability and improving well-being and development conditions (OECD, 2020). As part of this concept, smart mobility refers to the integration of innovation and new technologies, such as Information and Communication Technologies (ICTs) (Benevolo et al., 2016), into the transport system to improve efficiency, inclusiveness, and sustainability. Other key aspects of smart mobility comprise: data sharing and connectivity; flexibility; safety and security; automation; and user-oriented, door-to-door service provision (Paiva et al., 2021). In this framework, smart mobility aims for the use of new technologies in transport to accelerate the shift to sustainable mobility.

6.3 Sustainable development goals and urban mobility

The 2030 Agenda for Sustainable Development introduced the Sustainable Development Goals (SDGs) and the corresponding Targets and Indicators. The SDG framework includes 17 SDGs, 169 Targets and 247 Indicators (United Nations,

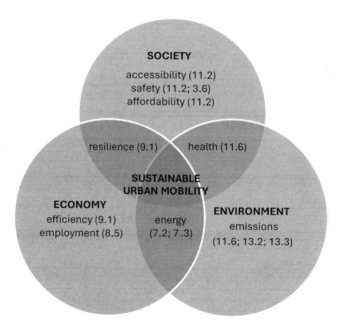

Figure 6.2 Priorities of sustainable urban mobility and related SDG Targets.
Source: Own elaboration

2015). "Sustainable transport" is a topic related to SDG 11: Sustainable cities and communities. However, more links between the SDG Targets and sustainable urban mobility can be identified by considering its environmental, social, and economic dimensions (Figure 6.2). In the Figure, each dimension of sustainable urban mobility corresponds to specific priorities which are related to the respective SDG Targets. A common priority is included in the overlapping space of each pair of dimensions. The overlapping space of all three dimensions is where all priorities converge under the sustainable urban mobility concept. The identified SDGs and related Targets are listed in Table 6.1.

Table 6.1 List of SDG Targets related to sustainable urban mobility dimensions and priorities

Sustainable development goal		*Target*	
3	Good health and well-being	3.6	By 2020, halve the number of global deaths and injuries from road traffic accidents
7	Affordable and clean energy	7.2	By 2030, increase substantially the share of renewable energy in the global energy mix
		7.3	By 2030, double the global rate of improvement in energy efficiency
8	Decent work and economic growth	8.5	By 2030, achieve full and productive employment and decent work for all women and men, including for young people and persons with disabilities, and equal pay for work of equal value
9	Industry, innovation and infrastructure	9.1	Develop quality, reliable, sustainable and resilient infrastructure, including regional and transborder infrastructure, to support economic development and human well-being, with a focus on affordable and equitable access for all
11	Sustainable cities and communities	11.2	By 2030, provide access to safe, affordable, accessible and sustainable transport systems for all, improving road safety, notably by expanding public transport, with special attention to the needs of those in vulnerable situations, women, children, persons with disabilities and older persons
		11.6	By 2030, reduce the adverse per capita environmental impact of cities, including by paying special attention to air quality and municipal and other waste management
13	Climate action	13.2	Integrate climate change measures into national policies, strategies and planning
		13.3	Improve education, awareness-raising and human and institutional capacity on climate change mitigation, adaptation, impact reduction and early warning

Source: United Nations (2024).

6.4   Examples from international planning practice

The current section involves the presentation of concrete examples from international planning practice from the viewpoint of urban mobility and the promotion of sustainable urban mobility priorities. More specifically, the following examples are presented:

- The EU Sustainable Urban Mobility Plan (SUMP) approach, as an example of integrated strategic planning for sustainable urban mobility.
- The Finger Plan of Copenhagen (Denmark) and the BRT (Bus Rapid Transit) system of Curitiba (Brazil), as examples of Transit Oriented Development (TOD). TOD refers to urban development based on public transport, land-use mix and compact development in the vicinity of public transport stations, where active transport is facilitated (Delft University of Technology et al., 2016; Cervero et al., 2002).
- The Supeblocks of Barcelona (Spain), as an example of neighbourhood planning for reclaiming the streets from cars though traffic calming and access restriction. Traffic calming can be defined as "the combination of mainly physical measures that reduce the negative effects of motor vehicle use, alter driver behavior and improve conditions for non-motorized street users" (Lockwood, 1997).

6.4.1   Strategic planning for sustainable urban mobility: sustainable urban mobility plans

The Sustainable Urban Mobility Plan (SUMP) approach aims to guide strategic transport planning in European cities. The official definition of SUMP is:

> A Sustainable Urban Mobility Plan is a strategic plan designed to satisfy the mobility needs of people and businesses in cities and their surroundings for a better quality of life. It builds on existing planning practices and takes due consideration of integration, participation, and evaluation principles.
>
> (Rupprecht Consult, 2019)

The need to develop a common framework for integrated urban transport planning in Europe was highlighted by the 2007 Green Paper on Urban Mobility (European Commission, 2007). The policy document proposes the conduction of Sustainable Urban Transport Plans (SUTPs) to improve accessibility "through balanced coordination of land use and an integrated approach to urban mobility". The SUMP concept was announced by the European Commission as part of the 2013 Mobility Package (European Commission, 2013). The first edition of the SUMP guidelines was published in the same year (Rupprecht Consult, 2013), while the second edition was published in 2019 (Rupprecht Consult, 2019). Since then, the SUMP approach has been at the core of Europe's urban mobility policy, such as the New EU Urban Mobility Framework (European Commission, 2021). In 2023 the EU Member States were recommended to establish a national help office to support their cities with sustainable urban mobility planning (Official Journal of the European Union, L73, Volume 66, 10.03.2023).

The SUMP concept is based on the eight principles (Rupprecht Consult, 2019): (i) plan for sustainable mobility in the Functional Urban Area (FUA), which can be broadly described as the city and its commuting zone; (ii) cooperate across institutional boundaries; (iii) involve citizens and stakeholders; (iv) assess current and future performance; (v) define a long-term vision and a clear implementation plan; (vi) develop all transport modes in an integrated manner; (vii) arrange for monitoring and evaluation; (viii) assure quality. The SUMP process (Figure 6.3) is circular, organised into four phases: (i) preparation and analysis of the current situation; (ii) assessment of scenarios and target setting; (iii) selection of specific measures and preparation for implementation; (iv) implementation and monitoring, as well as evaluation of impacts. The last step, i.e. the review of the process, marks the launch of an updated Plan.

SUMPs provide a realistic analysis of the city's transport system as their spatial reference, namely the FUA, is defined by daily accessibility. They combine expert-based and public participation practices, such as scenario assessment, monitoring and evaluation indicators, stakeholder engagement and cooperation, and participatory planning. Their target setting incorporates all dimensions of sustainable urban mobility and climate change, in line with SDG Target 13.2.

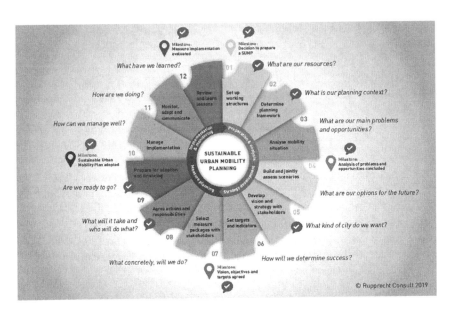

Figure 6.3 Steps of the SUMP process.

Source: Rupprecht Consult (2019).

Intra-city clean smart and sustainable mobility 101

6.4.2 Urban planning based on sustainable mobility

City plans driven by sustainable urban mobility aim to reduce private car dependency and promote sustainable urban development. The examples presented below were selected according to the criteria of Table 6.2.

6.4.2.1 Finger plan of Copenhagen, Denmark

The Finger Plan for the Greater Copenhagen Area in Denmark was developed in 1947 and is still considered a remarkable case of integrated planning for urban development, sustainable mobility, and preservation of green areas (Solly et al., 2021; Global Platform for Sustainable Cities (GPSC), 2018; Olesen, 2022). It was first published as the "Draft Proposal for a Regional Plan for Greater Copenhagen" (Danish Ministry of the Environment, 2015; Olesen, 2022; Copenhagen Regional Planning Offices, 1947). It is a radial development plan which aims to attract housing, commerce, business offices, public buildings, and similar facilities around five transport corridors of the "finger town", while reserving the areas in-between for green wedges with recreational and farming facilities, as well as small urban communities (Danish Ministry of the Environment, 2015; Erhvervsstyrelsen, 2019). Four types of geographical areas are identified (Erhvervsstyrelsen, 2019): The inner metropolitan area, corresponding to the "palm"; the outer metropolitan area, corresponding to the "fingers" which extend radially from the "palm" along the transport corridors; the green wedges in between the "fingers"; and the rest of the metropolitan area.

Since its first edition, different parameters, such as population and economic growth, stakeholders' interests, administrative reforms, and policy priorities, resulted into supplementary provisions and revisions of the Finger Plan (Danish Ministry of the Environment, 2015; Olesen, 2022; Sørensen & Torfing, 2019). The original principles of the Finger Plan were re-established in 1989 by the "Regional Plan of the Greater Copenhagen Council" (with the motto: "better city, not more city") (Olesen, 2022). The Plan became a National Planning Directive in 2007. The

Table 6.2 Criteria for the selection of examples

Selection criteria	Examples		
	Finger Plan in Copenhagen, Denmark	*BRT in Curitiba, Brazil*	*Superblocks in Barcelona, Spain*
Different sustainable transport modes	Public transport (rail)	Public transport (bus)	Active transport
Different spatial levels	Metropolitan to city		Neighbourhood to city
Different periods of development	Late 1940s	Early 1970s	Early 2000s

Source: Own elaboration.

2019 version of the Finger Plan provided a statutory planning framework for 34 capital municipalities in the Greater Copenhagen Area (Erhvervsstyrelsen, 2019).

The Finger Plan is based on TOD along five rapid commuting corridors, which connect the outer metropolitan area with the inner metropolitan area. The corridors comprise five suburban railway lines (S-train) converging to the city centre (Knowles, 2012). Since the first implementation of the plan, new ring roads and public transport lines, such as metro and bus lines, were developed to connect the "fingers". The rail stations along the corridors, which were interconnected with the new lines, became multimodal hubs (Sørensen & Torfing, 2019). According to the Finger Plan directive, major urban development and regeneration schemes in the Great Copenhagen Area should coordinate with the development of public and collective transport infrastructure and services (Erhvervsstyrelsen, 2019; Danish Ministry of the Environment, 2015).

Focusing on public transport as the backbone of a collective transport system, the Finger Plan contributes to the promotion of sustainable mobility and, more specifically, to SDG Target 11.2. A direct impact from the Plan's TOD approach is less private car dependency with a positive effect on emissions and energy consumption. The combination of TOD with the preservation of green areas contributes even more to environmental sustainability. The Finger Plan also aims for a better quality of life through multimodal connectivity between the urban areas and proximity to recreational facilities in the green wedges. According to the benchmarking of European cities on creating the conditions for zero-emission mobility, Copenhagen is ranked fourth among 36 cities in the overall ranking and 5th in terms of access to climate-friendly mobility (Stoll et al., 2022).

6.4.2.2   The BRT system of Curitiba, Brazil

Curitiba is a city in Brazil with approximately 2 million people at the centre of a metropolitan area of about 3.5 million people. Aiming to address the pressures from urbanisation and urban sprawl in the 60s and despite the global trend of increasing private car use, the city adopted a TOD model (ICLEI – Local Governments for Sustainability, 2016). The initial plan to develop a Light Rail Transit (LRT) system was abandoned due to high costs and a Bus Rapid Transit (BRT) system was chosen instead (Duarte & Rojas, 2012). This was the first complete BRT system in the world, launched in the early 1970s (Lindau et al., 2010). Curitiba's network is known as the Integrated Transit Network (Rede Integrada de Transporte, RIT). A BRT system is an integrated system of vehicles, infrastructure, services, and technologies based on the bus as a rapid transit mode, combining the flexibility of road transport with the reliability of LRT. BRT and LRT systems have similar attributes regarding service levels, while the cost of BRT is potentially lower (Levinson et al., 2002). In this context, BRT systems are often considered by planners as a transition phase to integrate higher capacity LRT systems into the urban transport network (Henke, 2012).

The city of Curitiba has adopted a radial pattern of development by implementing the trinary (trinario) system. The trinary system (Figure 6.4) is formed by a main axis with two-way BRT lanes in its core and local access roads on each side.

Intra-city clean smart and sustainable mobility 103

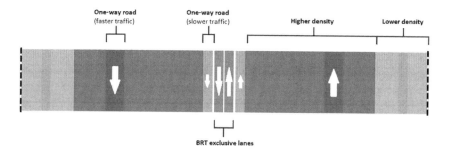

Figure 6.4 The trinary system of Curitiba, Brazil.
Source: Own elaboration.

A single row of high-density mixed land use is located along each side of the central axis. Next to that, a pair of one-way main arteries with opposite directions are located, followed by lower density, mainly residential, land uses (Pierer & Creutzig, 2019; Suzuki et al., 2013).

Curitiba's BRT network has managed to play a key role in promoting sustainable mobility and urban development during the last five decades. In this respect, the examined case is a good example of developing resilient and sustainable infrastructure, as described by SDG Target 9.1. More specifically, because of the integrated transport and land use planning of Curitiba, the share of public transport is around 45%, with buses accounting for only 1% of the vehicle fleet (KTH Royal Institute of Technology, 2018). The share for walking is also relatively high (20%), but slightly lower than the share of the private car (22%). The modal share for cycling is about 5% (ICLEI-Local Governments for Sustainability, 2024). According to these statistics, daily mobility in Curitiba is mostly serviced by sustainable transport modes. However, car ownership in Curitiba has been rising and it is now the highest in Brazil (de Souza & Mulaski, 2018).

6.4.2.3 The Supeblocks of Barcelona, Spain

City planning in Barcelona evolved over the centuries to address the daily life and mobility needs of citizens, starting from the Cerdá plan in the second half of the 19th century (Amati et al., 2024). The concept of Superblocks for Barcelona was proposed by Salvador Rueda in the 1980s (Roberts, 2019; Amati, et al., 2024; World Health Organization, 2021). The first Superblock was created in 2003 in Vila de Gràcia. Superblocks (Superilla) were officially adopted in 2016 as a measure of Barcelona's local government to cope with the current environmental challenges and to improve health and quality of life (Barcelona City Council – Commission for Ecology, Urban Planning and Mobility, 2016). Superblocks were also adopted by the city's Climate Plan 2018–2030 to reduce car traffic, decrease GHG emissions and reclaim urban space from transport (Barcelona City Council, 2018).

According to Rueda (2019), more than 60% of public space and more than 85% of roads are occupied by motorised traffic. At the same time, availability of green space is relatively low with variations between the city's regions. Air pollution levels are sometimes above the maximum levels, while more than 40% of the residents are exposed to noise levels above the maximum limit (65 dBA). Improvement of road safety and opportunities for more physical activity are also considered important priorities for the city (Barcelona City Council – Commission for Ecology, Urban Planning and Mobility, 2016). Superblocks aim to redistribute public space in a more balanced way between people and vehicles by removing motorised traffic from neighbourhoods and replacing it with green spaces. They became a fundamental component of the road's hierarchy and a main contributor to the promotion of sustainable mobility in Barcelona (Ajuntament de Barcelona, 2022).

The Superblock is a block cell of approximately 400 m × 400 m (Figure 6.5) with 5,000–6,000 inhabitants. Traffic calming measures are implemented along the local roads within the block cell, where the speed limit is 10 km/hour. These roads are used for local access, service, and emergency vehicles, but also for active transport. Car traffic across the cell is prohibited. Thus, the interior (intervia) of the cell, where these roads converge, can be used to develop green and public spaces. The streets surrounding the block cell function as one-way streets, forming pairs of opposite directions. These streets are tasked with channelling road traffic (Rueda, 2019; Amati, et al., 2024; Barcelona City Council – Commission for Ecology, Urban Planning and Mobility, 2016).

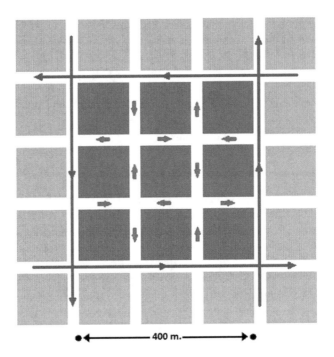

Figure 6.5 The Superblock concept in Barcelona, Spain.

Source: Own elaboration.

Superblocks present benefits for well-being and health (Mueller et al., 2020). Their implementation has the potential to reduce the exposure to noise for 25%–40% of the residents (Amati et al., 2024). It can also contribute to the improvement of air quality, in line with SDG Target 11.6, and address related health concerns. For example, the assessment of pollution levels at the superblock of Sant Antoni showed a decrease in the concentration of NO_2 by 25% and of PM10 by 17% (Ajuntament de Barclona, 2021). However, for Superblocks to be fully effective, it is estimated that a reduction of 21% in car and moped traffic should be achieved (Barcelona City Council – Commission for Ecology, Urban Planning and Mobility, 2016; Amati et al., 2024; Ajuntament de Barcelona, 2022).

6.5 New mobility services and planning for sustainable urban mobility

The unprecedented technological advancement of Industry 4.0 offers new opportunities for smart mobility, capitalising on digital connectivity, artificial intelligence, and flexible automation (World Economic Forum, 2018). New services are available for cities to address their mobility needs through shared mobility, on-demand intermodal transport and autonomous transport solutions (Dotteret al., 2019). These new mobility services (NMS) are defined by ITF (2023) as "intraurban passenger mobility services and vehicles enabled by digital technology". From the perspective of planning, New Mobility Services have the potential to reduce private car dependency and accelerate the shift to sustainable urban mobility. However, this potential is coupled with uncertainty due to (i) the scarcity of historical data and experience from the implementation of NMS and the assessment of the wider impacts; (ii) the disruptive character of NMS which may affect mobility patterns, accessibility conditions and, through the land use and transport interaction, urban development.

Already in 2007, Banister argued that planners and policy makers should make "the best use of technology", in terms of policies for guiding industry and investment, raising public awareness, sharing information, and motivating behavioural change. The author also draws attention to the rebound effects from the increase in travel demand due to the improved services provided by smarter mobility options. Another interesting statement is that these options are not "controversial" for the user, as adopting them is expected to bring minimum change to their everyday activity (Banister, 2007). However, recent research shows that NMS may bring disruptive changes to travel choices and affect daily activities (Sopjani et al., 2020). On this basis, the potential contribution of NMS to each dimension of sustainable urban mobility and the challenges related to uncertainty are discussed in the next subsection, by using examples of new services, i.e. shared mobility and MaaS, and new vehicles, i.e. AVs. A brief description of these types of NMS is presented below:

- *Shared mobility* is the shared use of a vehicle (car, van, bicycle, scooter etc.) by enabling short-term access without having to own the vehicle (Shaheen & Cohen,

2021). Shared mobility services may refer to: (i) vehicle sharing (short-term renting of a vehicle); (ii) ride-sharing (short-term sharing of a ride in a privately owned vehicle with other passengers); and (iii) ride-hailing (short-term hiring of a personal driver and vehicle) (Guyader et al., 2021; FHWA, 2016).

- *Mobility as a service* is the provision of user-oriented, on-demand, "door-to-door" mobility services which combine different (shared and public) transport modes by different operators in a single trip, through a common digital platform that enables the user to remotely plan, book and pay for the trip (UNECE Inland Transport Committee, 2020; MaaS Alliance, 2017; UITP, 2019).
- *Autonomous road vehicles* are road vehicles equipped with telecommunication systems, sensors and other technologies that enable self-driving without the driver's intervention (Li et al., 2016; Gordon & Lidberg, 2015). The globally accepted framework of driving automation comprises six levels, from no automation (level 0) to full autonomy under all driving conditions (level 5) (SAE International, 2021). Large-scale implementation of fully AVs is estimated to become feasible by the end of the decade (ERTRAC Working Group "Connectivity and Automated Driving", 2019).

6.5.1   The environmental dimension

Policy makers and planners promote NMS to reduce emissions, enhance decarbonisation and upgrade the quality of the urban environment (Storme et al., 2021).

6.5.1.1   Environmental concerns of shared mobility and MaaS

The deployment of shared mobility and MaaS can reduce the overall vehicle fleet in a city, as car ownership is decoupled from mobility service. The preliminary analysis of a sample of 15,666 respondents in the Region of Madrid shows that approximately 25% (42% among those not owning a car) believe that car ownership will no longer be required in the future due to shared mobility (Vega-Gonzalo et al., 2024). However, as motorisation rates are still high, further policy interventions will be needed towards this direction (Soares Machado et al., 2018). Shared vehicles, in general, are newer than the average personal vehicle and, thus, have higher energy efficiency and environmental performance (Mubiru & Westerholt, 2024). On the other hand, they are used more intensively and have a shorter lifespan. A full life-cycle assessment is needed for the better understanding of the environmental potential of shared mobility and MaaS (Storme et al., 2021; Oliver Wyman, 2024).

6.5.1.2   Environmental concerns of autonomous vehicles

The large-scale penetration of AVs into the city's road network will probably lead to more regular traffic flows and less congestion, with a positive impact on emissions and energy consumption (Taiebat et al., 2018). On the other hand, the shared use of roadway space by driver-less and human-operated vehicles during the transition to autonomous mobility may have adverse effects on congestion (Soteropoulos et al., 2019). AVs are also able to search for parking away from central areas and contribute to the decrease of parking-related congestion (Tettamanti et al., 2019). Combined benefits can be achieved from the use of AVs in a shared mobility environment.

6.5.2 Social dimension

The implementation of NMS in urban areas has already started to generate social benefits and trade-offs (Gompf et al., 2020).

6.5.2.1 Social concerns of shared mobility and MaaS

Shared mobility and MaaS allow users to make informed decisions about the planning and cost of a trip, based on their current needs and preferences (Soares Machado et al., 2018; Mubiru & Westerholt, 2024). In the case of ride-sharing, cost savings can be obtained due to the more efficient use of the vehicle and the sharing of travel costs (Chen et al., 2022). MaaS systems, which combine shared and public transport services, can offer mobility solutions of high quality with lower cost than using the private car. They can also be more inclusive towards households that cannot afford to purchase a car (Oliver Wyman, 2024). However, a precondition for a citizen to use shared mobility and MaaS is the ability to access and use digital devices (Davidson et al., 2017). It should also be highlighted that capacity constraints apply for NMS, as for conventional transport services (Oliver Wyman, 2024).

6.5.2.2 Social concerns of autonomous vehicles

One of the main competitive advantages of autonomous vehicles compared to conventional ones is the removal of human error in driving, which is expected to significantly improve road safety (European Commission, 2018). In terms of inclusiveness, AVs can be accessible by all users, including those who are permanently or temporarily unable to drive. In terms of comfort, AVs allow for the "driver" to engage to other activities instead of driving. An adverse effect from the above may be the surge in the number of daily trips (Metz, 2018) and the increase of the distance that people are willing to travel, affecting location choices and urban sprawl (Gavanas, 2019). Furthermore, data security and vulnerabilities to cyber-attacks are identified as challenges which may affect the social acceptance of AVs (Parkinson et al., 2017).

6.5.3 Economic dimension

New economic opportunities for people and businesses are expected to derive from the deployment of NMS in cities (Oliver Wyman, 2024).

108 Nikos Gavanas

6.5.3.1 *Economic concerns of shared mobility and MaaS*

The adoption of NMS presents a two-fold opportunity for cities: i. Reduction of the external costs from transport through the above discussed benefits for the environment and society, and ii. New opportunities for entrepreneurship and stakeholder cooperation (Storme et al., 2021). In the case of MaaS, the aggregation of different transport services from different operators creates the opportunity for new business models and the need for efficient collaboration between stakeholders (Hensher et al., 2021). Shared mobility accounts for more than 9 million workers, with an estimated increase of another 7 million by the end of the decade. In addition to the above, the reduction of personal travel costs and the ability to reach previously under-serviced areas can improve the access to employment opportunities (Oliver Wyman, 2024).

6.5.3.2 *Economic concerns of autonomous vehicles*

The implementation of AVs enables new forms of cooperation between the automotive and the telecommunication sectors and affects other sectors, such as automobile repair and maintenance (due to vehicle technologies) and insurance (due to accident liability issues) (Clements & Kockelman, 2017). New job opportunities in technology intensive sectors will be created. However, driver-less vehicles, especially as part of shared mobility and public transport, are expected to decrease the demand for professional drivers. Upskilling schemes are considered important to address this challenge (ITF, 2017).

6.6   Conclusion

The current chapter presents examples of integrated urban transport planning and cases of new mobility services and modes. Regarding integrated transport planning, the SUMP approach offers a citizen-oriented and target-based methodology that covers the assessment of alternative scenarios, the development of a common strategy and its implementation through specific measures. The Finger Plan of Copenhagen and the BRT system of Curitiba showcase the ability of public transport and TOD to address the negative effects of urbanisation. The case of the Superblocks of Barcelona refers to the role of active transport in improving the citizens' health and quality of life. These city plans aim to decrease the use of private cars in specific areas or corridors, without compromising the ability of the urban transport network to service mobility needs. Another common feature of these plans is the need for adaptation to the changing conditions and development goals of the corresponding cities. Regarding the examined cases of NMS, i.e. shared mobility, MaaS and AVs, a main conclusion is that their implementation can be guided by transport planning to contribute the city's goals for sustainable and smart mobility. Towards this direction, planners should consider the possible disruptions that NMS may bring to the current organisation and operation of the city's transport system and the overall conditions of sustainable urban development.

Table 6.3 Revisiting the "alternative approach to sustainable mobility"

The conventional approach – transport planning and engineering	An alternative approach – sustainable mobility	Components of planning for clean, smart, and sustainable mobility
Physical dimensions	Social dimensions	Addressing mobility needs, but also broader social aspects, such as equity, quality of life and employment
Mobility	Accessibility	Considering the spatial pattern of transport networks – Accessibility to under-serviced areas
Traffic focus, particularly on the car	People focus, either in (or on) a vehicle or on foot	Citizen-oriented planning and services for safe, effective, inclusive and healthy mobility – Central role of public participation in SUMP
Large in scale	Local in scale	Integration of scales from a common large-scale vision and strategy to local-scale planning, adapted to specific needs and conditions
Street as a road	Street as a space	Using the street to accommodate different mobility options and public/green space
Motorised transport	All modes of transport often in a hierarchy with pedestrian and cyclist at the top and car users at the bottom	Prioritising public transport, active mobility and intermodality – Introducing new forms of mobility – Discouraging car use
Forecasting traffic	Visioning on cities	Considering transport-land use interaction, SDGs and smart city development
Modelling approaches	Scenario development and modelling	Scenario development and assessment in SUMP – Uncertainty in forecasting NMS impact
Economic evaluation	Multicriteria analysis to take account of environmental and social concerns	Assessing and monitoring environmental, social and economic impacts in SUMP
Travel as a derived demand	Travel as a valued activity as well as a derived demand	Designing sustainable mobility ecosystems which value effectiveness and travel experience
Demand based	Management based	Better use of existing network capacity by space-efficient planning and time-efficient services
Speeding up traffic	Slowing movement down	Planning for effective commuting and on-demand transport, as well as for active transport
Travel time minimisation	Reasonable travel times and travel time reliability	Providing flexible and reliable on-demand services to best serve each trip purpose
Segregation of people and traffic	Integration of people and traffic	Designing for local mixed traffic environments – Collective use of shared mobility services

Source: Adaptation from Banister (2007), as adapted from Marshall (2001).

110 *Nikos Gavanas*

The synthetic analysis of these cases can be used to identify the fundamental planning components for clean, smart, and sustainable urban mobility. In order to frame these components in a solid context, the "alternative approach to sustainable mobility", as Banister (2007) has adapted from Marshall (2001), is used for validation and elaboration (Table 6.3).

Sustainable urban mobility is a constant pursuit for transport planning. Based on the same fundamental components, different planning approaches, such as the above presented examples of Copenhagen, Curitiba, and Barcelona, evolve to address the specific characteristics, as well as the dynamic needs and objectives of each city. Other cities can benefit from these examples by adjusting them to their own planning purposes and using them as inspiration to develop new approaches. In addition, the SUMP approach integrates the fundamental components and the current practices into a common methodological framework for strategic planning.

Nowadays, the shift to sustainable urban mobility is key for addressing global challenges, such as urbanisation, ageing population, and climate change, and achieving the SDGs. Smart mobility and NMS can accelerate this process. However, the long-term impacts from the deployment of NMS are still unknown. In this complex environment, there is a need to introduce the fundamental planning components for clean, smart and sustainable mobility into an interdisciplinary planning process for sustainable and smart urban development.

References

Ajuntament de Barcelona. (2022). *Pla de mobilitat urbana 2024.* Barcelona: Ajuntament de Barcelona.

Ajuntament de Barclona. (2021). *Superilles.* Retrieved from: https://ajuntament.barcelona.cat/superilles/en/noticia/superblocks-are-having-positive-effects-on-health-and-wellbeing

Alves, B. B., Mjahed, L. B., & Moody, J. (2023). *Decarbonizing Urban Transport.* Washington, DC: International Bank for Reconstruction and Development/The World Bank.

Amati, M., Stevens, Q., & Rueda, S. (2024). Taking play seriously in urban design: The evolution of Barcelona's superblocks. *Space and Culture,* 27:2, 156–171, https://doi.org/10.1177/12063312231159229.

Banister, D. (2007). The sustainable mobility paradigm. *Transport Policy,* 15: 73–80, https://doi.org/10.1016/j.tranpol.2007.10.005.

Barcelona City Council. (2018). *Climate Plan 2018–2030.* Barcelona: Barcelona City Council.

Barcelona City Council – Commission for Ecology, Urban Planning and Mobility. (2016). *Let's Fill Streets with Life. Establishing Superblocks in Barcelona.* Barcelona: Barcelona City Council.

Benevolo, C., Dameri, R. P., & D' Auria, B. (2016). Smart mobility in smart city: Action taxonomy, ICT intensity and public benefits. In T. Torre, A. Braccini, & R. Spinelli (Eds.), *Empowering Organizations. Lecture Notes in Information Systems and Organisation,* 11. Berlin: Springer.

Cervero, R., Ferell, C., & Murphy, S. (2002, October). *Transit Cooperative Research Program,* 52, pp. 144. https://onlinepubs.trb.org/onlinepubs/tcrp/tcrp_rrd_52.pdf

Clements, J. L., & Kockelman, K. M. (2017). Economic effects of automated vehicles. *Transportation Research Records,* 2606:1, 106–114. https://doi.org/10.3141/2606-14.

Copenhagen Regional Planning Offices. (1947). *Draft Proposal for a Regional Plan for Greater Copenhagen*. Copenhagen: Copenhagen Regional Planning Offices.

Danish Ministry of the Environment. (2015). *The Finger Plan. A Strategy for the Development of the Greater Copenhagen Area*. Copenhagen: The Danish Nature Agency.

Davidson, A., Peters, J., & Brakewood, C. (2017). Interactive travel modes: Uber, transit, and mobility in New York city. *Transportation Research Board 96th Annual Meeting*. Washington, DC: TRB.

de Souza, H. P., & Mulaski, P. P. (2018). Curitiba Walk City: Revitalization of city center by making the city walking friendly, and sustainable. *European Journal of Sustainable Development*, 7: 4, 445–450, https://doi.org/10.14207/ejsd.2018.v7n4p445.

Delft University of Technology, Nordregio and Austrian Institute for Spatial Planning. (2016). *Transitoriented development and sustainable urban planning, Casual Policy Brief, No 2*. Retrieved from: https://www.nordregio.org/wp-content/uploads/2018/09/CASUAL-PB-2.pdf

Dotter, F., Lennert, F., & Patatouka, E. (2019). *Smart Mobility Systems and Services (STRIA) Roadmaps 2019*. Brussels: European Commission.

Duarte, F., & Rojas, F. (2012). Intermodal connectivity to BRT: A comparative analysis of Bogotá and Curitiba. *Journal of Public Transportation*, 15:2, 1–18, https://doi.org/10.5038/2375-0901.15.2.1.

Erhvervsstyrelsen. (2019). *Fingerplan 2019 – landsplandirektiv for hovedstadsområdets planlægning*. Copenhagen: Erhvervsstyrelsen.

ERTRAC Working Group "Connectivity and Automated Driving". (2019). *Connected automated driving roadmap*. Retrieved from: https://www.ertrac.org/wp-content/uploads/2022/07/ERTRAC-CAD-Roadmap-2019.pdf

European Commission. (2007). *Green Paper. Towards a new culture for urban mobility, COM(2007) 551 final*.

European Commission. (2013). *Together towards competitive and resource-efficient urban mobility, COM(2013) 913 final*.

European Commission. (2018). *Autonomous vehicles & road safety 2018*. Retrieved from: https://road-safety.transport.ec.europa.eu/document/download/b624f334-a7f0-4c46-809a-6ddd8e33aee2_en?filename=ersosynthesis2018-autonomoussafety.pdf

European Commission. (2021). *The new EU urban mobility framework, COM(2021) 811 final*.

European Commission. (2023). *Urban transport. Sustainable urban mobility*. Retrieved from: https://transport.ec.europa.eu/transport-themes/urban-transport_en

European Commission, Directorate-General for Mobility and Transport. (2018). *Transport in the European Union – Current Trends and Issues*. Brussels: European Commission.

FHWA. (2016). *Shared Mobility. Current Practices and Guiding Principles*. Washington, DC: U.S. Department of Transportation, Federal Highway Administration.

Gavanas, N. (2019). Autonomous road vehicles: Challenges for urban planning in European cities. *Urban Science*, 3:2, 61, https://doi.org/10.3390/urbansci3020061.

Glaeser, E. L., & Kahn, M. E. (2004). Sprawl and urban growth. In J. V. Henderson & J.- F. Thisse (Eds.), *Handbook of Regional and Urban Economics* (pp. 2481–2527). Amsterdam: Elsevier.

Global Platform for Sustainable Cities (GPSC). (2018). *Urban Sustainability Framework (USF)*. Washington, DC: International Bank for Reconstruction and Development/The World Bank.

Gompf, K., Traverso, M., & Hetterich, J. (2020). Towards social life cycle assessment of mobility services: Systematic literature review and the way forward.

112   *Nikos Gavanas*

The International Journal of Life Cycle Assessment, 25, 1883–1909, https://doi.org/10.1007/s11367-020-01788-8.

Gordon, T. J., & Lidberg, M. (2015). Automated driving and autonomous functions on road vehicles. *Vehicle System Dynamics,* 53:7, 958–994, https://doi.org/10.1080/00423114.2015.1037774.

Guyader, H., Friman, M., & Olsson, L. E. (2021). Shared mobility: Evolving practices for sustainability. *Sustainability,* 13:21, 12148. https://doi.org/10.3390/su132112148.

Henke, C. (2012). Bus rapid transit and light rail transit systems: State of discussion. In R. A. Meyers (Ed.), *Encyclopedia of Sustainability Science and Technology* (pp. 1810–1818). New York: Springer.

Hensher, D. A., Mulley, C., & Nelson, J. D. (2021). Mobility as a Service (MaaS) – Going somewhere or nowhere? *Transport Policy,* 111, 153–156, https://doi.org/10.1016/j.tranpol.2021.07.021.

ICLEI – Local Governments for Sustainability. (2024, 19 March). *Sustainable mobility.* Retrieved from: https://sustainablemobility.iclei.org/ecomobility-alliance/curitiba-brazil/

ICLEI – Local Governments for Sustainability. (2016). *Curitiba, Brazil. A model for transit oriented development. ICLEI Case Studies 2016, No 190.* Retrieved from: https://www.thegpsc.org/tod/knowledge/model-transit-oriented-development-curitiba-brazil

IEA. (2023). *Tracking Clean Energy Progress 2023.* Paris: IEA.

ITF. (2017). *Managing the Transition to Driverless Road Freight Transport.* Paris: OECD Publishing.

ITF. (2023). *Measuring New Mobility: Definitions, Indicators, Data Collection, ITF Policy Papers, No. 114.* Paris: OECD Publishing.

Knowles, R. D. (2012). Transit oriented development in Copenhagen, Denmark: From the finger plan to Ørestad. *Journal of Transport Geography,* 22, 251–261, https://doi.org/10.1016/j.jtrangeo.2012.01.009.

KTH Royal Institute of Technology. (2018). *Smart City Concepts in Curitiba. Innovation for Sustainable Mobility and Energy Efficiency. Executive Summary.* KTH Energy and Climate Studies, Stockholm.

Levinson, H. S., Zimmerman, S., Clinger, J., & Scott Rutherford, H. S. (2002). Bus rapid transit: An overview. *Journal of Public Transportation,* 5:2, 1–30, https://doi.org/10.5038/2375-0901.5.2.1.

Li, L., Huang, W. L., Liu, Y., Zheng, N. N., & Wang, F. Y. (2016). Intelligence testing for autonomous vehicles: A new approach. *IEEE Transactions on Intelligent Vehicles,* 1:2, 158–166, https://doi.org/10.1109/TIV.2016.2608003.

Lindau, L. A., Hidalgo, D., & Facchini, D. (2010). Bus rapid transit in Curitiba, Brazil. A look at the outcome after 35 years of bus-oriented development. *Transportation Research Record: Journal of the Transportation Research Board,* 2193, 17–27, https://doi.org/10.3141/2193-03.

Lockwood, I. (1997, July). ITE traffic calming definition. *ITE Journal, Institute of Transportation Engineering,* 22–24. https://www.scirp.org/reference/referencespapers?referenceid=2252887

MaaS Alliance. (2017). *White Paper. Guidelines and recommendations to create the foundations for a thriving MaaS ecosystem.* Retrieved from: https://maas-alliance.eu/homepage/what-is-maas/

Maibach, M., Schreyer, C., Sutter, D., van Essen, H. P., Boon, B. H., Smokers, R., Doll, C., Pawloska, B. & Bak, M. (2008). *Handbook on Estimation of External Costs in the Transport Sector.* Delft: CE Delft.

Marshall, S. (2001). The challenge of sustainable transport. In A. Layard, S. Davoudi, & S. Batty (Eds.), *Planning for a Sustainable Future* (pp. 131–147). London: Spon.

Metz, D. (2018). Developing policy for urban autonomous vehicles: Impact on congestion. *Urban Science*, 2:2, 33. https://doi.org/10.3390/urbansci2020033.

Morris, R. L. (1977). Traffic as a function of supply and demand. *Traffic Quarterly*, 31:4, 591–603.

Mubiru, I., & Westerholt, R. (2024). A scoping review on the conceptualisation and impacts of new mobility services. *European Transport Research Review*, 16:12, https://doi.org/10.1186/s12544-024-00633-5.

Mueller, N., Rojas-Rueda, D., Khreis, H., Cirach, M., Andrés, D., Ballester, J., Bartoll, X., Daher, C., Deluca, A., Echave, C., Mila, C., Marquez, S., Palou, J., Perez, K., Tonne, C., Stevenson, M., Rueda, S., & Nieuwenhuijsen, M. (2020). Changing the urban design of cities for health: The superblock model. *Environment International*, 134, 105132. https://doi.org/10.1016/j.envint.2019.105132.

Newman, P. W., & Kenworthy, J. R. (1996). The land-use transport connection. An overview. *Land Use Policy*, 13:1, 1–22.

OECD. (2020). *Smart cities and inclusive growth. Building on the outcomes of the 1st OECD Roundtable on smart cities and inclusive growth.* Retrieved from OECD: https://www.oecd.org/en/about/programmes/the-oecd-programme-on-smart-cities-and-inclusive-growth0.html.

Olesen, K. (2022). Unsettling the Copenhagen Finger Plan: Towards neoliberalization of a planning doctrine? *International Planning Studies*, 27:1, 77–90, https://doi.org/10.1080/13563475.2021.1945913.

Oliver Wyman. (2024). *Shared mobility's global impact. An economic, social and environmental analysis.* Retrieved from: https://www.oliverwyman.com/our-expertise/insights/2023/nov/shared-mobility-global-impact.html

Paiva, S., Ahad, M. A., Tripathi, G., Feroz, N., & Casalino, G. (2021). Enabling technologies for urban smart mobility: Recent trends, opportunities and challenges. *Sensors*, 21:6, 1–41, https://doi.org/10.3390/s21062143.

Parkinson, S., Ward, P., Wilson, K., & Miller, J. (2017). Cyber threats facing autonomous and connected vehicles: future challenges. *IEEE Transactions on Intelligent Transportation*, 18:11, 2898–2915, https://doi.org/10.1109/TITS.2017.2665968.

Pierer, C., & Creutzig, F. (2019). Star-shaped cities alleviate trade-off between climate change mitigation and adaptation. *Environmental Research Letters*, 14:8, 5011, https://doi.org/10.1088/1748-9326/ab2081.

Roberts, D. (2019). *Superblocks. Barcelona's Plan to Free Itself from Cars*. Philadelphia: Kleinman Center for Energy Policy.

Rodrigue, J. P. (2024). *The Geography of Transport Systems*, 6th edition. New York: Routledge.

Rueda, S. (2019). Superblocks for the design of new cities and renovation of existing ones: Barcelona's case. In M. Nieuwenhuijsen & H. Khreis (Eds.), *Integrating Human Health into Urban and Transport Planning* (pp. 135–153). Berlin: Springer International Publishing.

Rupprecht Consult. (ed.). (2013). *Developing and Implementing a Sustainable Urban Mobility Plan Guidelines*. EU Urban Mobility Observatory, Brussels.

Rupprecht Consult. (ed.) (2019). *Guidelines for Developing and Implementing a Sustainable Urban Mobility Plan*, Second Edition.

SAE International. (2021). *SAE levels of driving automation™ refined for clarity and international audience.* Retrieved from: https://www.sae.org/blog/sae-j3016-update

Shaheen, S., & Cohen, A. (2021). Shared mobility: An overview of definitions, current practices, and its relationship to mobility on demand and mobility as a service. *International Encyclopedia of Transportation*, 2021, 155–159, https://doi.org/10.1016/B978-0-08-102671-7.10420-8.

Soares Machado, C. A., de Salles Hue, N. P., Berssaneti, F. T., & Quintanilha, J. A. (2018). An overview of shared mobility. *Sustainability,* 10:12, 4342. https://doi.org/10.3390/su10124342.

Solly, A., Berisha, E., & Cotella, G. (2021). Towards sustainable urbanization. Learning from what's out there. *Land,* 10:4, 356, https://doi.org/10.3390/land10040356.

Sopjani, L., Stier, J. J., Hesselgren, M., & Ritzen, S. (2020). Shared mobility services versus private car: Implications of changes in everyday life. *Journal of Cleaner Production,* 259, 120845. https://doi.org/10.1016/j.jclepro.2020.120845.

Sørensen, E., & Torfing, J. (2019). The Copenhagen Metropolitan 'Finger Plan'. A robust urban planning success based on collaborative governance. In M. Compton & P. 't Hart, *Great Policy Successes* (pp. 218–243). Oxford: Oxford University Press.

Soteropoulos, A., Berger, M., & Ciari, F. (2019). Impacts of automated vehicles on travel behaviour and land use: An international review of modelling studies. *Transport Reviews,* 39, 29–49, https://doi.org/10.1080/01441647.2018.1523253.

Stoll, B., Müller, J., Giaconi, M., & Azdad, Z. (2022). *Benchmarking European cities on creating the right conditions for zero-emission mobility.* Retrieved from: https://cleancitiescampaign.org/wp-content/uploads/2022/09/Clean-Cities_-City-Ranking-Rating-briefing-2.pdf.

Storme, T., Casier, C., Azadi, H., & Witlox, F. (2021). Impact assessments of new mobility services: A critical review. *Sustainability,* 13:6, 3074, https://doi.org/10.3390/su13063074.

Suzuki, H., Cervero, R., & Iuchi, K. (2013). *Transforming Cities with Transit: Transit and Land-Use Integration for Sustainable Urban Development.* Washington, DC: World Bank.

Taiebat, M., Brown, A. L., Safford, H., & Xu, M. (2018). A review on energy, environmental, and sustainability implications of connected and automated vehicles. *Environmental Science & Technology,* 52:20, 11449–11465, https://doi.org/10.1021/acs.est.8b00127.

Tettamanti, T., Horcher, D., & Varga, I. (2019, 09 June). The impact of autonomous vehicles on urban traffic network capacity: an experimental analysis by microscopic traffic simulation. *Transportation Letters. The International Journal of Transportation Research*, 12:8, 540–549, https://doi.org/10.1080/19427867.2019.1662561

The World Bank. (2023, 04 March). *Urban development.* Retrieved from: https://www.worldbank.org/en/topic/urbandevelopment/overview

UITP. (2019). *Mobility as a Service.* Brussels: International Association of Public Transport (UITP).

UN Habitat. (2022). *Envisaging the Future of Cities. World Cities Report 2022.* Nairobi: United Nations Human Settlements Programme.

UNECE Inland Transport Committee. (2020). *Transport Trends and Economics 2018–2019. Mobility as a Service.* Geneva: United Nations.

United Nations. (1987). *Our Common Future. Report of the World Commission on Environment and Development.* https://sustainabledevelopment.un.org/content/documents/5987our-common-future.pdf

United Nations. (2015). *Transforming Our World: The 2030 Agenda for Sustainable Development, A/RES/70/1.* https://sdgs.un.org/2030agenda

United Nations. (2016). *Mobilizing sustainable transport for development. Summary of the Report by the United Nations Secretary-General's High-Level Advisory Group on*

Sustainable Transport. Retrieved from: https://sustainabledevelopment.un.org/index.php ?page=view&type=400&nr=2375&menu=1515

United Nations. (2021). *Fact Sheet. Climate Change.* Sustainable Transport Conference, Beijing, 14–16 October 2021.

United Nations. (2022). *The sustainable development goals report 2022.* Retrieved from: https://unstats.un.org/sdgs/report/2022/

United Nations. (2023). *World Social Report 2023: Leaving Noone Behind in an Ageing World.* United Nations, New York.

United Nations. (2024). *Sustainable Urban Mobility.* Retrieved from: https://sdgs.un.org/ partnerships/sustainable-urban-mobility#targets-tab

United Nations Economic Commission for Europe. (2020). *A Handbook on Sustainable Urban Mobility and Spatial Planning. Promoting Active Mobility.* Geneva: United Nations.

Vega-Gonzalo, M., Gomaz, J., Christidis, P., & Vassalo, J. M. (2024). The role of shared mobility in reducing perceived private car dependency. *Transportation Research Part D,* 126, 104023, https://doi.org/10.1016/j.trd.2023.104023.

Verhoef, E. (1994). External effects and social costs of road transport. *Transportation Research Part A,* 28A:4, 273–287.

Wegener, M., & Fürst, F. (1999). *Land-Use Transport Interaction: State-of-the-art. Deliverable 2a of the project TRANSLAND (Integration of Transport and Land Use Planning) of the 4th RTD Framework Programme of the European Commission.* Dortmund: Institut für Raumplanung, Universität Dortmund, Fakultät Raumplanung.

World Economic Forum. (2018). *White paper. The next economic growth engine. Scaling fourth industrial revolution technologies in production.* Retrieved from: https://www. weforum.org/publications/the-next-economic-growth-engine-scaling-fourth-industrial-revolution-technologies-in-production/

World Health Organization. (2021). *Using urban desgin for health. Barcelona, Spain.* Retrieved from: https://cdn.who.int/media/docs/default-source/urban-health-documents/ barcelona-urban-design-case-study.pdf?sfvrsn=4c91dc2d_5

World Inequality Lab. (2021). *World inequality report 2022.* Retrieved from: https:// wir2022.wid.world/

Part III

Regional planning for self-sufficient cities

7 Solutions to achieve electricity self-sufficiency in regional planning

Comparing São Paulo and Ceará's Brazilian States

Flávia Mendes de Almeida Collaço,
João M. M. Pavanelli, Mariah Pires Carramillo
and Mônica Cavalcanti Sá de Abreu

7.1 Introduction

Energy self-sufficiency encompasses a range of concepts and dimensions, each contributing to a region's ability to meet its energy needs without relying on external resources. Synonymous terms such as self-sufficiency (Park et al., 2013), energy dependence/independence (Covenant of Mayors, 2014), energy autonomy (Rae & Bradley, 2012), energy autarky (Müller et al., 2011), and energy safety index (Liu et al., 2011) all revolve around the central theme of achieving a condition where a region can sustainably fulfill its energy requirements.

At its core, energy self-sufficiency entails achieving a balance between energy demand and energy supply. This can be manifested in various forms, including zero energy resource imports, where the region generates all its required energy locally, or where the energy supply equals the demand. The degree of energy self-sufficiency can be defined as the proportion of locally generated energy to the local energy demand. In contrast, absolute energy self-sufficiency refers to the ability of a region to fully supply itself with its own energy resources without the necessity of a grid connection or external resources (Schmidt et al., 2012).

Both forms of self-sufficiency are often, but not necessarily, based on renewable energy technologies. This reliance on renewable sources is often coupled with decentralized energy systems, which empower communities to generate and manage their energy locally. However, in this study, in one of our case studies, renewable insertion, and self-sufficiency were strongly linked to wind-centralized generation. Nevertheless, relative energy self-sufficiency only indicates a local energy supply, but not necessarily for direct self-consumption, in this case is common that the region also relies on electricity from the grid.

In this study, we argue that the dimensions of energy self-sufficiency should extend beyond mere supply and demand considerations. Factors such as the type of final energy consumption (electricity, heat, fuel, etc.), spatial extent (e.g., municipality or region), type of self-sufficiency (relative vs. physical), and degree of self-sufficiency all play crucial roles in defining the energy landscape of a region. Understanding and addressing these dimensions are essential for crafting effective

DOI: 10.4324/9781003498216-11

energy policies and strategies that promote sustainability, resilience, and local empowerment. Therefore, this research aims to address the comparative analysis of the electricity systems of São Paulo State and Ceará State in Brazil, focusing on renewable production, demand, and self-sufficiency from 2010 to 2022. This investigation seeks to understand the key factors influencing the transition toward electricity self-sufficiency in these regions, and how regional or local system analyses can guide the formulation of coherent and integrated public policies to address climate change challenges and promote self-sufficiency.

To achieve this objective, a mixed-method approach (Creswell, 2007) will be adopted, combining literature on integrated policy, descriptive analysis of energy data with qualitative examination of policy documents and literature review. The primary data sources included historical energy consumption and production data for São Paulo and Ceará States. The databases deployed in this study were obtained from the Energy Research Company (EPE), through the Brazilian Energy Balance Report from 2015 until 2023. The findings were synthesized to inform recommendations for policy interventions aimed at promoting sustainable energy self-sufficiency. By bridging the gap between technical approaches and societal realities, this research aims to contribute to the development of effective and inclusive energy policies at the regional and local levels, ultimately fostering a transition toward a more sustainable, self-sufficient, and resilient energy future.

7.2   Methodology

The methodology employed in this study aimed to discuss and compare two Brazilian States' renewable energy production on its energy resources for generating the useful energy required to sustain the society within that region: São Paulo State in the Southeast of Brazil and Ceará State in the Northeast region of Brazil.

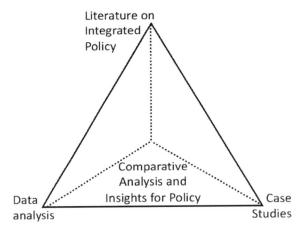

Figure 7.1 Methodological main steps.
Source: Own elaboration with the ideas of Creswell (2007).

Solutions to achieve electricity self-sufficiency 121

To do so, we relied on a mixed-method approach using: (a) the historical trends in the electricity supply and demand for both States' Energy Systems, (b) integrated policy literature, and (c) case studies of each State. The results were analyzed, compared, and displayed with a focus on the informational aspects of policies for promoting energy self-sufficiency. Figure 7.1 displays an illustration of the methodology deployed in this study.

The case studies for each State covered the period from 2010 to 2022, with a specific emphasis on characterizing their respective energy systems. The time clipping was chosen due to the first relevant experiences of renewable energy generation in Brazil. Given the scope of this study, which primarily aimed to explore the potential for energy self-sufficiency in the two States rather than conduct scenario modeling, our data collection and analysis focused solely on electricity generation and demand.

The state of Ceará was chosen for three main reasons: Firstly, it is the third most populous and wealthiest state in the Northeast, with persistent economic growth over the last 12 years. Secondly, Ceará has stood out in terms of the energy transition. From 2021 to 2022, there was a significant reduction of 42% in thermal energy generation, while solar energy production increased by 14% and wind energy by 27%. Finally, when analyzing energy self-sufficiency, Ceará has been registering positive outcomes, demonstrating a reduction in dependence on energy imports from other states, enhancing energy security.

Comparatively, São Paulo, was chosen because is the Brazil's most populous state and the country's economic center. Despite its economic importance, São Paulo faces a considerable deficit in electricity production, consuming significantly more energy than it produces internally. This deficit puts the state in a position of dependence on energy imports from other regions, which not only increases the associated costs but also exposes weaknesses in the energy supply.

For the elaboration of this analysis, all relevant data were sourced from the database of the EPE, through the Brazilian Energy Balance Report from 2015 until 2023, ensuring accuracy and consistency throughout our analysis. Policy literature relied on the approach proposed by Collaço et al. (Collaço, Dias, et al., 2019; Collaço et al., 2020; Collaço, Simoes, et al., 2019; Collaço & Lazaro, 2021), understanding that local policy should integrate social, economic, physical, and environmental drivers while formulating and implementing energy policies. This methodological approach allowed us to offer insights into the electricity self-sufficiency outlooks of São Paulo and Ceará, shedding light on opportunities and challenges in their journey toward sustainable energy transitions and self-sufficiency.

7.3 Grappling on the theory of local energy governance and integrated policy

Collaço, Simoes, et al. (2019) demonstrated the importance of integrating energy considerations into urban planning processes, particularly in megacities like

São Paulo, Brazil. By uncovering synergies between energy efficiency, renewable energy adoption, and sustainable urban growth, the study underscored the potential for enhancing energy self-sufficiency at the regional level. Their findings highlighted the need for holistic approaches to regional planning that prioritize energy sustainability and resilience.

In a similar vein, Collaço, Dias, et al. (2019) explored the potential of transitioning São Paulo toward renewable and endogenous energy sources to enhance energy autonomy and reduce dependency on external resources. By envisioning a renewable energy-based future for the megacity, the study offered valuable insights into the pathways for achieving energy self-sufficiency at the regional level. The research emphasized the importance of diversifying energy sources and reducing reliance on fossil fuels, aligning with the principles of regional energy self-sufficiency.

Additionally, Collaço and colleagues (2020) conducted a comprehensive analysis of the energy system within the Paulista Macrometropolis, emphasizing the importance of local action in promoting energy sustainability and mitigating climate change. Their findings underscored the role of collaborative efforts between stakeholders in driving initiatives to enhance energy self-sufficiency at the regional level. By identifying opportunities for energy efficiency improvements, renewable energy integration, and carbon emissions reduction, the study contributed to the discourse on regional planning strategies for achieving energy self-sufficiency.

In essence, energy self-sufficiency represents a multifaceted concept transcending mere energy production figures. It encompasses economic, environmental, and social dimensions, highlighting the importance of holistic approaches to regional energy planning and management. By embracing the principles of self-sufficiency and leveraging renewable energy technologies, regions can chart a course toward a more sustainable and resilient energy future.

While numerous studies have explored the technical aspects of renewable energy production and its integration into energy systems (Jones & Brown, 2018; Smith et al., 2020), there remains a gap in the literature regarding the holistic examination of energy systems at the subnational level. Specifically, there is a lack of comprehensive analyses that consider the interplay between technical solutions, societal needs, and policy frameworks in the context of regional energy self-sufficiency (Johnson, 2019; Garcia & Martinez, 2021). Existing research often overlooks the human dimension of energy transitions, treating it as an ancillary issue rather than an integral aspect of the planning and implementation process (Thomas & Clark, 2017). Thus, there is a need for studies that bridge the gap between technical approaches and societal realities to inform the development of effective and inclusive energy policies at the regional level.

7.4   Energy system at the subnational levels

More and more, subnational spheres such as cities, States, and regions are encouraged to adopt measures to reduce CO_2 emissions by implementing actions, strategies, and energy planning policies. In this context, local authorities and inhabitants need to gain

Solutions to achieve electricity self-sufficiency 123

experience and consider the analysis of energy systems and energy planning strategies in the regions' planning process. Since fossil fuel consumption is one of the main causes of climate change on subnational scales (Webb et al., 2016), there is a growing interest in increasing the potential for energy self-sufficiency in cities and regions and in promoting the transition from current energy systems to more sustainable ones.

However, there is still a lack of knowledge about the energy systems of each territory and energy demand needs by sector and end-use. Similarly, there is a lack of understanding of the detailed energy supply profile in neighborhoods, metropolitan cities, etc., especially regarding their potential for developing endogenous energy systems (e.g., the energy resources available within the perimeter of the urban or territorial area under analysis, including solar, wind, biomass, local hydrological possibilities, waste, and industrial waste heat).

The territorials' energy demands, along with their respective emissions of atmospheric pollutants and Greenhouse Gases (GHGs), are strongly linked to the physical, social, economic, and environmental aspects of cities (Yazdanie et al., 2017). Therefore, recent literature on local energy systems advocates that the systemic characteristics of energy use are more important for achieving energy efficiency than individual consumer habits and/or technological artifact characteristics (Grubler, 2012).

There is a wide range of territorial planning parameters relevant to energy conservation (Torabi Moghadam et al., 2017), such as urban form and mobility infrastructure. However, most current scientific literature addressing energy planning focuses only on a few components, such as specific economic sectors of cities (residential, industrial, or transportation) specific end-use energy services (heating, cooking, among others), or even specific energy technologies for end-use (such as smart grids and electric vehicles, for example).

The specialized bibliography on energy systems modeling generally suggests sectoral solutions (preferably in urban mobility and buildings) focused on demand, with an emphasis on technological substitution, including building retrofitting (e.g., Simoes et al., 2018). These works also concern themselves with the integration and promotion of local generation through renewable sources. Other bibliographies, such as Marins and Roméro (2014), present a methodology for integrating strategies and solutions in urban morphology, mobility, buildings, energy, and the environment for planning new neighborhoods (or neighborhoods undergoing revitalization).

As mentioned earlier, there is a lack of systematic information on regional energy-use drivers and their interrelations (Grubler, 2012; Grubler et al., 2012). These drivers can be understood as the aspects of territories that most influence the mode and quantity of energy demanded by an area. Each driver can be impacted by a series of social, economic, natural, or even engineering parameters, which, in this case, represent all the variables that characterize any system (related or unrelated to energy aspects). Therefore, it is proposed to structure the territorial energy-use drivers into groups of parameters, as follows:

- *Physical and historical drivers of the region aggregate the following parameters:* urban form (including the built urban environment, mobility infrastructure, and density), together with the region's economic structure and national and international function and integration (i.e., seeking to understand the role that the analyzed region plays within the national and global division of labor from production and consumption perspectives, for example, a more tourist-oriented State may have lower energy demand than a State that concentrates technological or industrial hubs). These physical and historical aspects play an important role in determining regional energy consumption patterns and needs.

- *Current and future socioeconomic and demographic development drivers present as main parameters:* the socioeconomic situation, human capital resources, and behavioral aspects (culture, consumption patterns, and lifestyles), which strongly influence energy consumption levels, as well as economic sectors (residential, commercial and services, industrial, etc.), also determining energy demand in regions.
- *Institutional environment deployed as main parameters:* the normative and political drivers and past and present governance aspects (laws, policies, and current and past programs).
- *Location drivers, endogenous natural resources, and import needs:* include the bioclimatic aspects of regions, as well as the availability of local resources (endogenous) and access to exogenous resources (or import needs of resources for the city, considering that cities belong to a larger context within their region or country). Such parameters influence the region's degree of energy dependence, as well as energy consumption needs.

The interactions between these energy-use drivers may vary from region to region. Furthermore, although the presented drivers are different, they are interconnected and mutually influence each other with strong feedback and synergies. By considering the elements of energy drivers and their interconnections, it is possible to identify a comprehensive and holistic list of strategies to promote development that is more concerned with sustainability, aiming to increase or maintain well-being, energy conservation (EC), energy efficiency (EE), as well as greater inclusion of renewables, through a quest for self-sufficiency.

7.5   Results and discussion

Case study 1: Ceará

Ceará stands out as a leading contributor to renewable electricity generation among the 26 Brazilian States, securing the seventh position in 2022 (EPE, 2023). The State boasts a vast expanse, covering an area larger than countries like Portugal and Greece, spanning 148,000 km^2, and is home to approximately 9 million people, a population akin to that of Austria and Switzerland.

Over the past decade, Ceará has undergone a profound electricity supply transformation, marked by a remarkable surge in renewable energy adoption. Despite the escalating demand for electricity, renewable sources have surged as the primary suppliers, skyrocketing from 27% in 2015 to an impressive 98% in 2022 (EPE, 2016, 2022), see Figure 7.2.

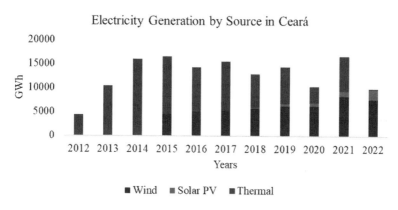

Figure 7.2 Electricity historical generation by source in Ceará State
Source: Own elaboration with data from EPE (2023).

During the preceding ten years (2012–2022), following the inception of pioneering onshore wind projects and regulatory advancements like RN482,[1] Ceará has witnessed a substantial increase in electricity generation from renewable sources, coupled with a decline in thermal power production. In 2022, 77% of the State's energy supply is sourced from wind farms, complemented by 21% from photovoltaic plants (EPE, 2023). This shift has been propelled by incentivized programs promoting renewable energy generation, such as the PROINFA.

Despite facing socioeconomic challenges, Ceará has emerged as a frontrunner in the realm of energy transition and diversification of electricity generation sources. Notably, the State has successfully reduced its reliance on thermal power plants in favor of less polluting alternatives such as wind and photovoltaic energy. This transition is evident in the period spanning 2015 to 2022. Primarily driven by the widespread adoption of wind energy from centralized wind farms and the proliferation of photovoltaic systems across rooftops (ANEEL, 2024).

From 2012 to 2022, the supply side in Ceará fluctuated between 4,424 GWh in 2012 to a peak of 16,609 GWh in 2021 (Table 7.1). The greater variability in energy supply suggests that Ceará may face challenges in ensuring a consistent and reliable energy supply to meet demand fluctuations. Factors such as weather variability affecting renewable energy generation (e.g., intermittence of wind and solar irradiation) or disruptions in traditional energy sources (e.g., fossil fuels) could contribute to the observed supply-side fluctuations. The data indicates fluctuations in self-sufficiency performance, with some years exhibiting surplus generation (exporting electricity) and others showing deficits (importing electricity). The variability in self-sufficiency is influenced by factors such as renewable energy production, demand patterns, and external electricity trade.

Table 7.1 Ceará supply, demand and self-sufficiency historical performance in GWh

Ceará	Supply	Demand	Import/export (%)	Self-sufficiency
2012	4,424	10,024	−127	−5,599
2013	10,396	10,808	−4	−412
2014	15,956	11,356	29	4,600
2015	16,519	11,325	31	5,193
2016	14,343	11,913	17	2,429
2017	15,547	11,424	27	4.122
2018	12,957	11,265	13	1,691
2019	14,395	12,279	15	2,115
2020	10,345	11,947	−15	−1,602
2021	16,609	13,200	21	3,408
2022	9,872	12,884	−31	−3,012

Source: Own elaboration with data from EPE (2023).

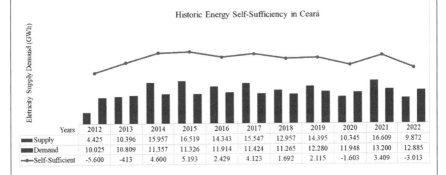

Figure 7.3 Ceará's historical self-sufficiency performance.
Source: Own elaboration with data obtained from EPE (2023).

For the demand side, the relatively stable energy demand, ranging from 10,024 up to 13,200 GWh, may indicate consistent patterns in energy consumption within Ceará, possibly driven by factors such as population growth, industrial activity, and residential consumption habits. Ceará, and Brazil in general, still lack infrastructure, access to fundamental rights, and conditions for effectively realizing local/regional vocations. This electricity demand necessary to ensure a good quality of life for the population is not adequately addressed by public policies, which has kept demand growth constant with demographic changes.

Figure 7.3 shows the import/export dynamics of Ceará and indicates whether Ceará is a net importer or exporter of electricity. For most years, Ceará appears to be a net exporter, with positive values indicating a surplus of around 13% up to 31% of its electricity production. However, there are a few years, such as 2012 and 2022, where Ceará becomes a net importer, indicating a deficit in energy supply, since demand did not present significant variation.

The degree of self-sufficiency in energy production fluctuates over the years (Figure 7.3). Positive values indicate that Ceará is producing more energy than it consumes, while negative values indicate a deficit. The degree of self-sufficiency varies, reaching a peak of 5,193.27 GWh in 2015 and a low of -5,599.84 GWh in 2012. Overall, the data suggests that while Ceará experiences fluctuations in energy supply, it generally maintains a degree of self-sufficiency in electricity production, with occasional periods of surplus and deficit.

The data shows significant contributions from renewable energy sources, particularly wind and solar photovoltaic (PV) energy, in electricity generation. Wind energy has been consistently increasing over the years, becoming a substantial component of Ceará's energy mix. Solar PV energy has also shown remarkable growth, albeit from a smaller base.

Overall, there has been an upward trend in total electricity generation in Ceará over the years, with fluctuations attributed to variations in renewable and thermal energy production. The increasing role of renewable sources, especially wind and solar, is notable. Furthermore, the discrepancy between supply and demand variations underscores the importance of adopting a holistic approach to energy planning and management in Ceará, considering both supply-side and demand-side dynamics to ensure a stable and sustainable energy system for the region's residents and industries.

Policymakers and energy planners in Ceará may need to focus on strategies to enhance the reliability and resilience of the energy supply infrastructure to mitigate the impacts of supply-side variability. This could involve investing in diversified energy sources, improving energy storage capabilities, and implementing demand-side management measures, such as efficiency programs, to better match supply and demand patterns.

Case study 2: São Paulo

São Paulo State, located in the southeastern region of Brazil, stands as a prominent economic and cultural hub within the country. With a land area of approximately 248,209 km^2, it is similar in size to the State of Illinois in the United States or the country of Romania in Europe.

São Paulo State boasts a significant demographic presence, housing over 45 million inhabitants according to the latest census data from the Brazilian Institute of Geography and Statistics (IBGE, 2022). As the powerhouse of Brazil's economy, São Paulo State contributes significantly to the nation's Gross Domestic Product (GDP), with a robust and diversified economy encompassing sectors such as manufacturing, services, agriculture, and technology. In the ranking of the largest economies, São Paulo State's economy ranks 21st in the world (US$ 603.4 billion) for the year 2019.

The energy system of São Paulo, unlike what we have just analyzed about the state of Ceará, did not undergo many changes in the period analyzed. Throughout this period, hydroelectric power remained a steadfast contributor to São Paulo's energy portfolio, maintaining consistent generation levels despite minor fluctuations. With generation figures ranging from 32,961 GWh in 2015 to 28,311 GWh in 2022, hydroelectric power emerged as a cornerstone of the State's renewable energy strategy, reflecting its abundant water resources and historical investments in hydroelectric infrastructure (both centralized and small hydroelectric).

However, amidst the subdued performance of wind energy, solar PV generation experienced remarkable growth, emerging as an important player in São Paulo's energy state expansion. Although timidly, the share of solar energy grew from 3 GWh in 2015 to 3,491 GWh in 2022, reflecting São Paulo's implementation of supportive policies and incentives to promote renewable energy development and investment, such as the RN482.

Thermal power maintained a significant presence in São Paulo's energy landscape, comprising both fossil fuel-based and renewable sources mainly because of the State's strong incentives to the sugar and ethanol industry, as we observe in Figure 7.4.

The analysis of electricity supply, demand, and self-sufficiency in São Paulo State reveals a consistent and concerning trend of growing dependence on external sources to meet energy needs (Table 7.2).

Over the period from 2012 to 2022, there is a clear and significant deficit between electricity supply and demand, resulting in negative self-sufficiency values each year. The gap between electricity supply and demand has widened over time, indicating a progressive imbalance in the State's energy ecosystem. This imbalance poses significant challenges to

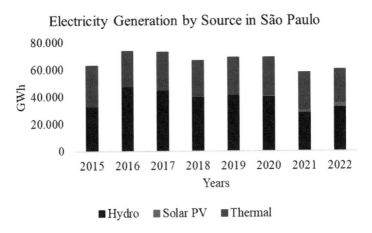

Figure 7.4 Electricity historical generation by source in São Paulo State.
Source: Own elaboration with data obtained from EPE (2023).

Table 7.2 São Paulo Supply, Demand and Self-sufficiency historical performance in GWh

São Paulo	Supply	Demand	Import/export (%)	Self-sufficiency
2012	78,539	133,742	−70	−55,202
2013	75,517	136,244	−80	−60,727
2014	65,506	136,481	−108	−70,974
2015	62,654	130,814	−109	−68,160
2016	73,460	127,170	−73	−53,710
2017	72,576	129,607	−79	−57,031
2018	66,494	132,435	−99	−65,941
2019	68,717	132,848	−93	−64,131
2020	68,607	129224	−88	−60,617
2021	57,659	133,273	−131	−75,614
2022	59,887	138,022	−130	−78,135

Source: Own elaboration with data obtained from EPE (2023).

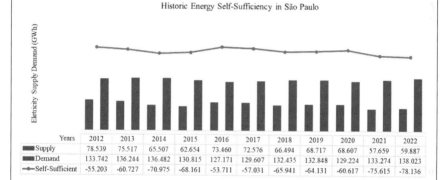

Figure 7.5 São Paulo's historical self-sufficiency performance.
Source: Own elaboration with data obtained from EPE (2023).

energy security, reliability, and affordability, as São Paulo relies increasingly on external sources to bridge the shortfall in domestic electricity production. This threat posed by electricity dependence gains even more relevance considering that the State is responsible for 25% of the national GDP and 22% of the national population (IBGE, 2022).

Despite fluctuations in both supply and demand, the overall trend is one of widening disparity, with demand consistently outstripping supply in the long term, as shown in the moving average tendency curve in Figure 7.5 (dotted gray line) where the black curve represents the deficit per year from 2012 to 2022.

This suggests underlying structural issues in the State's energy infrastructure, planning, and policies that must be addressed to ensure a more balanced and sustainable energy system. The negative self-sufficiency values underscore the urgency of implementing measures to enhance energy resilience and reduce dependency on external energy sources. Strategies such as diversifying energy sources, investing in renewable energy infrastructure, improving EE, and promoting demand-side management are essential to mitigate the risk of energy shortages and disruptions (Figure 7.5).

By promoting renewable energy deployment in a decentralized manner, improving energy infrastructure, and enhancing energy conservation efforts, São Paulo can reduce its dependence on external energy sources and enhance its energy security and sustainability in the long term.

In conclusion, the data on electricity supply, demand, and self-sufficiency highlight the importance of proactive measures to address energy security challenges and promote sustainable energy development in São Paulo State. By adopting a comprehensive and integrated approach to energy planning and management, São Paulo can build a more resilient and sustainable energy future for its residents and businesses.

7.5.1   Ceará and São Paulo similarities and differences

Both cases analyzed were under the same regulatory environment. The PROINFA in 2002, incentivized Wind, small hydroelectric, and biomass electricity generation, and the RN482 from 2012, which regulated distributed generation. Those regulatory measures are defined at the federal level, and therefore, set the same condition for both States analyzed.

According to Figure 7.6, one can observe in the case of Ceará, the population consistently grew at a rate of approximately 1% per year, reaching 8,794,957 in 2021, with a decrease of 5% in 2022. GDP and industrial GDP also showed growth over the years, with a notable increase of 28% in industrial GDP in 2021. However, the supply of electricity had significant fluctuations, peaking in 2015 and sharply declining in 2022, resulting in a 68% reduction from the previous year. Electricity demand, on the other hand, remained relatively stable, with minor variations year-on-year, indicating some consistency in per capita energy consumption patterns.

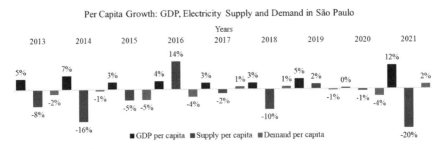

Figure 7.6 São Paulo and Ceará's historical self-sufficiency performance (2013–2021).
Source: Own elaboration with data obtained from EPE (2023).

Solutions to achieve electricity self-sufficiency 131

In the case of São Paulo, we observe a similar pattern of population growth, GDP, and industrial GDP, with annual growth rates ranging from 1% to 4%. The supply of electricity, however, showed a downward trend from 2012, with a 19% decrease in 2021 compared to the previous year. This contrasts with electricity demand, which exhibited smaller fluctuations but still recorded a 3% increase in 2022.

When analyzing these data, it is evident that both Ceará and São Paulo face challenges in ensuring an adequate supply of electricity to meet the growing demand of their populations and expanding economies. These challenges can be attributed to a range of factors, including variations in energy production, changes in consumption patterns, and underdeveloped energy infrastructure. Thus, proactive measures are necessary to ensure a reliable and sustainable energy supply for both regions. In conclusion, when comparing the growth of electricity supply and demand between the states of Ceará and São Paulo, we can observe similar patterns of population, economic, and industrial growth over the years. Both states experienced consistent increases in key indicators, such as GDP and industrial GDP, reflecting positive economic development.

However, in terms of electricity supply, there are significant disparities between the two states. While Ceará experienced sharp fluctuations in electricity supply, with a steep decline in 2022, São Paulo demonstrated a consistent downward trend over the years. In contrast, electricity demand remained relatively stable in both states, with minor year-on-year variations. This demand stability can be attributed to factors such as consistent population growth and similar energy consumption patterns. However, fluctuations in electricity supply highlight the need for proactive measures to ensure a reliable and sustainable electricity supply in both regions, especially in the face of continued population and economic growth.

However, the wind availability is not the same for the States. Ceará has much more wind and solar potential to be explored and pent-up demand for energy (Governo do Estado do Ceará, 2019), meanwhile, São Paulo is a state with much higher energy consumption, a much more disputed territorial use of land and with an industrial vocation focused on historical biomass and encouraged by programs such as Pro-alcool (1975).

The case studies of renewable energy supply in São Paulo and Ceará exemplify the prioritizing of renewable energy policies, but they also still need external energy sources to safeguard their electricity supply. While both States have made strides in adopting renewable energy, their outcomes in terms of import/export needs vary considerably, especially in shorter periods.

The cases show how policies to encourage renewables in two very different contexts were in fact successful in increasing the installed capacity of renewables, as well as electricity generation through renewables for each of the states, contributing positively to a "cleaner" national grid. However, such policies have not advanced the understanding of their regional energy systems. Even the state of CE, which transitioned its matrix, had self-sufficiency problems in recent years (2020), electricity generation remained at a relatively constant volume over the years, while demand remained stable, which is a problem since the state of Ceará has significant cases of energy poverty.

132 *Flávia Mendes de Almeida Collaço et al.*

The state of São Paulo, in turn, has fewer options to expand its matrix and therefore must focus mainly on solutions based on demand management, and there are no policies in force in the state in this regard.

Finally, this study suggests that comprehensive and integrated policy could support more rapid electricity transitions. This can be done by encompassing self-sufficiency and universal, perennial, and affordable access and boosting local participation in crafting and adapting federal regulations to better cope with local institutional features.

7.6 Conclusion

The analysis of electricity self-sufficiency serves as a critical lens through which various stakeholders can assess and address energy challenges effectively. By highlighting the gap between energy supply and demand, self-sufficiency metrics provide valuable insights for policymakers, decision-makers, civil society, and environmental agencies. Understanding the dynamics of energy production and consumption supports stakeholders to develop informed strategies and initiatives to enhance energy security, reliability, and sustainability.

The results, analysis, and comparison from the case study of Ceará reveal a State that has made significant strides in renewable electricity generation, positioning itself as a leader among Brazilian States. Renewable energy sources have surged to the forefront. This transition has been chiefly driven by the proliferation of wind farms and photovoltaic plants, which now contribute with 77% and 21% of the State's energy supply, respectively. Despite socioeconomic challenges, Ceará has successfully reduced its reliance on thermal power plants, marking a significant achievement in its energy transition journey.

The data analysis also sheds light on fluctuations in energy supply, demand, and self-sufficiency within Ceará's energy system. While renewable energy adoption has surged, leading to increased electricity generation, the State still faces challenges in ensuring a consistent and reliable energy supply. Import/export dynamics reveal Ceará's status as a net exporter of electricity in most years, with occasional deficits observed in 2012 and 2022. Besides the difficulty of self-maintaining sustainability over electricity supply, there is other negligence, such as accompanying the energy poverty conditions and considering local social impacts.

Turning to São Paulo State, the analysis uncovers a contrasting energy landscape characterized by growing dependence on external sources to meet energy needs. Despite boasting a significant demographic presence and economic prowess, São Paulo faces a widening disparity between electricity supply and demand, resulting in negative self-sufficiency values each year from 2012 to 2022. This trend underscores structural challenges in the State's energy infrastructure, planning, and policies, necessitating urgent measures to enhance energy resilience and reduce dependency on external sources. Strategies such as diversifying energy sources, investing in decentralized renewable energy infrastructure, improving EE, and promoting demand-side management are crucial to mitigate the risk of energy shortages and disruptions. By adopting a comprehensive and integrated approach to energy planning and management, São Paulo can build a more resilient and sustainable energy future, ensuring the well-being of its residents and businesses in the years to come.

São Paulo's deficit in electricity self-sufficiency underscores the need for targeted interventions to boost demand-side management strategies. In contrast, Ceará's success in achieving high levels of renewable energy deployment also did not necessarily guarantee the State's self-sufficiency in all years analyzed in this chapter. This can be related to the learning curve necessary to deal with intermittent energy primary sources, such as the sun's irradiance and the wind patterns.

However, it is important to acknowledge certain limitations within this study. Firstly, the analysis primarily focuses on the electricity sector, neglecting other essential aspects of energy systems such as transportation, heating, and industrial processes. Consequently, the broader concept of energy self-sufficiency, encompassing various energy sources and sectors, remains unexplored. Additionally, while the paper discusses renewable energy potential a more in-depth analysis of these factors could provide valuable insights into the feasibility and sustainability of energy transitions.

Moreover, the study does not delve into the specific drivers of energy demand within different sectors of São Paulo and Ceará States. Understanding the unique energy consumption profiles of residential, commercial, industrial, and transportation sectors is crucial for developing targeted strategies to enhance EE and self-sufficiency. Furthermore, the analysis overlooks the broader contextual factors influencing energy systems, including political, geographical, and economic dynamics. A more holistic approach that considers these multifaceted drivers could offer a comprehensive understanding of the challenges and opportunities for achieving energy self-sufficiency.

In light of these limitations, future research endeavors should strive to adopt a more integrated and comprehensive approach to analyzing energy systems. By incorporating a broader range of energy sources, sectors, and contextual factors, researchers can generate more robust insights and recommendations to guide policy-making and decision-making processes toward a sustainable and self-sufficient energy future.

Note

1 Normative Resolution from 2012, that established the general conditions for micro-generation and distributed minigeneration access to the electrical energy distribution systems and the electrical energy compensation system for Brazil.

References

ANEEL - Agência Nacional de Energia Elétrica (2024). SiGAA - Sistema de Gestão de Atividades Acadêmicas. ANEEL, ano de publicação. Disponível em: < https://app.powerbi. com/view?r=eyJrIjoiNjc4OGYyYjQtYWM2ZC00YjllLWJlYmEtYzdkNTQ1MTc1NjM 2IiwidCI6IjQwZDZmOWI4LWVjYTctNDZhMi05MmQ0LWVhNGU5YzAxNzBlMSIs ImMiOjR9>. Acesso em: 10 fev.

134 *Flávia Mendes de Almeida Collaço et al.*

Collaço, F. M. de A., Dias, L. P., Simoes, S. G., Puksec, T., Seixas, J., & Bermann, C. (2019a). What if São Paulo (Brazil) would like to become a renewable and endogenous energy – Based megacity? *Renewable Energy*, *138*, 416–433. https://doi.org/10.1016/J. RENENE.2019.01.073

Collaço, F. M. de A., & Lazaro, L. L. B. (2021). A governança multinível do planejamento energético – limitações e potencialidades para a atuação subnacional. *Cadernos de Campo: Revista de Ciências Sociais*, *31*, 95–120. https://doi.org/10.47284/2359-2419. 2021.31.95120

Collaço, F. M. de A., Schirmer Soares, R., Benites-lazaro, L. L., Berejuk, G., Mott Pavanelli, J., Lampis, A., & Bermann, C. (2020). Identificação do Sistema Energético da Macrometrópole Paulista: primeiro passo para atuação local em Mudanças Climáticas. *Ambiente & Sociedade,* São Paulo, *23,* 1–24.

Collaço, F. M. de A., Simoes, S. G., Dias, L. P., Duic, N., Seixas, J., & Bermann, C. (2019b). The dawn of urban energy planning – synergies between energy and urban planning for São Paulo (Brazil) megacity. *Journal of Cleaner Production*, *215*, 458–479. https://doi. org/10.1016/J.JCLEPRO.2019.01.013

Covenant of Mayors. Reducing Energy Dependence in European Cities. Brussels: Covenant of Mayors, 2014. Disponível em: https://www.covenantofmayors.eu/IMG/pdf/Covenant_ of_Mayors_Brochure.pdf. Acesso em: 9 jul. 2024.

Creswell, J. W. (2007). *Projeto de pesquisa: métodos qualitativo, quantitativo e misto*. 2. ed. Porto Alegre: Artmed.

Empresa de Pesquisa Energética (EPE). Balanço Energético Nacional: Ano Base 2015. Disponível em: https://www.epe.gov.br/pt/publicacoes-dados-abertos/publicacoes/balanco-energetico-nacional-ben. Acesso em: 10 fev. 2024.

Empresa de Pesquisa Energética (EPE). Balanço Energético Nacional: Ano Base 2016. Disponível em: https://www.epe.gov.br/pt/publicacoes-dados-abertos/publicacoes/balanco-energetico-nacional-ben. Acesso em: 10 fev. 2024.

Empresa de Pesquisa Energética (EPE). Balanço Energético Nacional: Ano Base 2017. Disponível em: https://www.epe.gov.br/pt/publicacoes-dados-abertos/publicacoes/balanco-energetico-nacional-ben. Acesso em: 10 fev. 2024.

Empresa de Pesquisa Energética (EPE). Balanço Energético Nacional: Ano Base 2018. Disponível em: https://www.epe.gov.br/pt/publicacoes-dados-abertos/publicacoes/balanco-energetico-nacional-ben. Acesso em: 10 fev. 2024.

Empresa de Pesquisa Energética (EPE). Balanço Energético Nacional: Ano Base 2019. Disponível em: https://www.epe.gov.br/pt/publicacoes-dados-abertos/publicacoes/balanco-energetico-nacional-ben. Acesso em: 10 fev. 2024.

Empresa de Pesquisa Energética (EPE). Balanço Energético Nacional: Ano Base 2020. Disponível em: https://www.epe.gov.br/pt/publicacoes-dados-abertos/publicacoes/balanco-energetico-nacional-ben. Acesso em: 10 fev. 2024.

Empresa de Pesquisa Energética (EPE). Balanço Energético Nacional: Ano Base 2021. Disponível em: https://www.epe.gov.br/pt/publicacoes-dados-abertos/publicacoes/balanco-energetico-nacional-ben. Acesso em: 10 fev. 2024.

Empresa de Pesquisa Energética (EPE). Balanço Energético Nacional: Ano Base 2022. Disponível em: https://www.epe.gov.br/pt/publicacoes-dados-abertos/publicacoes/balanco-energetico-nacional-ben. Acesso em: 10 fev. 2024.

Empresa de Pesquisa Energética (EPE). Balanço Energético Nacional: Ano Base 2023. Disponível em: https://www.epe.gov.br/pt/publicacoes-dados-abertos/publicacoes/balanco-energetico-nacional-ben. Acesso em: 10 fev. 2024.

Garcia, F., & Martinez, G. (2021). Policy frameworks for regional energy self-sufficiency. *Journal of Sustainable Development, 32*(1), 45–56.

Governo do Estado do Ceará; FIEC; SEBRAE. Atlas Eólico e Solar do Ceará. Fortaleza: Governo do Estado do Ceará, 2019. Disponível em: https://atlas.adece.ce.gov.br. Acesso em: 9 jul. 2024.

Grubler, A. (2012). Energy transitions research: Insights and cautionary tales. *Energy Policy, 50*, 8–16. https://doi.org/10.1016/j.enpol.2012.02.070

Grubler, A., Bai, X, Buettner, T., Dhakal, S., Fisk, D. J., Ichinose, T., Keirstead, J. E., Sammer, G., Satterthwaite, D., Schulz, N. B., Shah, N., Steinberger, J., Weisz, H. (2012). Urban energy systems. In: Global Energy Assessment: Toward a Sustainable Future. Cambridge: Cambridge University Press, p. 1307–1400. Disponível em: https://doi.org/10.4324/9780203066782. Acesso em: 9 jul. 2024.

INSTITUTO BRASILEIRO DE GEOGRAFIA E ESTATÍSTICA (IBGE). Participação das atividades econômicas no valor adicionado bruto, por Unidades da Federação – 2002–2021. Rio de Janeiro: IBGE, 2021. Disponível em: https://www.ibge.gov.br. Acesso em: 9 jul. 2024.

Johnson, E. (2019). Local-level energy system analysis: Bridging the gap. *Energy Economics, 15*(4), 210–225.

Jones, D., & Brown, K. (2018). Integrating renewable energy into energy systems. *Renewable and Sustainable Energy Reviews, 28*(2), 67–78.

Liu, D., Yang, X., Tian, X., Wu, R., & Wang, L. (2011). Study on integrated simulation model of economic, energy and environment safety system under the low-carbon policy in Beijing. *Procedia Environmental Sciences, 5*, 120–130. https://doi.org/10.1016/j.proenv.2011.03.057

MARINS, K. R. D. C. C.; ROMÉRO, M. de A. Urban and Energy Assessment from a Systemi Approach of Urban Morphology, Urban Mobility, and Buildings: Case Study of Agua Branca in Sao Paulo. Journal of Urban Planning and Development, Reston, v. 140, n. 3, p. 402–408 2014.

Müller, M. O., Stämpfli, A., Dold, U., & Hammer, T. (2011). Energy autarky: A conceptual framework for sustainable regional development. *Energy Policy, 39*(10), 5800–5810. https://doi.org/10.1016/j.enpol.2011.04.019

Park, M., Kim, Y., Lee, H., Han, S., Hwang, S., & Choi, M. J. (2013). Modeling the dynamics of urban development project: Focusing on self-sufficient city development. *Mathematical and Computer Modelling, 57*(9–10), 2082–2093. https://doi.org/10.1016/j.mcm.2011.05.058

Rae, C., & Bradley, F. (2012). Energy autonomy in sustainable communities – A review of key issues. *Renewable and Sustainable Energy Reviews, 16*(9), 6497–6506. https://doi.org/10.1016/j.rser.2012.08.002

Schmidt, J., Schönhart, M., Biberacher, M., Guggenberger, T., Hausl, S., Kalt, G., Leduc, S., Schardinger, I., & Schmid, E. (2012). Regional energy autarky: Potentials, costs and consequences for an Austrian region. *Energy Policy, 47*, 211–221. https://doi.org/10.1016/j.enpol.2012.04.059

Simoes, S. G., Dias, L., Gouveia, J. P., Seixas, J., De Miglio, R., Chiodi, A., Gargiulo, M., Long, G., & Giannakidis, G. (2018). INSMART – Insights on integrated modelling of EU cities energy system transition. *Energy Strategy Reviews, 20*, 150–155. https://doi.org/10.1016/j.esr.2018.02.003

Smith, A., Johnson, B., & White, C. (2020). Exploring technical aspects of renewable energy production. *Energy Policy, 45*(3), 123–135.

Torabi Moghadam, S., Delmastro, C., Corgnati, S. P., & Lombardi, P. (2017). Urban energy planning procedure for sustainable development in the built environment: A review of available spatial approaches. *Journal of Cleaner Production, 165*, 811–827. https://doi.org/10.1016/j.jclepro.2017.07.142

Thomas, R., & Clark, L. (2017). The human dimension of energy transitions. *Energy Transition, 10*(2), 89–102.Instituto Brasileiro De Geografia E Estatística (IBGE). PIB pela Ótica da Renda (2010–2021).

Webb, J., Hawkey, D., & Tingey, M. (2016). Governing cities for sustainable energy: The UK case. *Cities, 54*, 28–35. https://doi.org/10.1016/j.cities.2015.10.014

Yazdanie, M., Densing, M., & Wokaun, A. (2017). Cost optimal urban energy systems planning in the context of national energy policies: A case study for the city of Basel. *Energy Policy* (Accepted), *110*(June), 176–190. https://doi.org/10.1016/j.enpol.2017.08.009

8 Promoting local autonomy through the circular economy

Rethinking regional development

Sébastien Bourdin

8.1 Introduction

We live on a planet with limited resources. Since the beginning of the industrial revolution, we have extracted and used these resources at an unprecedented rate, often without considering their renewal or sustainability. For instance, fossil fuel consumption has increased exponentially since the industrial revolution began, going from nearly nothing in the early 20th century to approximately 100 million barrels a day in 2022. Extraction of minerals like gold, copper, and other rare metals has also significantly increased since the 19th century, resulting in ecosystem degradation, pollution, and other environmental problems. Consequently, global CO_2 emissions have risen by over 400% since the start of the industrial revolution, reaching around 36.8 gigatonnes in 2022 (IPCC, 2023).

Alongside the resource exploitation, our current linear economic model – which involves extraction, manufacturing, consumption, and disposal – has produced an enormous amount of waste (Voukkali et al., 2023). This waste, whether non-biodegradable plastics, industrial chemicals, or greenhouse gases, has devastating implications for the environment, biodiversity, and ultimately, humanity. Furthermore, our current concept of economic growth is heavily reliant on increased and sustained consumption. For instance, according to the World Bank, global gross domestic product (GDP) was approximately 11.34 trillion US dollars in 1980. By 2019, prior to the COVID-19 pandemic, global GDP had soared to nearly 88 trillion US dollars. Despite the economic and health crisis that followed, growth quickly rebounded, reaching a global GDP of 96.51 trillion US dollars only two years later.

This GDP growth signifies a significant increase in the production and consumption of goods and services. However, in a world with finite resources, infinite growth is not only impossible but also harmful (Stahel, 2016). Climate change, biodiversity loss, and pollution are clear warnings that our current trajectory is unsustainable (IPCC, 2023). The severity of the situation demands a complete reevaluation of our economic approach. It is not merely about minor improvements or slight adjustments; it is about entirely rethinking how we produce, consume, and dispose of (Stahel, 2019). In this context, the circular economy emerges as an alternative (Hachaichi & Bourdin, 2023). Rather than following a linear model, the circular economy promotes a system where nothing is wasted. Products are

DOI: 10.4324/9781003498216-12

designed to be durable, repairable, reusable, and recyclable. The waste from one process becomes the resources for another, creating a cycle of production and consumption that can, theoretically, continue indefinitely without depleting resources or overwhelming the planet with waste (Desing et al., 2020). Ultimately, the circular economy not only offers an alternative to a failing economic model but also presents a new vision of how we want to live on Earth (Korhonen et al., 2018) and hence is a critical element for implementing urban and regional self-sufficiency development strategies. Additionally, Hartley et al. (2023) suggest that the circular economy concept can help manage major systemic crises.

While the challenges of climate change and resource scarcity are global, regions also play a crucial role in facing these problems and may encounter increasingly critical resource management issues. Ineffective recycling and reuse strategies result in many resources, once extracted and used, becoming waste instead of assets reintegrated into the local economy. This 'take-make-throw' model not only depletes natural resources quickly but also incurs significant environmental costs, including water and air pollution and soil degradation (Arsova et al., 2022). Moreover, the linear model accentuates the vulnerability of regions to external economic shocks. By heavily relying on global supply chains for essential materials, regions question their economic resilience and reduce their adaptability. The COVID-19 pandemic (Jeanne et al., 2023) and the recent crisis in Ukraine (Steinbach, 2023) have highlighted this issue, emphasizing the urgent need to reevaluate not only our economic model but also our approach to regional development, aiming for greater autonomy (Bourdin et al., 2022).

In this context, this chapter aims to emphasize the importance of transitioning from a linear economic model to a circular model, where resources are reused, recycled, and redistributed. We will discuss innovative strategies and best practices that regions can adopt to promote the implementation of the circular economy. Additionally, this chapter will explore the role of regional policies and governance in facilitating this transition. We will emphasize the economic, social, and environmental benefits of implementing circular economy policies at the regional level, demonstrating how these measures contribute to self-sufficiency, build resilience, and promote environmentally sustainable regional planning. In conclusion, we will advocate for a paradigm shift in planning and development practices, encouraging regions to adopt a long-term perspective that prioritizes sustainability and circularity over the linear economy, whose limitations are now evident.

8.2   Conceptualizing the circular economy

The concept of a circular economy, although considered a contemporary phenomenon, has its roots in various theories and disciplines that date back several decades. One of the first thinkers to introduce ideas similar to the circular economy was economist Kenneth Boulding. In 1966, Boulding wrote an influential essay titled "The Economics of the Coming Spaceship Earth". He proposed a new perspective on the Earth, suggesting that we view it as a spaceship rather than an infinite, inexhaustible entity. By likening the Earth to a spaceship, Boulding emphasized that it possesses limited resources, just like a spaceship has to work with what it has onboard for its entire journey. This viewpoint challenged the traditional belief that the Earth is an unlimited source from which we can extract endlessly without consequences. Boulding used this analogy to advocate for more sustainable and responsible resource management. Therefore, he argued for the adoption of a closed economy that prioritizes sustainability, recycling, and preservation instead of unrestrained extraction.

Several decades later, in the 1990s, architect William McDonough and chemist Michael Braungart (1994) introduced the concept of "Cradle to Cradle". They challenged the prevalent cradle-to-grave approach to production and proposed designing products that could be fully recycled or composted at the end of their useful life. In this way, these products would either return to nature or reenter the industry, beginning a new life cycle.

Building upon these ideas, the concept of a more regenerative economy emerged. Initially viewed as a concept derived directly from practical applications, the circular economy gradually gained acceptance in academic circles. Researchers from various disciplines began embracing the concept, leading to a proliferation of studies and analyses since the early 2000s. Rooted in different theories, the circular economy progressed from a practical concept to a fully-fledged academic research field (Geissdoerfer et al., 2017; Hachaichi, 2023). The importance of the circular economy has also been reflected in the establishment of specialized academic journals dedicated to this field, solidifying its position as an independent discipline, according to some researchers (Kirchherr et al., 2023). Like in any evolving idea, however, the definition of the circular economy has continued to change. As a result, there are now more than 220 definitions of the concept, created by various experts and organizations around the world (Kirchherr et al., 2023). To consolidate these interpretations, we can define the circular economy as a "regenerative economic system that requires a paradigm shift to replace the end-of-life concept with the reduction, reuse, recycling, and recovery of materials". The circular economy highlights the need to reconsider our traditional economic systems and transition to more sustainable models, especially in a world with finite resources (Velenturf & Purnell, 2021).

The circular economy is opposed to the linear economy, which follows a consumption model of extract, produce, consume, and dispose. This approach has several drawbacks. Firstly, it relies on a constant supply of raw materials. However, this is not guaranteed for two reasons. Natural resources are being depleted, and even if they were infinite and abundant, their distribution across the Earth is uneven, leading to issues of resource access and geopolitical concerns (Le Billon, 2004). Additionally, the production and disposal of products contribute to pollution and environmental harm. Furthermore, waste is inherent in this system, resulting in the loss of energy, labor, and resources (MacArthur, 2013). When comparing these two systems, the linear economy appears to be a short-term model focused on rapid consumption and disposal, while the circular economy takes a forward-looking approach, aiming to balance consumption and resource conservation (Schroeder et al., 2019). The circular economy not only addresses environmental challenges

140 *Sébastien Bourdin*

but also presents economic opportunities. Recovering waste and extending the lifespan of products can lead to savings and the creation of new markets (Krikke, 2020).

8.3 Implementing the principles of the circular economy at regional and local level

As part of the transition to more sustainable economic systems, the circular economy offers guiding principles for reshaping production and consumption. Initially focused on the three fundamental pillars known as the "3Rs" – Reduce, Reuse, Recycle – these principles set the foundation for circular thinking. However, as knowledge and needs have evolved, the vision has expanded to include other essential dimensions, resulting in a more comprehensive approach with the "9Rs" (Hartley et al., 2023). This shift from 3Rs to 9Rs recognizes that achieving a true circular economy requires more than just reducing, reusing, and recycling. The expanded concept of the 9Rs provides a holistic view of how to integrate circular economy principles into all aspects of consumption and production, emphasizing each stage of a product's life cycle, from design to end-of-life. It is important to understand that these 9Rs follow a specific hierarchy. This hierarchy is designed to prioritize waste prevention first (in other words, the best waste is the waste we don't produce), followed by optimal use, and finally efficient disposal. Each additional "R" introduces specific strategies for resource management. In Table 8.1, we have provided a brief definition for each R, along with concrete examples of how the principle is implemented at the local and regional level.

Each principle, from "Refuse" unsustainable products and services to "Recover" the usable elements of waste, is exemplified by local and regional initiatives. These initiatives include laws against the use of pesticides in Piedmont, Italy, San Francisco's efforts to eliminate plastic water bottles, and Stockholm's program that turns food waste into energy. The table illustrates the diversity of approaches to minimizing environmental impact and implementing the circular economy, going well beyond simple recycling, which is often emphasized as the most important (Chioatto & Sospiro, 2023). It also highlights the importance of locally adapting circular economy strategies. The table demonstrates how concrete examples, such as bike-sharing schemes in Oslo to reduce reliance on motorized vehicles, or energy retrofit initiatives in Portland, contribute to a more circular and efficient management of the world's resources.

8.4 The circular economy as an opportunity to move toward regional self-sufficiency

The circular economy provides an opportunity to decrease reliance on imports by prioritizing local production. By adding value to local resources, such as raw materials or transformed waste, territories can minimize the need for external resources (Tapia et al., 2021). This stimulates the local economy by creating jobs and strengthening regional industrial capacity. For instance, the City of Vancouver has

Promoting local autonomy through the circular economy 141

Table 8.1 The nine guiding principles of the circular economy and their application at regional and local level

Principle	Definition	Implementation and the regional and local scale	Concrete examples
Refused	Avoid unsustainable or unnecessary products or services	Encouraging the establishment of stores that offer goods without packaging, where consumers bring their own containers, can significantly reduce packaging waste.	San Francisco, USA: *In 2014, the city banned the sale of plastic water bottles on city property.* Piedmont Region, Italy: *In 2019, the region introduced a law banning the use of synthetic pesticides in public parks and gardens.* Walloon Region, Belgium: The region has introduced a deposit scheme for glass and plastic bottles, where consumers pay a deposit for the bottles they buy and are refunded when they return them.
Rethink	Rethink the way we consume	Local education initiatives on buying products in bulk to avoid packaging. Development of parks and green spaces using ecological materials.	Vancouver, Canada: *The city has introduced a green mobility plan to become a cycling city. The plan includes the construction of new cycle paths, car-free zones, and a self-service bicycle system.* Île-de-France region, France: The region has implemented a plan to combat food waste, which includes raising consumer awareness, supporting food banks, and promoting the use of unsold food.
Reduce	Minimize resource consumption	Local bicycle sharing schemes to reduce individual use of motorized vehicles. Water reduction programs in public administrations.	Oslo, Norway: *The city has introduced a waste collection program that encourages residents to separate their waste by charging for residual waste based on weight.* Catalonia, Spain: *The region has implemented a water management program to reduce water consumption by raising consumer awareness, repairing water leaks, and investing in water-saving irrigation technologies.*
Reuse	Reuse without significant processing	Flea markets organized by the local authority to encourage the reuse of items. Community composting programs to reuse organic waste. Reuse of greywater in municipal facilities.	Amsterdam, Netherlands: *The city has established a building materials reuse program that allows contractors to recover and reuse materials from demolition sites.* Flanders Region, Belgium: *The region has established a clothing reuse program that allows consumers to donate their old clothes to charity or sell them in second-hand shops.*

(Continued)

142 Sébastien Bourdin

Table 8.1 (Continued)

Principle	Definition	Implementation and the regional and local scale	Concrete examples
Repair	Repair rather than throw away or replace	Initiatives for repairing toys and tools in libraries of things. Establishment of free repair stations for bicycles. Community workshops to teach residents how to repair electronic devices.	Berlin, Germany: *The city has established a bicycle repair program that offers free repairs to residents.* Région Nouvelle-Aquitaine, France: *The region has established an appliance repair program that offers reduced-price repairs to residents.*
Recycle	Convert waste into new products	Install recycling collection points in neighborhoods to make sorting easier. Awareness campaigns for textile recycling in schools.	Seoul, South Korea: *The city has established a food waste recycling program that allows residents to compost their food waste in special bins.* Lombardy Region, Italy: *The region has established a plastics recycling program that allows residents to recycle their plastics in special bins.*
Renovate	Renovate old products to make them new again	Subsidy programs for renovating old furniture offered by local authorities. Energy renovation of social housing to improve efficiency.	Portland, United States: *The city has established an energy renovation program to help homeowners improve the energy efficiency of their homes.* Occitanie region, France: *The region has established a program to renovate public buildings and improve their energy efficiency.*
Repurpose	Use an object for a purpose other than its original use	Projects to transform old industrial buildings into coworking spaces. Conversion of old buses into mobile cafes or community spaces.	London, United Kingdom: *The city has established a program to repurpose old shipping containers into commercial and community spaces.* Auvergne-Rhône-Alpes region, France: *The region has established a program to convert old buses into mobile libraries.*
Recover	Extract components from objects that cannot be recycled to produce energy	Use of wood waste for community heating.	Stockholm, Sweden: *The city has established a food waste-to-energy program that converts food waste into energy.* Brittany, France: *The region has established a forestry waste-to-energy program that converts forestry waste into biogas.*

Source: Author's own elaboration.

embraced a circular economy strategy with the objective of becoming the greenest city in the world by 2050. This strategy is based on multiple pillars, including waste reduction, promoting the circular economy in the construction sector, and developing new circular business models. An example of this is the Zero Waste Vancouver project, which aims to reduce waste by 50% by 2030.

One of the fundamental principles of the circular economy is the utilization of waste as a resource. For example, organic waste can be transformed into compost for local agriculture, diminishing the need for imported chemical fertilizers and lessening the environmental impact. Moreover, this waste-to-resource conversion contributes to more sustainable waste management and reduces associated costs. Bio-waste can also be converted into biogas, utilizing biomass waste (e.g., food industry waste, green waste, agricultural waste) to produce energy that can be consumed locally (Vinci et al., 2017). This promotes local self-sufficiency (Bourdin et al., 2020). The Nordhackstedt methanization plant in Germany exemplifies how the circular economy can enhance resource efficiency and local self-sufficiency. Opened in 2013, the facility converts local organic waste, such as slurry, manure, and waste from the food industry, into biogas and digestate. The biogas generated is then used for electricity generation or injected into the natural gas network, diversifying the energy mix and reducing reliance on fossil fuels locally. The digestate is utilized as a natural fertilizer, enriching local soils and decreasing the need for imported chemical fertilizers. This waste-to-energy cycle reduces greenhouse gas emissions and optimizes the management of waste from local biomass resources increased efficiency in resource use is crucial in the circular economy.

The circular economy promotes practices like repair, remanufacture, and reuse, which extend product lifespans. This reduces the need for importing new products, keeping more resources in the local economic cycle and reducing waste. Return systems, where products are sent back to manufacturers for refurbishment or recycling, also help keep materials within the local economy (Veyssière et al., 2022). These systems reduce the flow of raw materials and promote an economy less reliant on external markets. Pôle R, located in Grenoble, France, is a prime example. This 8,000 m² site brings together around 15 companies and associations dedicated to repairing, reusing, and recycling everyday objects. It also combats food waste and unnecessary packaging. Within Pôle R, repair workshops extend the lifespan of broken or worn items, reducing waste. A reuse shop gives new life to objects that would have otherwise ended up in landfills, and a recycling platform sorts and recycles waste to recover reusable materials for new products. Initiatives to combat food waste, such as a community grocery shop and a collective composter, optimize the use of available food resources. Pôle R has a significant impact on the local community. It reduces waste production, stimulates the local economy by creating jobs, and raises public awareness of eco-responsible practices. Through repair, reuse, recycling, and the development of return systems, Pôle R keeps resources within the local economy, reduces the need for new product imports, and promotes greater autonomy from external markets. This project illustrates how the circular economy can enhance the efficient use of local resources while offering sustainable solutions that benefit the environment and the community.

8.5   What local strategy for rolling out the circular economy?

To promote the adoption of circular practices that aim to enhance regional autonomy and efficient use of local resources, local and regional governments can implement incentive policies such as tax breaks or subsidies. These measures can help reduce the initial costs associated with transitioning to circular production processes and encourage investments in recycling and reuse technologies. For instance, tax reductions can be offered to companies that incorporate recycled materials in their production or successfully reduce waste generation. Additionally, local and regional governments can provide grants for research and development projects that focus on enhancing recycling and waste management technologies (Aranda-Usón et al., 2019). Simultaneously, local authorities can drive the circular economy's implementation through public procurement (Rainville, 2021).

Educational programs and awareness campaigns are also crucial to ensure widespread adoption of circular economy principles. Authorities can introduce initiatives in schools to educate young people about the significance of reuse and recycling (Del Vecchio et al., 2021). Moreover, businesses can benefit from awareness campaigns and workshops that help them comprehend the economic and environmental advantages of embracing circular practices (Whalen et al., 2018). Such endeavors can raise public awareness and foster active participation from local communities in implementing the circular economy and pursuing greater territorial self-sufficiency. Furthermore, as Burger et al. (2019) elucidate, the circular economy necessitates novel skills. For instance, product design has to envision easy dismantling and reusability (Sumter et al., 2020). As a result, dedicated training courses must be created to enhance employees' skill sets.

Another crucial aspect of implementing the circular economy at the local level is the establishment of effective territorial governance. Research has shown that the success of the circular economy depends on the ability of local stakeholders to collaborate and optimize resources within a specific territory (Chembessi et al., 2024; Niang et al., 2022a). This type of governance is particularly important in circular economy approaches, where the exchange and shared use of resources between different entities, such as businesses, public administrations, and educational institutions, are vital. The interaction between these players allows for the creation of synergies where one activity's by-products can be used as resources for another, forming an interconnected network that promotes rational and sustainable use of raw materials and waste (Vahidzadeh et al., 2021).

Territorial governance becomes an essential pillar in coordinating and orchestrating these interactions, ensuring that industrial symbiosis efforts occur within a structured framework that benefits all participants by facilitating cooperation and minimizing barriers (Cerceau et al., 2018). To establish effective industrial symbiosis, which involves one company's waste or by-products becoming resources for another, an intermediary player is crucial in facilitating these exchanges (Niang et al., 2022). Often, this intermediary is a dedicated body within local government, or a specific entity created for this purpose, acting as a mediator and catalyst for collaboration between businesses, public institutions, and other entities (Bourdin, 2024).

Promoting local autonomy through the circular economy 145

The active governance provided by this intermediary helps identify synergistic opportunities, resolve logistical challenges, and overcome regulatory or economic obstacles. Through organizing forums, workshops, and regular meetings, the territorial intermediary ensures that all stakeholders are informed, committed, and motivated to participate in this circular dynamic (Jambou et al., 2022).

Lastly, for the successful implementation of the circular economy, it is crucial to establish strong policy and regulatory frameworks that support and facilitate this transition. These frameworks should encompass clear policies and tailor-made regulations that encourage practices such as reduction, reuse, recycling, and resource recovery (Maitre-Ekern, 2017). For instance, the implementation of stringent environmental standards and the requirement for companies to adhere to sustainable production principles can incentivize the adoption of circular methods.

8.6   Conclusion

The transition to the circular economy is imperative for regions facing the dual pressures of environmental degradation and resource scarcity. The principles of the circular economy, which include reducing, reusing, recycling, and recovering resources, provide a strong framework for rethinking our production and consumption models. This approach not only minimizes negative impacts on the environment but also offers a regenerative vision that promotes long-term sustainability and is a critical avenue for implementing effective urban and regional self-sufficiency development strategies.

Regions that adopt circular economy strategies enjoy several tangible benefits. These strategies strengthen regional autonomy, stimulate the local economy by creating green jobs, and reduce dependence on imported resources and external supply chains. Additionally, they promote more efficient management of local resources by transforming waste into valuable assets that support other local industries and services.

In the face of climate challenges and resource pressure, it is crucial for regional planners and decision-makers to embrace a paradigm shift toward the circular economy. This requires a profound transformation of regional planning and development practices. Policies need to be redefined to incorporate circularity right from the design stage of projects and infrastructure and actively support innovations that close production and consumption loops. The circular economy should not be seen as just a local waste management strategy but as a long-term economic development strategy.

Rethinking local economic development through the prism of the circular economy represents a fundamental transformation in the way territories approach their growth and resilience. Traditionally, the focus has been on the linear exploitation of resources – extract, manufacture, consume, and throw away. However, the local economic development model is now facing increasing ecological and economic limits. On the other hand, embracing the circular economy encourages regions to design systems where resources are kept in circulation for as long as possible, maximizing their value. This involves developing local infrastructures that support the recycling and reuse of materials, as well as promoting innovation in production processes that minimize waste. From this perspective, the transition to a circular economy represents a paradigm shift in territorial development. It is no longer simply a question of managing environmental impacts after the fact but of integrating them preventively into local planning and the local economy.

It is also essential that this paradigm shift is supported by strong policy and regulatory frameworks, economic incentives for businesses that adopt circular practices, and strong political will to promote this new model. Only through collective commitment to regional planning based on the principles of the circular economy can the vision of sustainable, self-sustaining, regenerative, and resilient development be realized.

References

Aranda-Usón, A., Portillo-Tarragona, P., Marín-Vinuesa, L. M., & Scarpellini, S. (2019). Financial resources for the circular economy: A perspective from businesses. *Sustainability,* 11(3), 888.

Arsova, S., Genovese, A., & Ketikidis, P. H. (2022). Implementing circular economy in a regional context: A systematic literature review and a research agenda. *Journal of Cleaner Production,* 368, 133117.

Boulding, K. E. (1966). The economics of the coming spaceship earth. In H. Jarrett (Ed.), *Interdisciplinary Economics* (pp. 335–344). Routledge, London.

Bourdin, S. (2024). The interplay of politics and space: How elected decisions shape place-based policies and outcomes. *The Geographical Journal,* 12591, 1–23.

Bourdin, S., Galliano, D., & Gonçalves, A. (2022). Circularities in territories: Opportunities & challenges. *European Planning Studies,* 30(7), 1183–1191.

Bourdin, S., Raulin, F., & Josset, C. (2020). On the (un)successful deployment of renewable energies: Territorial context matters. A conceptual framework and an empirical analysis of biogas projects. *Energy Studies Review,* 24(1), 1–23.

Burger, M., Stavropoulos, S., Ramkumar, S., Dufourmont, J., & van Oort, F. (2019). The heterogeneous skill-base of circular economy employment. *Research Policy,* 48(1), 248–261.

Cerceau, J., Mat, N., & Junqua, G. (2018). Territorial embeddedness of natural resource management: A perspective through the implementation of Industrial Ecology. *Geoforum,* 89, 29–42.

Chembessi, C., Bourdin, S., & Torre, A. (2024). Towards a territorialisation of the circular economy: The proximity of stakeholders and resources matters. *Cambridge Journal of Regions, Economy and Society,* rsae007. https://academic.oup.com/cjres/advance-article-abstract/doi/10.1093/cjres/rsae007/7624798?redirectedFrom=fulltext#no-access-message

Chioatto, E., & Sospiro, P. (2023). Transition from waste management to circular economy: The European Union roadmap. *Environment, Development and Sustainability,* 25(1), 249–276.

Del Vecchio, P., Secundo, G., Mele, G., & Passiante, G. (2021). Sustainable entrepreneurship education for circular economy: Emerging perspectives in Europe. *International Journal of Entrepreneurial Behavior & Research*, 27(8), 2096–2124.

Desing, H., Brunner, D., Takacs, F., Nahrath, S., Frankenberger, K., & Hischier, R. (2020). A circular economy within the planetary boundaries: Towards a resource-based, systemic approach. *Resources, Conservation and Recycling,* 155, 104673.

Geissdoerfer, M., Savaget, P., Bocken, N. M., & Hultink, E. J. (2017). The Circular Economy-A new sustainability paradigm?. *Journal of Cleaner Production,* 143, 757–768.

Hachaichi, M., & Bourdin, S. (2023). Wheels within wheels: Mapping the genealogy of circular economy using machine learning. *Circular Economy and Sustainability,* 3(4), 2061–2081.

Hartley, K., Baldassarre, B., & Kirchherr, J. (2023). Circular economy as crisis response. *Journal of Cleaner Production,* 434, 140140.

IPCC. (2023). *Sixth Assessment Report.* IPCC.

Jambou, M., Torre, A., Dermine-Brullot, S., & Bourdin, S. (2022). Inter-firm cooperation and local industrial ecology processes: Evidence from three French case studies. *The Annals of Regional Science,* 68(2), 331–358.

Jeanne, L., Bourdin, S., Nadou, F., & Noiret, G. (2023). Economic globalization and the COVID-19 pandemic: Global spread and inequalities. *GeoJournal,* 88(1), 1181–1188.

Kirchherr, J., Urbinati, A., & Hartley, K. (2023a). Circular economy: A new research field?. *Journal of Industrial Ecology,* 27(5), 1239–1251.

Kirchherr, J., Yang, N. H. N., Schulze-Spüntrup, F., Heerink, M. J., & Hartley, K. (2023b). Conceptualizing the circular economy (revisited): An analysis of 221 definitions. *Resources, Conservation and Recycling,* 194, 107001.

Korhonen, J., Nuur, C., Feldmann, A., & Birkie, S. E. (2018). Circular economy as an essentially contested concept. *Journal of Cleaner Production,* 175, 544–552.

Krikke, H. (2020). Value creation in a circular economy: An interdisciplinary approach. In *Decent Work and Economic Growth.* Springer Nature, 1–15.

Le Billon, P. (2004). The geopolitical economy of 'resource wars'. *Geopolitics,* 9(1), 1–28.

MacArthur, E. (2013). Towards the circular economy. *Journal of Industrial Ecology,* 2(1), 23–44.

Maitre-Ekern, E. (2017). *The Choice of Regulatory Instruments for a Circular Economy* (pp. 305–334). Springer International Publishing.

McDonough, W., & Braungart, M. (1994). Remaking the way we make things: Creating a new definition of quality with cradle-to-cradle design. In *The International Handbook on Environmental Technology Management,* 33, Edward Elgar Publishing, Cheltenham.

Niang, A., Torre, A., & Bourdin, S. (2022a). How do local actors coordinate to implement a successful biogas project? *Environmental Science & Policy,* 136, 337–347.

Niang, A., Torre, A., & Bourdin, S. (2022b). Territorial governance and actors' coordination in a local project of anaerobic digestion. A social network analysis. *European Planning Studies,* 30(7), 1251–1270.

Rainville, A. (2021). Stimulating a more circular economy through public procurement: Roles and dynamics of intermediation. *Research Policy,* 50(4), 104193.

Schroeder, P., Anggraeni, K., & Weber, U. (2019). The relevance of circular economy practices to the sustainable development goals. *Journal of Industrial Ecology,* 23(1), 77–95.

Stahel, W. R. (2016). The circular economy. *Nature,* 531(7595), 435–438.

Stahel, W. R. (2019). *The Circular Economy: A User's Guide.* Routledge.

Steinbach, S. (2023). The Russia-Ukraine war and global trade reallocations. *Economics Letters,* 226, 111075.

Sumter, D., De Koning, J., Bakker, C., & Balkenende, R. (2020). Circular economy competencies for design. *Sustainability,* 12(4), 1561.

Tapia, C., Bianchi, M., Pallaske, G., & Bassi, A. M. (2021). Towards a territorial definition of a circular economy: Exploring the role of territorial factors in closed-loop systems. *European Planning Studies,* 29(8), 1438–1457.

Vahidzadeh, R., Bertanza, G., Sbaffoni, S., & Vaccari, M. (2021). Regional industrial symbiosis: A review based on social network analysis. *Journal of Cleaner Production, 280*, 124054.

Velenturf, A. P., & Purnell, P. (2021). Principles for a sustainable circular economy. *Sustainable Production and Consumption, 27*, 1437–1457.

Veyssière, S., Laperche, B., & Blanquart, C. (2022). Territorial development process based on the circular economy: A systematic literature review. *European Planning Studies, 30*(7), 1192–1211.

Vinci, G., Musarra, M., Esposito, A., & D'Ascenzo, F. (2017). Industrial symbiosis: A sustainable approach for territorial development through the reuse of biomass. In Collins, M. (Ed.), *Organic Waste: Management Strategies, Environmental Impact and Emerging Regulations* (141–160), Nova Science Publishers, New York.

Voukkali, I., Papamichael, I., Loizia, P., Lekkas, D. F., Rodríguez-Espinosa, T., Navarro-Pedreño, J., & Zorpas, A. A. (2023). Waste metrics in the framework of circular economy. *Waste Management & Research, 41*(12), 1741–1753.

Whalen, K. A., Berlin, C., Ekberg, J., Barletta, I., & Hammersberg, P. (2018). 'All they do is win': Lessons learned from use of a serious game for circular economy education. *Resources, Conservation and Recycling*, 135, 335–345.

9 Clean, smart, and sustainable regional mobility

Eloísa Macedo and Jorge M. Bandeira

9.1 Introduction

In the ever-evolving landscape of any sector, the goal of sustainability is a fundamental challenge and urges to an effective collaborative work (Robèrt, 2017). As the population continues to concentrate in urban centres, the pressure on resources, infrastructure, and ecosystems becomes increasingly evident. European regions are facing numerous challenges related to transport and mobility, requiring new solutions, technologies, and business models (Myrovali & Morfoulaki, 2021). At the centre of sustainability is the relationship between urban and rural areas – a dynamic interaction that has implications for regional development, economic viability, and environmental integrity. Transport systems play a fundamental role in a city and region, contributing to the development of society. However, it is well known that these systems can also affect communities with negative effects such as noise, air pollution, as well as congestion and accidents (Maeder et al., 2023; Pisoni et al., 2019).

At a time when climate change concerns have put pressure on regional authorities to achieve ambitious sustainable mobility targets, it is important to understand what potential good practices can be transferred and applied in regions in order to mitigate harmful effects on the transport system, as well as to improve the quality of life and mobility needs of communities (Pisoni et al., 2019). In this context, the concept of accessibility also emerges as an essential factor, encompassing not only physical mobility but also the social and economic dimensions of connectivity. Additionally, the transport system is not just about passenger transport. A large part of the operation of logistics networks involves the transport of goods. It is therefore desirable to recognise the transport system as a whole, encompassing the specificities of passenger transport as well as goods (Hrelja, 2015).

As far as logistics is concerned, the sector has seen numerous changes in order to mitigate its negative impact on the environment and communities and has been seeking to implement improvements in order to facilitate the transition to greener logistics (Mommens et al., 2021). All these challenges do not present a unique fit-of-all solution. Regional approaches and transformative solutions allow for tailored solutions that address the specific barriers and think about enablers to sustainable mobility within a particular area or community. Furthermore, the recent

DOI: 10.4324/9781003498216-13

shifting in mobility patterns (Cawood et al., 2023; Correia & van Arem, 2017; Hamidi et al., 2019; Lopez-Carreiro et al., 2021; Zheng & Pantuso, 2023), with changing demographics (Pavanini et al., 2023), evolving consumer preferences (Aquilué Junyent et al., 2024; Curtale & Liao, 2023; Matyas & Kamargianni, 2019), and technological advancements influencing travel choices (Anund et al., 2022; Liljamo et al., 2020; Richter et al., 2022; Smith & Hensher, 2020), demand effective regional planning that should be adjusted and responsive to the ongoing trends to ensure long-term sustainability. Mobility is evolving to meet new demands for both passengers and freight. Greening mobility and logistics and digitalisation should be planned in a sustainable and effective way, considering different geographical and demographic contexts (European Commission, 2024). This means that all mobility-related measures should be implemented also considering vulnerable citizens, either from urban or rural areas.

In essence, this chapter is devoted to better understand challenges and discuss potential solutions through the lens of driving sustainability of transport systems, with a specific focus on reducing the urban-rural gap. By focusing on passenger and freight transport, we aim to unravel the complexities of regional mobility and explore innovative strategies that hold promise for promoting sustainable development.

Policymaking is essential for driving systemic changes needed to address sustainability challenges, mitigate environmental adverse effects, and transition towards a more resilient and equitable future mobility. These policy aspects are key to implementing self-sufficient cities and regions. There has been a need to find effective strategies that combine accessibility-focused planning with more traditional mobility-focused planning (Straatemeier & Bertolini, 2020), opening up a holistic approach to tackle mobility issues. Basic pillars within the mobility umbrella include policies that encourage modal shifts in transport, reduce transport-related emissions, and promote behavioural changes towards more eco-friendly practices. In particular, the ASI approach (Maeder et al., 2023), offers a framework for addressing sustainability challenges in transport by focusing on three main points:

- Avoid and reduce unnecessary trips, which can also be reinforced at the policy level by reorganising the spatial layout to reduce the distance people need to travel for daily activities;
- Shift to more sustainable mobility options, which can be achieved by policies and incentives that promote travel behaviour change and modal shifts, such as transitioning from private vehicle to public transport, cycling, or walking;
- Improve the environmental performance of transport, which can harness the emerging technology (e.g., cleaner vehicles) and digitalisation (e.g., improving operational practices) of the transport sector, in which the cooperation of stakeholders is crucial to achieving higher goals.

Bearing in mind such issues can ensure that transport systems contribute to a more sustainable and resilient society. Following the new European Urban Mobility

Clean, smart, and sustainable regional mobility 151

Framework, which outlines a common list of measures and initiatives to move towards more sustainable mobility by setting the higher goal of improving the transport of passengers and goods, specific initiatives can be considered, including:

- Promoting a coherent and integrated approach to ensure high-quality sustainable urban mobility plans;
- Fostering the integration of innovative mobility services into urban transport systems and increased digitalisation for sustainable urban mobility;
- Increasing the support for, and share of, sustainable transport modes (in particular public transport and active mobility such as walking and cycling) as well as zero-emission urban logistics.

The purpose of this chapter is to provide knowledge-sharing and insights to inspire policy change, focusing on innovative and sustainable mobility measures to improve mobility, by also taking action to tackle climate change through a modal shift, curb emissions, and promote behavioural change. In this chapter, we selected a broad sample of good practices collected from the Interreg Europe project database that have proved successful when implemented either at a local or regional level.

The chapter is structured as follows. The first section presents an introduction to the thematics addressed in the chapter and the second section provides a brief description of the focus of the European funding programme Interreg Europe and its role in the development of this chapter. The third section delves into initiatives on enhancing and optimising the movement of people within urban, suburban, and inter-city environments, while the fourth section is devoted to presenting a glimpse of current initiatives implemented to make the logistics ecosystem more sustainable and efficient. The final remarks are drawn in the fifth section.

9.2 Promoting interregional cooperation across Europe

The current chapter will mainly focus on presenting a selection of initiatives that have been identified and proposed as good practices within the thematic related to sustainable mobility between urban and rural areas. In particular, we will dig into good practices highlighted through projects financed by the Interreg Europe Programme (*Interreg Europe|Interreg Europe – Sharing Solutions for Better Policy*, n.d.). The Interreg Europe Programme is a collaborative initiative funded by the European Union aimed at promoting interregional cooperation, in which its main goal is to address disparities in development, growth, and quality of life among European regions and through capacity building and knowledge transfer seeks to help local, regional, and national governments across Europe to develop and implement more effective policies. Interreg Europe provides a platform for sharing solutions to regional development challenges and facilitates the exchange of good practices and policy learning among European regions. By fostering collaboration and knowledge exchange, the programme aims to contribute to the EU's broader objective of promoting cohesion and sustainable development across Europe.

9.3 Building a better passenger transport system

Bearing in mind the disruption caused by the COVID-19 pandemic and an analysis of the needs and effects derived from the situation and consequent change in mobility patterns, public transport authorities realise the need to improve the perceived value of public transport and shared services, while ensuring that cost-effective, sustainable solutions are provided to meet citizens' mobility needs (UITP, 2022).

Urban mobility challenges have been at the core of multiple research, and from a long time have attracted the attention of policymakers and transport planners. Challenges include pressure to meet mobility needs of an increasing population in urban centres, traffic congestion and high reliance on private vehicles, noise and pollutant emissions mostly derived from road transport, inefficient public transport network, the need to reshape the existing infrastructure, and the boom in online shopping that implied an increase of the number of commercial deliveries in the roads often contributing to a degradation in safety perception. Policy authorities have been putting efforts into managing such challenges and seeking to come up with measures and initiatives that can minimise such negative impacts, not only in urban environments, but also in the surrounding and rural areas.

In what follows, we will present various good practices that have been implemented around European corners in an attempt to make a step forward to more sustainable and inclusive mobility, bridging the gap found in transport systems between the urban and rural areas.

9.3.1 *Regulations and incentives for behavioural change and promoting sustainable mobility*

While innovative technologies and infrastructure can play an important role in achieving sustainable mobility, a well-established and robust regulatory framework is equally important. This section delves into good practices that focus on conceiving and defining regulations and incentives to encourage a shift towards more sustainable transport choices and to meet the citizens mobility needs.

The first initiative we will describe comes from the PriMaaS Project. The "PART program (Program of Support to Fare Reduction in Public Transport) in Coimbra Region" is a financing initiative aimed at supporting transport authorities in implementing measures to reduce fares in public passenger transport systems while expanding service supply and network coverage. PART offers various typologies for its application, including general fare reductions for all users, targeted fare reductions or free tariffs for specific groups such as people with disabilities, the creation of family ticket card, and tariff adjustments due to network redesigns. In 2022, the implementation of PART included a 30% fare reduction for all users in passenger rail and road services, subsidised by kilometre and applied to various transport titles. This initiative not only contributes to reducing carbon emissions but also enhances accessibility. The program's automatic fare reduction mechanism simplifies the process for passengers, further incentivising the use of public transport. Besides the incentives for improving public transport network coverage in underserved areas, this initiative is an appealing way of using public funds to drive behavioural change by focusing on an economic dimension for the citizens, which immediately has the advantage of encouraging the use of public transport rather than individual transport.

A good practice identified in the MATCH-UP Project, "Boosting Multimodality: Universal and Inclusive Mobility for Pedestrians", presents a holistic approach to urban mobility, with a focus on reshaping the city's infrastructure to prioritise pedestrians and promote intermodality. The initiative is emphasised in the Sustainable Urban Mobility Plan in Funchal. Specific measures include enlarging pedestrian lanes, implementing road markings for better accessibility, and restricting access for private vehicles, encouraging intermodality. The initiative includes urban furniture to improve the area's attractiveness and boost the local economy while reducing road traffic and greenhouse emissions. Despite initial resistance, the intervention is now perceived positively by the community. This type of initiative can be implemented in other regions provided that stakeholder involvement, tailored communication, and funding assessment for successful implementation need to be ensured.

Some cities have been experiencing uneven service coverage and overcrowding in certain areas due to a lack of a coordinated public transport service, with many different sharing mobility companies usually offering either car-, moto-, or bike-sharing services. The initiative conducted by the Barcelona City Council, "Regulation framework for sharing mobility services", identified in the SMART-MR Project, aims to develop a regulatory framework to define operational rules and ensure equitable access to public space. The new regulations establish that sharing mobility companies need to obtain licences through tender procedures and meet safety and sustainability criteria (e.g., e-bikes, vehicles with geolocation systems). It is also requested that the sharing systems must be compatible with private use by providing reserved parking spaces for individual users in specific busy areas. By implementing this regulatory framework, the city seeks to optimise the benefits of sharing mobility while managing public space more efficiently. Evidence of success includes the reduction and renovation of the shared vehicle fleet, improved management of parking facilities, reorganisation of public space, and promotion of bicycle and electric vehicle usage. Municipalities can develop similar regulatory frameworks tailored to their sustainable mobility goals, serving as facilitators for sharing mobility while maintaining control over public space occupation.

Mobility-as-a-service (MaaS) is rapidly transforming urban transport, aiming to facilitate the transition from privately owned vehicles to integrated transport services. Policymakers have been gathering efforts to harness its full potential for promoting ease use of public transport, integrating it with other transport modes, improving the passenger travel experience, and ultimately, reducing pollutant emissions and congestion in urban centres. The MaaS concept generally reflects a single app that seamlessly integrates various transport modes (e.g., buses, trains, car rentals, bike-sharing) and allows for booking and payment of the transport service.

Since the core idea behind MaaS implies a collaborative service, specific and clear regulations should be placed to promote trust between all involved stakeholders. Learnings from the PriMaaS good practice "The Act on Transport Services" represents a groundbreaking shift in transport legislation. The Finnish Act on Transport Services provides a technology-neutral framework for digitalising transport services and implementing new transport models. By viewing the transport system as a single entity, the Act promotes fairness of competition in the passenger transport market and supports the competitiveness of service providers. Key elements of the legislation include the promotion of digitalisation, combined transport modes, and interoperability of ticket and payment systems for MaaS. An important item on the framework is related to open data, which is considered essential to ensure real-time information on the transport mode offer and interoperability to support MaaS. This legislation presents wide-reaching implications, benefiting businesses with new opportunities, municipalities with improved service offerings, and citizens with enhanced transport services. While this initiative cannot be directly transferred to other regions, its principles, such as open data, user-centricity, and public-private collaboration, can serve as an inspiring step for establishing a more general understanding and acceptance of MaaS, facilitating its implementation at higher scales.

Some initiatives to encourage more sustainable mobility choices have been proposed across European cities. Nevertheless, the use of gamification platforms to boost sustainable mobility deserves special attention due to its out-of-the-box concept. Concretely, gamification platforms under the umbrella of mobility are IT-based tracking tools that are specially conceived to motivate people to choose more sustainable means of transport, introducing points, prizes, or rewards as the personal journey is a gaming competition. One such initiative, "Use of Gamification platforms to boost Sustainable Mobility", was identified in the TRAM Project, and was sought to contribute to encouraging behaviour change towards more active and sustainable modes of transport with the Public Works Agency company, while simultaneously guiding infrastructure development to meet the actual needs of citizens through the data gathered through the use of the app. It started with a mobility plan for the company staff to improve their quality of life and promote environmental sustainability by using a gamification platform. Staff members used the tracking app and were incentivised through gamification elements such as rankings, points, challenges, and rewards for using sustainable transport modes. This approach increased productivity and at the same time, promoted local businesses, which collaboratively offered discounts to app users, leading to benefits for both customers and businesses. Moreover, the tracking data were used to create "Mobility heat maps", allowing to spot popular cycling, walking, and public transport routes, which can help in understanding infrastructure needs such as addressing gaps in cycling networks, prioritise infrastructure investments, and improving pedestrian safety and public transport services. With a strong commitment and a collaborative mindset, this initiative can motivate and can be replicated in other institutions and regions to change and shape travelling habits.

9.3.2 *Making mobility more accessible, inclusive and efficient*

In a period of enormous potential for major changes in order to achieve efficiency, climate and social objectives, from addressing barriers to accessibility for people with disabilities to promoting sustainable modes of transport in both urban and rural areas, the mobility ecosystem is undergoing a profound transformation. This section explores various initiatives aimed at tackling these challenges at local and regional levels and seizing opportunities to create more accessible, inclusive, and efficient mobility systems.

Policymakers are increasingly looking for efficient, sustainable and affordable mobility solutions. Among these, bike-sharing systems have emerged in countless corners of cities, offering a flexible and environmentally friendly alternative to traditional modes of transport. By providing convenient access to bicycles for short-term use, these systems have the potential to lighten traffic congestion, reduce carbon emissions and promote healthier lifestyles. The good practice "an effective bike sharing system as a mobility service in urban transport: the case of Easybike" identified in project INNOTRANS, explores the main components, benefits, challenges and the transformative impact a bike-sharing system can have on urban mobility. The EasyBike, developed by BrainBox, is a Greek bike-sharing system that integrates with MaaS initiatives, enabling last-mile trips and multimodal travel. It provides access to shared station-based bicycles through a user-friendly app, and is relevant to both residents and tourists. The system has to be seen as a "whole package" consisting of bicycles, rental stations, parking stands, software, and an app for users.

Monitoring studies on user behaviour and demand for the bike service are important to improve the network of stations. Results show a modal shift higher than 30% over private cars, leading to significant reductions in carbon dioxide (CO_2) emissions. The system can be tailored to each region's unique needs, and for that purpose, region-specific studies should be conducted to understand mobility parameters, demographics, and weather conditions so that the system design can be shaped according to the local needs. Overall, this type of bike-sharing integrated with MaaS fills the gap in first and last-mile connectivity, bridging the distance between public transport stations and final destinations, or being a complement to public transport. Integration with MaaS platforms allows users to seamlessly switch between different modes based on their specific needs and preferences, improving the journey experience. This initiative presents the features that allow for its transferability to other regions and has already been implemented in several countries (e.g., Bulgaria, Turkey, Cyprus, Norway, and Poland).

Another solution has been the introduction of electric minibuses, which represents a transformative and eco-friendly opportunity to redefine the way we move around cities. These compact and environmentally friendly vehicles have significant relevance in meeting the challenges of urban transport, while providing benefits both for users due to convenience and for urban planners, who design specific routes taking into account potential local constraints and impacts. The initiative highlighted in the InnovaSUMP project "Mobility on Demand service: The circuit of electric mini-buses of Viseu" comes from a joint collaboration with the General Direction of Land and River Transport, the Portuguese Association of Electric Vehicles, and 25 Portuguese Municipalities. The city of Viseu introduced a new integrated circuit in its urban public transport service using three electric minibuses, that rapidly gained public acceptance. The circuit of a fixed route of 2.3 km covers the historical centre, serving the main public facilities and operates on demand, providing free transport primarily to the older population of the city centre. Each minibus presents an energy autonomy for about 100 to 150 km, can accommodate up to 22 passengers, and operates daily with a frequency of 15 minutes. Policymakers are still focusing on improving the system service, thus, in the new mobility strategy, MUV – Urban Mobility of Viseu, the service will undergo slight changes, including a new image and the introduction of a fare system, with a 3-way ticket costing €1. This initiative aligns with the Sustainable Urban Mobility Plan (SUMP), promoting low-carbon urban transport and sustainable mobility, and follows from the straight collaboration between multiple municipalities. It demonstrated the effectiveness of on-demand mobility services, particularly for supporting the mobility of elderly citizens.

The initiative "EcoBus – flexible mobility in rural areas" from MATCH-UP Project, is jointly developed by the Max Planck Institute and local transport authorities. The EcoBus service implemented in Bad Gandersheim, provides on-demand rides within a 100 km² rural area, in which passengers can book their trips via a dedicated app, internet website, or by using a phone call. The routes are calculated in real-time and the service connects the railway hub, integrating tickets with scheduled bus and train services. The fleet consists of eight minibuses and the service aims to offer flexible public transport options in sparsely populated areas, addressing connectivity and cost concerns (e.g., each ticket price is the same as for a scheduled public line service). While widely accepted, the system requires ongoing public funding and faces challenges with peak hours and long-distance rides. Therefore, this type of practice requires efforts in terms of collaboration and investment but the benefits for the community are clear, especially for rural areas, where the traditional public transport is scarce.

Specific initiatives for fostering inclusivity, enhancing quality of life, and promoting sustainable mobility solutions have been tested and implemented at different regions. The REGIO-MOB Project identified the "Demand-Responsive Transport Service for Persons with Disabilities in Ljubljana Urban Region" as a good practice, that is especially focused on the concept of mobility for all. The proposed Demand-Responsive Transport (DRT) service, started to be implemented at a city level but was later expanded to regional public transport connections. The free service can be requested by a phone call. It has adapted low-floor vehicles and seeks to enhance the mobility and safety of disabled people. The service is complemented by the Kavalir network, providing small electric vehicles for people with limited mobility and the elderly, facilitating their easier access to services, shopping and social activities according to their needs. The implemented approach showed that communication between users, service providers and drivers is very important for smooth operations, assuring that all the needed assistance is satisfied, which turns out to lead to reduced stress and improved travel experience for people with disabilities and reduced mobility.

In the context of suburban areas lacking an efficient transport network, municipal authorities have been trying to implement adjacent services that can fill these gaps. One type of initiative is the implementation of a vehicle rental system, which more recently has taken the form of electric vehicles due to their lower environmental impact in terms of operation. The E-MOB Project good practice "Flexa: Connection of outlying areas through Demand Responsive Transport", provides a flexible travel solution that combines travel requests and provides customised rides tailored to individual preferences through a user-friendly app. The service offers direct connections within its coverage area and transfers to the public transport system if needed. The service of e-vehicles is implemented by the municipal transport company in partnership with GHT Mobility GmbH and has been expanding gradually, also motivated by the increasing number of service requests. This innovative approach was largely accepted in the regions where it has been implemented and demonstrates that this solution is suitable for both urban and rural settings. By enhancing connectivity between suburban areas and urban centres, this type of initiative improves access to public transport, meets citizens mobility needs, and saves costs on potential infrastructure construction.

In suburban and rural areas, access to flexible transport options or the public transport network can often be limited. Another good practice focusing on overcoming these challenges for residents in terms of mobility and connectivity was identified in the LAST-MILE Project. The "FLUGS e-carsharing" system was implemented in Lienz to promote e-mobility in rural areas and meet citizens mobility needs in an environmentally friendly way. The system offers an easy-to-use booking and payment system through an app or dedicated website, with a tariff structure including membership fees, kilometre costs, and hourly rates, yielding an affordable mobility solution. This can be regarded as a complement to public transport, focusing on the concept of "sharing instead of owning", contributing to reducing the number of cars in public spaces. The initiative involves collaboration between the private association "Energy ImPulse East Tyrol", as part of social projects aimed at improving regional quality of life, the Regional Management East Tyrol, private individuals interested in e-cars/carsharing, and the city of Lienz. Evidence of its success includes accessibility, ease of use, and contribution to environmental sustainability. Another aspect demonstrating the potential of this practice is related to its expansion to other seven municipalities, and policy authorities are planning to integrate the e-carsharing into the public transport service information systems. Flugs e-carsharing demonstrates that innovative approaches like carsharing in rural areas can be relevant to provide flexible mobility solutions and reduce private car ownership.

The integration of smart technologies is becoming increasingly common, offering new ways to improve information sharing, efficiency and accessibility of public transport systems. Numerous municipalities present challenges related with high car dependency and limited public transport options in the vicinity of cities and rural areas. In this context, smart technologies can also play a relevant role. Among the innovative approaches, the REGIO-MOB Project identified the "Smart Demand Responsive Transport App for public transport and taxis – SMARTA Project" as a good practice. The initiative involves a free online application to improve mobility for residents commuting from rural areas to the city centre in the municipality of Trikala. The app provides real-time information on city bus arrivals, reducing crowding at bus stops and enabling residents to plan their trips more efficiently. Additionally, it offers an on-demand service for requesting bus seats, allowing for better route planning based on actual demand, but also combining this with shared taxis. Key factors contributing to the success of the initiative include a relationship of collaboration with both public and private service providers, municipalities and taxi drivers. This is an example, like so many others across Europe, that the focus is to improve the transport options for a wide range of users and aims to reduce private car usage, while providing cost-effective alternatives for residents.

9.3.3 Innovative solutions for more sustainable passenger transport

To make passenger transport more sustainable, cities and regions are also investing in adopting innovative solutions to try to address and overcome the complex challenges in terms of accessibility and efficiency of urban mobility, while seeking to reduce the environmental impact and improve the overall quality of transport services. From taking advantage of and reinventing charging infrastructure to reshaping tourist mobility and integrating technologies to improve the travelling experience, a diverse range of initiatives are paving the way for a more sustainable and efficient future for passenger transport driven by technology. In what follows we will focus on initiatives that aim to revolutionise our notion of mobility.

Gathering multiple services and modes of transport under a single competence centre can help citizens planning better their trips. The good practice identified in e-smartec project "MOBITHESS: Urban Mobility Centre of Thessaloniki for the promotion of sustainable mobility" offers a range of services aimed at promoting sustainable urban mobility in Thessaloniki, Greece. Concretely, it was developed an Urban Mobility Centre integrating mobility-related services and information that can be considered as a centralised hub for promoting sustainable transport choices. The services include car routing based on speed or efficiency, environmentally friendly routing to minimise exposure to pollutants, trip planning using public transport, combined routing, pedestrian routing for walking trips, real-time traffic updates, public transport information, environmental impact data, points of interest, and Sustainable Urban Mobility (SUM) training. By providing these services, MOBITHESS encourages citizens and tourists to use sustainable modes of transport, such as public transport and walking, while actively contributing to the city's environmental improvement. The SUM training fosters a new vision of urban mobility, empowering citizens to make informed choices regarding low-carbon transport options. Evidence of success is reflected in its significant user engagement. Results also show that the public transport information feature was the most used, followed by the environmental trip planner and the training tool. This can be relevant for policymakers to promote data sharing among public transport operators. The initiative also conducted awareness campaigns about sustainable mobility practices in schools and public events. It shows that by combining stakeholder cooperation, user engagement, and awareness-raising initiatives, it is possible to effectively promote sustainable urban mobility.

Intermodal hubs have been playing a relevant role in supporting efficient and sustainable mobility, since these are transport nodes that interconnect different modes of transport in the same station. The good practice "Sustainable Tourism Mobility in Balatonfüred – Intermodal developments" from the DESTI-SMART Project focused on gathering efforts to modernise the railway station and integrate it with bus transport, benefiting all public transport users, including the large number of tourists. This intermodal development aimed to enhance energy efficiency, establish new functions, and strengthen connections between transport options. There was the need to reconstruct the railway station building, introduce parking facilities for Park and Ride and Bike and Ride, and improvements to accessibility for people with reduced mobility and visual disabilities. Collaboration between bus operators ensured the alignment of the local bus network with the railway timetable. Evidence of the success of such implementation includes the increase in ticket sales, and the high occupancy of the park/bike and ride, reflecting the behavioural change by choosing more sustainable transport modes. This intermodal development serves as a model for creating transfer-oriented transport systems in high-demand urban areas, which include tourist destinations. Its success highlights the importance of integrating low- and zero-emission transport modes and can serve as inspiration for policymakers seeking to reduce emissions while improving tourism mobility.

With the ever-increasing level of available technology, introducing Driverless Automated Shuttles in urban or rural areas represents a groundbreaking advancement in transport with a wide range of potential benefits. Some pilots have been implemented but the good practice selected in EMBRACER project "FLASH – Driverless Automated Shuttle arrives in Northern Saxony" stands out as it has emerged and grown from a pilot to become an integral part of the region's transport system. The initiative aimed to address the lack of reliable public transport in rural areas by providing an automated shuttle service in northern Saxony, with a focus on the Schladitzer See area. Partnerships with IAV GmbH, Fraunhofer Institute, TS Automotive Engineering GmbH, and AMCOM contribute to the project success and beneficiaries include residents of Northern Saxony and neighbouring regions. FLASH required converting a minibus to autonomous driving mode. In terms of operation, it presents operating costs similar to normal public transport and the self-driving bus can transport up to 20 passengers. The route takes around 15 minutes and it ends up by providing a connection with the public transport network. The initiative offers valuable insights that can be considered as a potential solution in other regions.

Another initiative that seeks to take advantage of data-driven information and technology to improve transport systems comes from the PriMaaS Project and the good practice "Tactrans ENABLE platform". The design of this initiative takes into account concerns about the efficiency and flexibility of the transport offer, but also its environmental and social impact. In fact, the ENABLE project, led by Tactran in partnership with many other service institutions, aims to develop a MaaS platform with the goal of improving access to essential services (e.g., education and healthcare) by maximising the awareness and ease of existing transport services. Initial steps around the app conception were made through different institutions, including NHS Tayside, Loch Lomond and Trossachs National Park Authority, and Dundee and Angus College. The selected platform offers real-time journey data, booking/ticketing, and payment systems, and presents an in-built feature capable of returning specific needs of patients, tourists, and students. The inclusive co-design process ensured that the needs of different client groups were considered, leading to improved promotion and marketing strategies. Moreover, the initiative clearly emphasises designing for inclusivity by addressing requirements such as accurate trip routing and accessibility information for users with additional needs. Collaboration among public and private transport operators and public transport authorities is crucial for its wide acceptance and implementation. In essence, through strategic partnerships and innovative solutions, ENABLE demonstrates the potential of MaaS to create inclusive, efficient, and environmentally friendly transport systems coupling it with societal goals by providing tailored routes/information for specific citizen needs.

The implementation of Real-Time Crowding Information represents a significant step towards enhancing the public transport experience. The CISMOB good practice "Real-time crowding information – positive impacts on metro trains" aims to address the issue of unevenly distributed passenger loads, particularly during peak hours. By providing real-time information about the load of metro trains through visual and vocal formats, passengers can make informed decisions about which train to board, improving the comfort of public transport users. The system is relatively easy to install and integrate, requiring a basic set of system solutions including crowding detection, information display, and data processing subsystems. Evidence of success includes a noticeable percentage of passengers finding the provided information useful and a reduction in the share of passengers in the most crowded trains. The relatively low cost and ease of installation, make this practice present a potential for transfer to other metro systems facing similar challenges, especially with crowded trains at peak hours with crowded trains during peak hours.

To address urban mobility challenges, cities can create innovative mobility solutions that enhance connectivity, and, at the same time, reduce environmental impact. One such initiative comes from Transport for London: the "Innovation in the air: teleferic/aerial cable cars as low-carbon sustainable tourism mobility". Aerial cable car systems are a long-proven technology and can be used as a low-carbon alternative for urban transport, particularly in tourist destinations or, for instance, in hilly areas where traditional public transport is inefficient. These systems can be constructed with minimal impact on the territory and consist of electrically-propelled steel cables that move suspended cabins between terminals at different elevations. Properly conceived systems can boost the environment around stations, promote urban development, and present a positive impact on users' well-being. In the planning process and implementation of such type of initiative, special attention should be given to the type of energy to use to translate this into an environmentally friendly transport option. Additional considerations are required regarding the financial sustainability and suitability for daily commuting. Besides these considerations, network integration, operations, and maintenance, as well as procurement must be ensured.

9.4 Transition to more sustainable deliveries

The last stage of the logistics process, also called the last-mile operation presents some challenges. As urbanisation accelerates and consumer expectations evolve, deliveries are expected to become more frequent, also due to the boom of e-commerce. Thus, more than ever, ensuring efficient last-mile delivery operations becomes crucial, either concerning economic and business growth or the associated traffic and environmental impacts. Moreover, this last step brings more challenges when the area is rural or sparsely populated, since there is little movement of people and goods, implying potential increases in delivery costs, time and environmental impacts. The importance of the last mile is evident both in terms of convenience and in socio-economic and environmental terms. Efficient last-mile logistics increases the competitiveness of businesses, promotes customer satisfaction, and plays a major role in reducing congestion, pollutant and noise emissions, and energy consumption, especially in urban environments where there is a higher demand. Thus, optimising last-mile distribution with environmental considerations represents a fundamental step for cities and regions, reinforcing efforts to balance economic growth with environmental responsibility, towards urban and regional self-sufficiency planning approaches. However, the challenges behind last-mile logistics are multi-levelled, often amplified by factors such as traffic congestion, limited infrastructure and spatial restrictions. To address these challenges, the importance of interregional collaborative efforts and stakeholder involvement are crucial. By fostering collaboration between municipalities, businesses and community stakeholders, regions can develop holistic solutions that mitigate the negative impacts of last-mile distributions, maximising efficiency and sustainability.

In what follows, we highlight and present an overview of a selection of good practices and innovative initiatives designed and implemented to optimise logistics and last-mile distribution operations. Our objective is to present initiatives that focus on the transformative potential of collaborative and targeted approaches to foster trust and ensure an efficient and engaging system for stakeholders, and the replication of these approaches in other regions with similar challenges, in the hope that this sharing of initiatives can spark and drive future policy efforts to improve logistics efficiency on a regional scale.

9.4.1 Enhancing logistics efficiency

Throughout this section, we will describe several initiatives that be regarded as practical experiences that can be easily transferred to other regions provided the challenges are similar. Through a synthesis of empirical evidence and practical insights, we want to underline what has been done to promote and make logistics operations more sustainable and efficient, by addressing the complex nature of improving logistics efficiency but also introducing initiatives that can be relevant to shape the future of last-mile delivery.

Strategic measures can also be applied to ease the logistics operations within city centres, contributing to mitigate the associated potential disruptions and unsafety maneuvres, pedestrian safety concerns, traffic congestion, and pollutant emissions. The "Harmonising logistic operation in city centres at a regional level" good practice identified in the RESOLVE Project was implemented in Emilia Romagna and addressed urban logistics challenges in its cities through strategic planning and collaborative agreements. The Regional Government established agreements with provinces and municipalities focusing on reducing the negative impacts of freight transport by optimising freight distribution at the regional level. For that purpose, harmonised city logistics rules were devised and implemented, focusing on freight vehicles under 3.5 tonnes and including regulations such as time windows, access restrictions to Limited Traffic Zones (LTZ), and benefits (incentives) for freight electric vehicles. For the success of this type of initiative, it is crucial to engage relevant stakeholders such as the Government Region, local public authorities (cities and mobility agencies), and logistics operators. The harmonised approach across the region brings improvements in the whole region, ensuring efficiency in logistics planning and operations. This approach can be considered as a model for regional coordination and strategic planning to improve environmental sustainability and transport efficiency in urban logistics over the long term.

Some initiatives have been put into practice concerning collaborative partnerships and free parking slots for logistics purposes. Regular meetings with delivery stakeholders allow quick issue resolution and feedback collection, facilitating policy adaptation to support initiatives or mitigate negative impacts. An example was found in the good practice identified in the SPOTLOG Project regarding a "Partnership between the municipality of Lille and La Poste about sustainable last mile delivery". This partnership facilitates regular discussions on projects and issues concerning logistics. This collaboration allows direct feedback when La Poste encounters difficulties due to changes in city policies. The continued feedback and discussion between decision-makers and on-the-ground players are relevant to improving the efficiency of the use of cargo bikes, logistics hub creation, first-time delivery improvement, delivery area plan enhancement, and best practice exchange. Under this initiative, the partnership addressed challenges related to the generalisation of paid parking, which often obstructs delivery spaces. As a short-term solution, the city introduced a subscription scheme for professionals to park in paid spaces, and avoid traffic disruptions and pollutant emissions.

Likewise, the good practice identified in the SMART-MR, it was implemented in Helsinki's city centre a "Pilot of free parking places for city logistics". A collaborative effort of the City of Helsinki, Forum Virium, and ten logistics companies developed an app for finding free parking spaces for city logistics. The app allows drivers to observe 22 parking spaces in real-time and includes features such as reporting stops and reserving time slots. The long-standing initiative involves stakeholders like logistics companies and technology providers. Due to its technology-driven features, it provides valuable data also for city planning.

Municipalities across regions often struggle with inefficient and environmentally harmful delivery systems, raising the need for effective initiatives and strategies to minimise the negative impacts of the last-mile operation. To overcome the city's long-standing issue of high concentrations of airborne pollutants, largely caused by traffic from logistics companies, and to optimise logistics, and enhance overall efficiency in goods delivery, regions have been exploring the implementation of urban logistics consolidation centres (ULCC). For instance, the RESOLVE Project good practice about the "Consolidation centre in Växjö" implemented in Finland, involves the establishment of a centralised distribution centre to expedite the delivery of goods within the municipality. Instead of individual suppliers delivering goods directly to various locations, the goods are co-loaded at the ULCC and then distributed to different destinations. In this initiative, regional and municipal authorities play an important role in managing and coordinating the establishment of the distribution centre and ensuring its smooth operation, while collaboration with cities in the vicinity of the logistics centre is relevant to expand the operations efficiently. The involvement of logistics operators and organisations like the Energy Agency for Southeast Sweden can provide operational-related knowledge, expertise and support in implementing sustainable transport solutions for the last-mile operation. It can be shown that consolidating deliveries at a ULCC, the energy consumption associated with transporting goods is reduced, the co-loading goods operation and optimising delivery routes contribute to a decrease in CO_2 emissions, leading to a reduction in the number of delivery trips required per week, thereby decreasing traffic congestion and mitigating the environmental impact of transport. Additionally, the ULCC may establish indirect effects that in turn, end up to directly impact local businesses, for instance, by incentivising the engagement of local suppliers, leading to an increase in their participation and contribution to the overall supply chain.

On this same page, a somewhat different approach was identified in the INNOTRANS Project, under the good practice "Ekologis – a City Logistics Project". This project was performed in Prague and focuses on a more integrated approach divided into two phases, with the ultimate goal of reducing harmful emissions and improve living conditions. The first phase involves promoting eco-driving practices among transport and logistics businesses, in the form of an awareness-raising campaign, putting some emphasis and responsibility on the logistics drivers to reshape their driving habits in a more environmentally friendly manner. In its second phase, the project aims to establish a ULCC, focused on small and medium-sized operators, in which environmentally friendly vehicles are used for the last-mile deliveries. The centre also promotes agreed-time deliveries, package storage, waste disposal, and repackaging so that the final logistics leg can be more sustainable and efficient. Different stakeholders benefit from the initiative, including end consumers, retailers, and transport companies. This initiative demonstrates the importance of integrated strategies combining communication campaigns to change behavioural aspects and concrete solutions for urban logistics challenges like logistics.

Another initiative comes from TRAM Project and focuses on the implementation of coordinated distribution of supplies to public buildings. This approach has demonstrated its potential for success, showing a reduction in deliveries of 60%–80% through efficient and coordinated logistics management. This initiative promotes the collaboration of municipalities in a region to establish a joint

164   *Eloísa Macedo and Jorge M. Bandeira*

distribution depot where individual suppliers deliver their products. The goods are then consolidated according to destination, significantly reducing the number of separate last-mile deliveries. In addition, the practice addresses the inefficiency of the traditional system, in which transport costs are often hidden in product prices. By taking control of distribution and implementing co-packed and coordinated distribution, municipalities can manage transport costs in a transparent way. It clearly presents socio-economic benefits alongside commercial considerations and environmental impacts, so it may well justify the initial investment in implementation.

One other initiative comes from Tampere, Finland, in which efforts have been made to make available a Living Lab to foster co-creation, research innovation and experiment-driven learning within the umbrella of sustainable urban logistics. The good practice identified in the SPOTLOG Project "Multi-stakeholder collaboration within logistics innovation ecosystem facilitates carbon-neutrality" focuses on the established Lyyli Living Lab, implemented within the Tampere Tramway system. The lab involves the Lyyli tram car equipped with cutting-edge technologies and incorporates a self-driving bus to bridge the last mile as a testbed for in-context trials during regular traffic. New services can be tested within the tram's operational context, allowing for practical experimentation and favours the discussion and potential actions to improve user-centric urban mobility and logistics solutions in a more sustainable and efficient manner. The centre provides learning opportunities and research potential since valuable data generated from many different experiments and scenarios, allowing to explore and analyse travel and drivers' behaviour, service and technology performance, and last-mile operational issues. The Lyyli Living Lab demonstrates how collaborative efforts can help achieve sustainability goals by optimising logistics and reducing environmental impact.

9.4.2   *Sustainable and innovative delivery solutions*

The initiatives described below inspire sustainable actions and strategies that prioritise environmental management and social responsibility with regard to the impacts of last-mile delivery, especially in urban environments. The increase in online shopping has also brought challenges for urban centres. While it can be regarded as convenient for consumers, the ever-increasing number of parcels translates to more delivery vehicles on the road, leading to traffic congestion and environmental pollution. This section seeks to provide an overview of a range of practices arising from interregional cooperation projects and focusing on innovative approaches to improving last-mile delivery. From the adoption of cutting-edge technologies to the use of more sustainable means of transport, these initiatives demonstrate the transformative potential of urban logistics to achieve direct environmental objectives. By highlighting these innovative solutions, this section aims to inspire, stimulate dialogue and drive action towards the definition and design of more resilient, efficient and environmentally friendly last-mile distribution systems.

With the aim of making parcel delivery more efficient and sustainable, many cities have been introducing cargo bike systems. The RESOLVE Project identified the good practice "Last mile delivery by electric cars and cargo bikes in urban areas".

To address the need for last-mile delivery services, a social enterprise was established, offering efficient cargo bike deliveries to grocers and retailers in the city centre. Surveys and adaptation processes have been crucial for all stakeholders involved, including the Municipality of Maribor, delivery companies, the cargo bike delivery social enterprise, retail stores, and restaurants. Delivery companies have also adapted by investing in environmentally friendly vehicles like light e-vehicles, promoted by municipality-related incentives and restrictions imposed in the city centre and pedestrian zones. This initiative of focusing on cargo bikes and e-vehicles for last-mile delivery minimises disruption to business value chains while promoting low-carbon transport, and can be easily transferred to other regions.

A public-private collaborative effort to improve logistics operations in isolated and sparsely populated regions was sought through the "GO RURAL: Logistic services for rural areas" initiative, identified in the RATIO Project. To overcome some logistical challenges faced by rural areas, particularly in terms of isolation and increased prices for logistics services, it was developed technology platforms to support logistics services to optimise transport, collection, and distribution services in these areas, benefiting not only end customers but also rural SMEs to remain competitive and innovative and logistic service providers. Joint work was required between two companies (one public and one private) and a technological centre in order to implement the platform for integrating logistics operations into a single system. Specific features needed to be taken into account as regional road mapping and route optimisation for efficient and coordinated transport. The innovative aspect of the good practice lies in the effective coordination of existing resources through ICT solutions, facilitating cooperation between different sectors and stakeholders. During its implementation, the number of truck shipments to rural areas was significantly decreased by optimising resources in real-time. Results also show a decrease in time and logistical problems.

Another initiative that has been at the municipalities attention across Europe is the implementation of automated parcel machine lockers. The initiative proposed in the SPOTLOG Project, "Last-mile delivery to Automated Parcel Machines – Poland" focuses on the strategic implementation of centralised pickup points in different spots of cities in Poland. The recent growth in e-commerce led to an increased number of deliveries and kilometres covered by logistics operators using a door-to-door delivery approach. This solution of lockers is quite convenient for customers. It requires a dedicated app for providing parcel information and for retrieving the package, customers only need to use a telephone number and a six-digit code sent via email or SMS, or scan a QR code. This approach reduces traffic congestion, emissions, and fuel consumption significantly compared to door-to-door delivery. The potential of this initiative is high due to its relatively easy deployment in any region, particularly low-density communities, offering convenience and environmental benefits. Upgrades can be considered for specialised automated parcel machines (e.g., refrigerated) for different types of business, such as food or flower pickup.

The initiative "The Mobile Depot: a logistic facilitation in the Turin City Centre", recently identified in the SPOTLOG Project, presents an inspiring action for reshaping the last-mile delivery system in urban environments. The Mobile Depot (MD) pilot in Turin consists of a truck trailer containing parcels and cargo bikes, operating as a single facility for last-mile delivery operations. The municipality provided road deployment and parking authorisations for the MD in different city corners. The MD can be regarded as a mobile micro-consolidation hub. Its implementation required a partnership between Turin Municipality and TNT, demonstrating higher goals can be achieved through collaboration among the public and private sectors. A progressive tax system to stimulate the registration of operators was also promoted. Evidence of success includes the increase in the average number of operations since bikers deliver more packages in less time, and the reduction of CO_2 emissions through the use of cargo bikes (each cargo bike saves 250 g of CO_2 per kilometre travelled).

From INNOTRANS Project comes a good practice that harnesses the full potential of new emerging technology. The Hellenic Post Group ELTA, the public company of postal services in Greece, implemented a fully automatic sorting system, leveraging automation and artificial intelligence (AI) technologies, to overcome the challenges related to buying behaviour set by the COVID-19 pandemic and meet the increasing demands of e-commerce. The system features robots guided by AI along a track with sensors, autonomously sorting objects with high speed and precision. These robots are equipped with collision avoidance sensors and can autonomously recharge, ensuring continuous operation. This initiative resulted in a 250% increase in the speed of processing the packages, the management capacity significantly increased, it was possible to ensure delivery on the same day, reduced errors, increased profitability, and improved customer service. ELTA also organised educational visits to familiarise students with the innovative system, part of their broader digital transformation plan. This practice demonstrates how combining technology and management innovation, can make a public company innovative, competitive, and efficient.

9.5   Conclusions

This chapter has sought to present a multitude of good practices with the ultimate aim of sharing what has been implemented and tested in various regions of Europe in the field of improving mobility systems to make them cleaner, sustainable and accessible. The selection of good practices presented covers a wide range of themes, all of which are innovative and success-oriented. It is clear that there is a need to foster collaboration between entities and authorities, the public and private sectors, as well as the mobilisation of communities, which play a fundamental role in accepting potential changes in the way the transport service is offered.

Although most movements of people and goods take place in urban environments, generating numerous challenges in terms of both operations and environmental and societal impacts, the outskirts and neighbourhoods of cities, as well as more remote and sparsely populated areas, require special attention from the authorities. In this latter case, such areas should not be "left in the dark" and efforts

Clean, smart, and sustainable regional mobility 167

should be made to improve the quality of life of citizens, who often have specific mobility needs, such as elderly people who need to use certain services occasionally or on a regular basis (e.g., health services, grocery).

By replicating the good practices adjusted to local and regional contexts, transport connections between different transport service providers can be strengthened, journey experience can be improved, travel behaviour can be reshaped to more sustainable options, and traffic-related impacts can be mitigated. Investment should be directed towards initiatives that actually benefit citizens and the environment, and ensure the long-term sustainability of transport services. The focus on the need to attract passengers to public transport is evident. To this end, it is clear from the good practices presented that it is essential to improve the accessibility, efficiency and comfort of mobility services. Policymakers can harness the potential of data and technology for better monitoring and future planning. Implemented practices allow to recognise that technology can be leveraged to optimise public transport, improve the travel experience, and set out innovative forms of transport. A coordinated and strategic involvement of all stakeholders can contribute to achieving the targeted goals set globally.

Therefore, enhancing the commuting experience requires cooperation and the transformative power of innovation for shaping the future of urban mobility and paving the way towards a more sustainable and inclusive transport system.

9.6 Acknowledgements

This chapter was supported by the projects UIDB/00481/2020 (DOI 10.54499/UIDB/00481/2020) and UIDP/00481/2020 (DOI 10.54499/UIDP/00481/2020) – Fundação para a Ciência e a Tecnologia, and Interreg Europe projects SPOTLOG P01C0055 and EMBRACER P01C0056.

References

Anund, A., Ludovic, R., Caroleo, B., Hardestam, H., Dahlman, A., Skogsmo, I., Nicaise, M., & Arnone, M. (2022). Lessons learned from setting up a demonstration site with autonomous shuttle operation – based on experience from three cities in Europe. *Journal of Urban Mobility, 2*, 100021. https://doi.org/10.1016/J.URBMOB.2022.100021

Aquilué Junyent, I., Martí Casanovas, M., Roukouni, A., Moreno Sanz, J., Roca Blanch, E., & Correia, G. H. de A. (2024). Planning shared mobility hubs in European cities: A methodological framework using MCDA and GIS applied to Barcelona. *Sustainable Cities and Society, 106*, 105377. https://doi.org/10.1016/J.SCS.2024.105377

Cawood, E. N., Fiorello, D., & Christidis, P. (2023). Mobility patterns after the pandemic: A survey in 20 European cities. *Transportation Research Procedia, 72*, 611–618. https://doi.org/10.1016/J.TRPRO.2023.11.446

Correia, G. H. de A., & van Arem, B. (2017). Estimating Urban Mobility Patterns Under a Scenario of Automated Driving: Results from a Model Application to Delft, the Netherlands. *Compendium of the Transportation Research Board 96th Annual Meeting,* Delft.

Curtale, R., & Liao, F. (2023). Travel preferences for electric sharing mobility services: Results from stated preference experiments in four European countries. *Transportation*

Research Part C: Emerging Technologies, 155, 104321. https://doi.org/10.1016/J.TRC.2023.104321

European Commission. (2024). *Social issues, equality and attractiveness of the transport sector – European Commission.* https://transport.ec.europa.eu/transport-themes/social-issues-equality-and-attractiveness-transport-sector_en

Hamidi, Z., Camporeale, R., & Caggiani, L. (2019). Inequalities in access to bike-and-ride opportunities: Findings for the city of Malmö. *Transportation Research Part A: Policy and Practice, 130,* 673–688. https://doi.org/10.1016/J.TRA.2019.09.062

Hrelja, R. (2015). Integrating transport and land-use planning? How steering cultures in local authorities affect implementation of integrated public transport and land-use planning. *Transportation Research Part A: Policy and Practice, 74,* 1–13. https://doi.org/10.1016/J.TRA.2015.01.003

Interreg Europe|Interreg Europe – Sharing solutions for better policy. (n.d.). Retrieved 10 May 2024, from https://www.interregeurope.eu/

Liljamo, T., Liimatainen, H., Pöllänen, M., & Utriainen, R. (2020). People's current mobility costs and willingness to pay for mobility as a service offerings. *Transportation Research Part A: Policy and Practice, 136,* 99–119. https://doi.org/10.1016/J.TRA.2020.03.034

Lopez-Carreiro, I., Monzon, A., Lois, D., & Lopez-Lambas, M. E. (2021). Are travellers willing to adopt MaaS? Exploring attitudinal and personality factors in the case of Madrid, Spain. *Travel Behaviour and Society, 25,* 246–261. https://doi.org/10.1016/J.TBS.2021.07.011

Maeder, S., Stauffacher, M., & Knaus, F. (2023). Zooming in and out on everyday mobility practices in a rural, mountainous area of Switzerland. *Journal of Transport Geography, 112,* 103680. https://doi.org/10.1016/J.JTRANGEO.2023.103680

Matyas, M., & Kamargianni, M. (2019). Survey design for exploring demand for mobility as a service plans. *Transportation, 46*(5), 1525–1558. https://doi.org/10.1007/s11116-018-9938-8

Mommens, K., Buldeo Rai, H., van Lier, T., & Macharis, C. (2021). Delivery to homes or collection points? A sustainability analysis for urban, urbanised and rural areas in Belgium. *Journal of Transport Geography, 94,* 103095. https://doi.org/10.1016/J.JTRANGEO.2021.103095

Myrovali, G., & Morfoulaki, M. (2021). *Sustainable urban mobility plans –A policy brief from the policy learning platform on low-carbon economy* (Issue October). https://doi.org/10.1007/978-3-030-67016-0_2

Pavanini, T., Liimatainen, H., Sievers, N., & Heemsoth, J. P. (2023). The role of DRT in European urban public transport systems—A comparison between Tampere, Braunschweig and Genoa. *Future Transportation, 3*(2), 584–600. https://doi.org/10.3390/FUTURETRANSP3020034

Pisoni, E., Christidis, P., Thunis, P., & Trombetti, M. (2019). Evaluating the impact of "sustainable urban mobility plans" on urban background air quality. *Journal of Environmental Management, 231,* 249–255. https://doi.org/10.1016/J.JENVMAN.2018.10.039

Richter, M. A., Hagenmaier, M., Bandte, O., Parida, V., & Wincent, J. (2022). Smart cities, urban mobility and autonomous vehicles: How different cities needs different sustainable investment strategies. *Technological Forecasting and Social Change, 184,* 121857. https://doi.org/10.1016/J.TECHFORE.2022.121857

Robèrt, M. (2017). Engaging private actors in transport planning to achieve future emission targets – Upscaling the climate and economic research in organisations (CERO) process to regional perspectives. *Journal of Cleaner Production, 140,* 324–332. https://doi.org/10.1016/J.JCLEPRO.2015.05.025

Smith, G., & Hensher, D. A. (2020). Towards a framework for mobility-as-a-service policies. *Transport Policy*, *89*, 54–65. https://doi.org/10.1016/J.TRANPOL.2020.02.004

Straatemeier, T., & Bertolini, L. (2020). How can planning for accessibility lead to more integrated transport and land-use strategies? Two examples from the Netherlands. *European Planning Studies*, *28*(9), 1713–1734. https://doi.org/10.1080/09654313.2019.1612326

UITP. (2022). *Managing the demand for mobility: A transformational policy instrument.* https://cms.uitp.org/wp/wp-content/uploads/2022/09/Policy-Brief-Demand-Management-Aug-2022.pdf

Zheng, M., & Pantuso, G. (2023). Trading off costs and service rates in a first-mile ride-sharing service. *Transportation Research Part C: Emerging Technologies*, *150*, 104099. https://doi.org/10.1016/J.TRC.2023.104099

Conclusion

Eduardo Medeiros

This book explored the concept and process of self-sufficiency at urban and regional levels. Pragmatically, this urban and regional self-sufficiency policy rationale entails a concrete solution to tackle the ongoing global climate crisis. Mainly, because a self-sufficient city/region would inevitably contribute to increasing environmental sustainability trends, as it entails increasing production of intra-city/region renewable sources of energy and food, as well as systems for clean water recycling. Ultimately, the positive ramifications of implementing urban and regional self-sufficiency processes for territorial development processes have the potential to extend the environmental positive gains. Here, for instance, at the urban level, self-sufficiency has the potential to positively foster innovative and transformational socioeconomic paths in the domains of intra-city food production, at a scale never seen in the world, with major implications in architecture/construction and specific food industries. Here, again, there are major potential environmental and human health benefits from the reduction of pesticides and pollution associated with mainstream agriculture and fisheries, via a circular economy path. Indeed, across all the book chapters, these and other critical aspects of urban and regional self-sufficiency are explored.

The first part of the book is focused on discussing the role of public policies towards urban and regional self-sufficiency. It starts with a first chapter dedicated to proposing a novel approach to implementing EU Cohesion Policy more focused on promoting territorial self-sufficiency development. Concretely, the author proposes concrete policy recommendations on how to allocate part of its funding to support urban and regional self-sufficiency development approaches in particular in the areas of energy and food production, as well as in the domains of transport mobility and circular economy. Based on the rationale that a self-sufficient city or region is fully independent of the outside world in providing the most basic needs for the survival of its dwellers, the author proposes a typology with distinct general levels of regional and urban self-sufficiency. At the first level is the production and consumption of basic food, clean water, and energy. In this stance, the proposed policy rationale supporting the implementation of future programming phases of EU Cohesion Policy should contemplate the financial support to intracity food production via vertical farming, the support to the production of renewable sources of

DOI: 10.4324/9781003498216-14

Conclusion 171

energy, and the support to water cleaning infrastructure, allowing constant access to clean water no matter the climate variations.

Chapter 2 provides a comprehensive theoretical discussion on how urban areas can adopt self-sufficiency as a pathway to sustainability. In essence, the author reveals the fundamental principles and strategies that underpin self-sufficiency planning in the urban context. Moreover, she clarifies the importance of integrating various dimensions such as energy, water, food, waste management, and transportation to foster resilient and self-reliant urban systems. Self-sufficiency planning advocates for the localization of resources and capabilities to enhance urban resilience and promote long-term territorial development viability. Put differently, self-sufficiency planning advocates for controlled growth that carefully considers ecological and social boundaries. As such, self-sufficiency planning necessitates the implementation of policies and practices that not only encourage urban densification but also seek to revitalize degraded areas and promote the development of sustainable infrastructure. Critically, self-sufficiency planning represents a profound paradigm shift in urban governance, emphasizing the importance of localized solutions, community engagement, and interdisciplinary collaboration in achieving sustainable urban futures. Ultimately, self-sufficiency planning has the potential to revolutionize urban governance and create more inclusive, resilient, and sustainable cities for future generations.

Chapter 3 focuses on debating just transition governance via self-sufficiency regional development. The author presents a case in which self-sufficiency refers to the ability of communities to independently fulfill their requirements for food, energy, and water at a local level, and that regional development policies might effectively reduce the risks associated with this transition. The author highlights that the effectiveness of ongoing urban and regional self-sufficient experiments, in particular in the domain of renewable energy, frequently arise from favourable policy frameworks, which are supported by strong community involvement, as well as innovative collaborations between the public and commercial sectors. More than 20 concrete ongoing case studies on self-sufficiency in the energy sector are presented from across the world engaging on climate, energy, and environmental justice and just transition principles. These can be replicated by interested regions and cities considering their place-placed characteristics. Critically, however, attaining self-sufficiency through renewable energy requires more than simply adopting technology. It requires a profound shift in humans' comprehension of and involvement with energy systems. On a positive note, it can help regions respond more effectively to crises during challenging times, acting as a buffer to provide resilience to local and regional communities, as well as preserving traditional livelihood strategies and promoting food sovereignty, which is essential for sustainable local systems.

Chapter 4 initiates the analyses of urban self-sufficiency processes, by highlighting the significance of intra-city renewable energy production in the green energy transition and sustainable city development. Indeed, in a global development context in which cities are increasingly important in terms of demography and

172 Eduardo Medeiros

economic competitiveness, there is a need that the future of renewable energy production is largely concentrated in these urban spaces to make them self-sufficient from an energy production and consumption standpoint. In this context, this chapter presents several potential intra-city renewable energy production possibilities, including: (i) solar photovoltaics; (ii) building-integrated photovoltaics; (iii) solar thermal technologies; (iv) photovoltaics-thermal hybrid systems; (v) bioenergy and waste-to-energy technologies; (vi) wind energy technologies; (viii) direct geothermal energy technologies; (ix) urban and coastal hydropower; (x) hydrogen and carbon capture and storage technologies; and (xi) district thermal energy networks. In all, "global cities are increasingly taking action to deploy renewable energy resources as part of their efforts to mitigate climate change and energy transition to carbon neutrality". However, these pro-urban environmentally sustainable trends in promoting the use of renewable energy sources are mostly concentrated in already socioeconomically developed countries, which leaves ample space for need increasing processes of intra-urban energy self-sufficiency globally.

Chapter 5 delves into the underlying motivations and the capacity of real estate actors' progression towards carbon-neutral urban settings. Moreover, it adopts a qualitative case-study approach to explore how stewardship informs and may help us understand the private sector's role in achieving net zero and advancing self-sufficiency. More particularly, it focuses on the London Landed Estates, representing some of the oldest and largest landowners and property developers. Especially, the author concludes that climate change and energy-efficient building legislation are key extrinsic factors to implementing net zero pledges in urban areas. This underscores the importance of regulation and the state's role in setting adequate legislation fostering self-sufficiency planning instruments. The findings indicate that motivations driving sustainable practices are both intrinsic and extrinsic. Here, the analysed case studies in the city of London demonstrate that they are in a favourable position to prioritize net zero goals, including exceeding the required standards.

Chapter 6 debates the importance of intra-city clean smart and sustainable mobility. For the author, a self-sufficient city is a city whose transport system can effectively address the constantly changing mobility needs of all, as well as the effects on socio-economic development and the environment. Hence, the planning for the city's transport system should incorporate all these elements into sustainable and smart mobility solutions. On a positive note, recent technological advancement offers new opportunities for smart mobility, such as New Mobility Services, available for cities that address their mobility needs through shared mobility, on-demand intermodal transport, and autonomous transport solutions. These services have the potential to reduce private car dependency and accelerate the shift to sustainable urban mobility. Ultimately, in the current complex environment, there is a need to introduce the fundamental planning components for clean, smart, and sustainable mobility into an interdisciplinary planning process for sustainable and smart urban development.

Chapter 7 discusses and compares renewable energy production among two Brazilian States: São Paulo, in the Southeast, and Ceará, in the Northeast. Written by four Brazilian authors, the research identifies the energy resources deployed for generating the useful energy required to sustain the society within each of these two Brazilian States. The authors conclude that local electricity systems analyses are critically important for the formulation of coherent and integrated public policies, which are necessary to cope with the effects of climate change and for the promotion of both demand-side and supply-side pathways for self-sufficiency urban and regional development strategies. Moreover, it was concluded that there is a need for increasing integrated policies and local adaptations to improve energy self-sufficiency and the sustainability of the electricity systems both at the urban and regional levels. Ultimately, energy self-sufficiency entails achieving a balance between energy demand and energy supply. The degree of energy self-sufficiency can be defined as the proportion of locally generated energy to the local energy demand. In contrast, absolute energy self-sufficiency refers to the ability of a region to fully supply itself with its energy resources without the necessity of a grid connection or external resources. In conclusion, the data on electricity supply, demand, and self-sufficiency highlight the importance of proactive measures to address energy security challenges and promote sustainable energy development in São Paulo State. By adopting a comprehensive and integrated approach to energy planning and management, São Paulo can build a more resilient and sustainable energy future for its residents and businesses. Likewise, policymakers and energy planners in Ceará may need to focus on strategies to enhance the reliability and resilience of the energy supply infrastructure to mitigate the impacts of supply-side variability. This could involve investing in diversified energy sources, improving energy storage capabilities, and implementing demand-side management measures, such as efficiency programs, to better match supply and demand patterns.

Chapter 8 discusses the relevance of circular economy in reinforcing the sustainability policies of cities and regions. The author highlights the economic, social, and environmental benefits of implementing circular economy policies at the regional level, demonstrating how it contributes to self-sufficiency, builds resilience, and promotes sustainable development. Critically, the circular economy offers an alternative to a failing economic model and is a critical policy element in implementing regional and urban self-sufficiency development strategies. Indeed, a circular economy not only addresses environmental challenges but also presents economic opportunities. To be fully implemented, a circular economy needs to consider nine principles: (i) refuse – avoid unsustainable or unnecessary products or services; (ii) rethink – rethink the way we consume; (iii) reduce – minimize resource consumption; (iv) reuse – re-use without significant processing; (v) repair – repair rather than throw away or replace; (vi) recycle – renovate old products to make them new again; (vii) renovate – renovate old products to make them new again; (viii) repurpose – use an object for a purpose other than its original use; (ix) recover – extract components from objects that cannot be recycled to produce energy. Ultimately, the transition to the circular economy is imperative for cities and regions facing the dual pressures of environmental degradation and resource scarcity. In this stance, circular economy is a critical component of urban and regional self-sufficiency development strategies.

The last chapter (9) addresses challenges and potential solutions through the lens of driving the sustainability of transport systems, with a specific focus on reducing the urban-rural gap. More particularly, it focuses on focusing on passenger and freight transport, to unravel the complexities of regional mobility and explore innovative strategies that hold promise for promoting sustainable development. From a policymaking perspective, the author proposes policies that encourage modal shifts in transport, reduce transport-related emissions, and promote behavioural changes towards more eco-friendly practices. To address urban mobility challenges, cities must create innovative mobility solutions that enhance connectivity and, at the same time, reduce environmental impact, which is a key policy element for a self-sufficient city. Following the presentation of several urban sustainable mobility good practices, the author concludes that there is a need to foster collaboration between entities and authorities, the public and private sectors, as well as the mobilization of communities, which play a fundamental role in accepting potential changes in the way the transport service is offered. Ultimately, enhancing the urban mobility experience requires cooperation and the transformative power of innovation and paving the way towards a more sustainable, self-sufficient, and inclusive transport system.

In conclusion, all the book chapters provide, in a complimentary manner, an academic guide on the advantages of critical domains of the concept of urban and regional self-sufficiency. It has long been acknowledged that human-induced planetary pressures can be mitigated by urban and regional sustainable and resilient planning and development processes. The question is: how far are human societies willing to go to save our planet from ongoing global climate change paths? In our view, the choice for urban and regional self-sufficiency development processes is the most effective development path to achieving the United Nations 2030 goal of making cities and human settlements inclusive, safe, resilient, and sustainable. At the same time, central to the urban and regional self-sufficiency policy development rationale is its potential positive contribution to transforming how societies generate energy and use materials in a circular manner, in a more effective manner. Moreover, the urban and regional self-sufficiency rationale, by concentrating food and energy production mostly in urban areas, could potentially free up wide territories to natural environmental spaces, thus dramatically contributing to another Agenda 2030 goal: protect, restore, and promote sustainable use of terrestrial ecosystems; sustainably manage forests; combat desertification; and halt and reverse land degradation and halt biodiversity loss. How far the urban and regional self-sufficiency policy development rationale is going to catch fire in global, national, and regional policy meanders is anyone's guess. What seems clear to us is that mainstream environmental policies, via the development of varying development strategies, can have positive impacts in certain territories over time. However, given rising environmental concerns, human societies' preparation to face environmental changes requires dramatic implementation of effective development solutions that can invert as fast as possible current global environmental trends in biodiversity, climate, and pollution. In this stance, the presented policy solution presented in this book of fostering urban and regional self-sufficiency policies should be regarded as a key policy priority to be implemented by regional, national, and international entities.

Index

Note: **Bold** page numbers refer to tables, *italic* page numbers refer to figures and page numbers followed by "n" refer to end notes.

2030 Agenda 8, 9, 97

actors 27–31, 33, 34, 43, 48, 78, 82, 87, 89, 172
Alaska 44, 46
Amiens 43, 44, 47
Ancien Régime village 43, 47
Australia 45, 47, 67
Austria 44, 46, 65, 124

Barcelona 32, 96, 99, 101, 103–105, *104*, 108, 110, 153
behavioural change 105, 150–154, 159, 174
bioenergy 11, 39, 43, 45, 48, 64–65, 70, 72, 73, 172
Brazil 2, 96, 99, 101–103, *103*, 119–133, 172, 173
building-integrated PV 63
buildings 1, 2, 27, 29, 32, 38, 43, 45, 51, 59, 61–64, 66–68, 70–74, 77–81, 83, 85, 86, 88, 90, 101, 123, 139, **141, 142**, 151, 152, 159, 163, 172
built environment 2, 24, 25, 27, 28, 31, 79, 90

Cadogan estate 83, 85–86, 88
Canary Islands 45, 46
capacity 1, 8, 9, 11, 13, **15**, 16, 19, 26, 27, 29, 31, 33, 36, 38, 39, 43, 47, 49, 51, 63, 64, 72, 74, 78, 81, 82, 88–89, 96, **98**, 102, 107, **109**, 131, 140, 151, 166, 172
carbon neutrality 31, 59, 62, 64, 69, 70, 73, 74, 77, 78, 82, 172
carbon-neutral 1, 3, 30, 59, 60, 63, 77, 78, 164, 172
carbon-neutral urban environment 77

Ceará 32, 119–133, 172, 173
circular economy 1–3, 16, 28, 32, 65, 68, 137–146, 170, 173
cities 1–4, 7–9, 12, 13, 16, 17, 18, 24–34, 59–74, 78, 81, 88, 94, 95, 96, 98–102, **98**, 105, 107–110, 121–124, 149, 150, 153–155, 157, 158, 160–166, 171–174
clean mobility 11
climate change 2, 8, 13, **15**, 16, 24, 25, 27, 30, 32, 37–42, 48, 59, 64, 65, 69, 74, 77, 85, 88, **98**, 100, 110, 120, 122, 123, 137, 138, 149, 151, 172–174
climate justice 24, 28, 31, 40–42, 46
collaborative partnerships 162
community engagement 24, 27, 29, 30, 44, 73, 171
congestion 11, 95, *95*, 96, 106, 107, 149, 152, 153, 155, 161–165
Copenhagen 32, 96, 99, 101, 102, 108, 110
cross-Sectoral Coordination 51
Curitiba 32, 96, 99, 102–103, *103*, 108, 110

decentralization 24, 29, 30, 33, 37, 38, 39, 51, 60, 61, 65
decentralization of electricity generation 60
decentralized government 37
Denmark 44, 46, 96, 99, 101–102
development 1–4, 7–9, 11–19, **14–15**, 23–34, 36–52, 60–62, 64, 67, 68, 73, 74, 78, 79, 83, 85, 87, 89, 94–99, **98**, 101–103, **101**, 105, 108, **109**, 110, 120, 122, 124, 128, 130, 131, 137–146, 149–151, 154, 159, 160, 170–174
direct geothermal energy technologies 66, 172
distributional justice 41, 42, 46, 47

176 *Index*

district thermal energy networks 68–69, 172
diversification 24, 29, 30, 33, 125

economic resilience 2, 49, 52, 138
El Hierro 45, 46
electricity self-sufficiency 32, 119–133
energy 1–4, 7, 9–13, 16–18, 23, 29, 31, 32, 33, 36, 37, 38–52, *49, 50,* 59–74, 77–80, 84, 85, 86, 88, 89, 90, 94, 96, 97, **98**, 102, 106, 119–133, 133n1, 140, **142**, 143, 156, 157, 159–161, 163, 170–174
energy autonomy 39, 44, 47, 119, 122, 156
energy governance 61, 121–122
energy infrastructures of cities 60–61
energy management systems 60, 79
energy policy 32, 37, 39, 41, 43, 50, 51, 59, 60, 74, 120, 121, 122, 131
energy self-sufficiency 17, 37, 38–40, 43, 44, 45, *49*, 50, *50*, 51, 119, 120, 121, 122, 123, 133, 172, 173
energy system 31, 32, 38, 42, 43, 45, 47–49, 52, 59–61, 63, 65–67, 69, 71, 73, 74, 90, 119, 121, 122–124, 127–129, 131–133, 171
energy transition 12, 41, 50, 59, 61–62, 68, 69, 70, 72, 74, 121, 122, 125, 132, 133, 171, 172
environmental justice 28, 29, 31, 37, 40–41, 42, 46, 171
environmental policies 51, 174
environmental sustainability 1, 2, 3, 4, 7, 8, 12, 13, **15**, 18, 30, 36, 38, 39, 68, 73, 84, 102, 154, 157, 162, 170
EU Cohesion Policy (ECP) 7–19, 30, 170
EU Green Deal 1, 9, 12, 13, 18, 19
European Union – (EU) 1, 3, 7–19, 30, 60, 79, 80, 94, 99, 100, 151

Feldheim 46, 47
food 1, 2, 4, 9, 10, 11, 12, 17, 18, 29, 36, 48, 65, 140, **141, 142**, 143, 165, 170, 171, 174
France 43, 44, 47, 65, 67, **141, 142**, 143

Germany 44–47, 65, **142**, 143
global energy transition 61–62
global urbanisation 4, 7
good practices 149, 151–153, 155–167, 174
governance 1, 2, 13, 23, 24, 26–27, 29, 30, 32, 36–52, 61, 78, 81, 121–122, 124, 138, 144, 145, 171
grassroots 37

green and digital transition 13
green infrastructure 12, 28, 30, 86
green transition 11
Güssing 44, 46

hydrogen and carbon capture and storage (CCS) technologies 68, 74, 172

incentives 12, 42, 45, 49, 51, 63, 77, 89, 128, 144, 146, 150, 152–154, 162, 165
innovative delivery solutions 164–166
innovative solutions 25, 26, 32, 63, 65, 67, 72, 89, 158–160, 164
integrated policy 8, 120–122, 132, 173
integrated solutions 51, 63, 72, 74
intermodal hubs 159
interregional cooperation **15**, 151, 164
intra-city 59–74, 94–110
Italy 45, 47, 140, **141, 142**

Jühnde 45, 46
Just Transition governance 2, 36–52, 171

King Island 45, 47
Kodiak Island 44, 46

local autonomy 39, 52, 137–146
local empowerment 32, 51, 120
locally available renewable sources 62
logistics efficiency 161–164
London Landed Estates 31, 77–90, 172

mobility 1–4, 9–13, **15**, 17, 18, 31, 32, 68, 72, 80, 94–110, 123, **141**, 149–167, 170, 172, 174
mobility services 32, 96, 105–108, 151, 153, 155, 156, 158, 167, 172
motivations 31, 78, 82, 84, 86, 87, 88, 89, 90, 172

net zero **15**, 77–90, 172
new mobility services 96, 105–108, 172
New Zealand 45, 46

Orkney Islands 44, 46, 67

place-based 1, 16, 17
planning 1–4, 7–9, 11–13, 17–19, 23–34, 42–44, 46, 49, 51, 66, 70, 71, 86, 96, **98**, 99–108, **109**, 110, 119–133, 138, 145, 146, 150, 157, 158, 160–162, 167, 171–174

Index 177

potable water 10, 17
procedural justice 41–43, 46, 47, 49, 50
public participation and transparency 51
public transport 9, 11, 12, 95, **98**, 99, **101**, 102, 103, 106–108, **109**, 150–160, 167
PV-thermal (PV-T) hybrid systems 64

real estate industry 78–80, 82
real-time crowding information 160
recognition justice 42, 43, 46, 47, 49
recover 52, 73, 139, 140, **141**, **142**, 143, 145, 173
recycle 2, 9, 12, 32, 138–140, **142**, 143, 144, 173
reduce 12, 13, 24, 36, 37, 39–41, 45, 47, 48, 51, 52, 61, 63–65, 67–69, 71, 73, 74, 78, 79, 86, 87, **98**, 99, 101, 103, 105, 106, 122, 125, 130, 132, 138, 140, **141**, **142**, 143–145, 150, 152, 155–160, 163, 165, 166, 171–174
refused **141**
regional development 1–3, 9, 12, 36–52, 137–146, 149, 151, 171, 173
regional self-sufficiency 2–4, 9–12, 17–19, 138, 140–143, 145, 161, 170, 171, 173, 174
regions 1–4, 7–10, 13, **14**, **15**, 16–18, 32, 37, 38, 39, 40, 42, 43, 47, 48, 49, 60, 65, 70, 73, 81, 82, 96, 104, 120–124, 131, 138, 145, 149–151, 153, 154, 155, 156, 157, 158, 159, 161, 162, 163, 165, 166, 171, 173
regulations 78–80, 84, 86, 88, 90, 132, 145, 152–154, 162, 172
renewable energy 1–4, 7, 9, 11, 16–18, 31–33, 37–52, *49*, *50*, 59–74, 79, 90, **98**, 119–122, 124, 125, 127, 128, 130–133, 171, 172
renewable energy for city districts 72
renewable energy in buildings 71–72
renewable energy in public lighting 72
renewable energy production 1, 2, 9, 17, 18, 31, 32, 47, 59–74, 120, 122, 125, 171, 172
renewable energy self-sufficiency 37, 38–40, *49*, 50, *50*, 51
renovate **142**, 173
repair 108, 138, **141**, **142**, 143, 173
repurpose **142**, 173
resilience 1, 2, 16, 23–27, 29, 30, 32, 33, 36, 37, 39, 40, 42, 43, 47–49, 52, 63, 67, 73, 74, 120, 122, 127, 130, 132, 138, 145, 171, 173

resource management 28, 30, 52, 81, 138–140
rethink 32, 38, 137–146, 173
reuse 2, 32, 138–140, **141**, 143–145, 173

Samsø Island 44, 46
São Paulo 32, 119–133, 172, 173
Scotland 44, 46, 67
self-sufficiency 1–4, 7–19, 23–34, 36–52, 59, 61, 78, 119–133, 138, 140–145, 161, 170–174
self-sufficiency planning 2, 3, 23–34, 161, 171, 172
self-sufficient urban and regional planning 3, 7
self-sustainable cities 7
self-sustainable regions 32, 138
Shaftesbury capital 83, 84–85, 87
smart energy management 60, 72
smart grids 73, 74, 123
smart mobility 3, 9, 96–97, 105, 108, 110, 172
social equity 24, 28, 31, 36, 38, 40, 51
social justice 2, 28
socioeconomic 12, 13, 17, 19, 25, 28–31, 43, 124, 125, 132, 170, 172
socio-technical transitions 32
solar photovoltaic 61, 62, 63, 73, 79, 127, 172
solar thermal technologies 63–64, 171, 172
Sonnen community 44, 47
Spain 45, 46, 67, 96, 99, 101, 103–105, *104*, **141**
stewardship 51, 77–90, 172
strategic planning 32, 96, 99–100, 110, 162
sustainable/sustainability 1–4, 7–13, **15**, 17, 18, 23–34, 36, 38–43, 45–49, 51, 52, 59, 61–74, 78–81, 83–85, 87–90, 94–110, 120–122, 124, 127, 129–133, 137–140, **141**, 143–146, 149–167, 170–174
sustainable cities 7, 8, 24, 27, 98, **98**, 101, 158, 171
sustainable city development 64, 74, 171
sustainable deliveries 161–166
sustainable development 3, 4, 7, 9, 11, 12, 23–34, 36, 38, 46, 48, 52, 60, 79, 96–98, **98**, 150, 151, 173, 174
sustainable economic systems 36, 140
sustainable land use 51
sustainable mobility 1–3, 9, 10, 18, 32, 72, 94–110, 149–154, 156, 158, 159, 172, 174
sustainable regions 2, 3, 32, 138, 149–167

178 Index

sustainable urban futures 23, 26, 27, 29, 171
sustainable urban mobility 11, 31, 32, 96, *97*, 98–100, **98,** 101, 105–108, 110, 151, 153, 156, 158, 172

Tasmania 45, 47
technological innovations 9, 73, 74
territorial cohesion 12, 13, **14, 15,** 16–18
territorial development 4, 12, 13, 18, 33, 146, 170, 171
territorial self-sufficiency policy 7–19, 144, 170
Tocco 45, 47
Tokelau 45, 46
transformative mobility 155, 167, 174
transport 2, 8, 9, 11–13, **15,** 16, 23, 24, 29, 32, 44, 62, 65, 68, 71, 72, 74, 78, 79, 94–108, **98, 101, 109,** 110, 123, 133, 149–167, 170–174
transport impacts 96, 152, 155, 158
transport system 11, 24, 94–97, **98,** 100, 102, 108, 149–160, 167, 172–174
transportation 2, 23, 24, 29, 32, 44, 62, 68, 71, 72, 74, 78, 94, 123, 133, 171

United Nations 1, 4, 8, 25, 37, 59, 60, 94, 96, 97, 174
urban and coastal hydro power 67
urban areas 2, 4, 7, 8, 10–12, 17–19, 23–25, 28, 30, 31, 33, 81, 95, 100, 102, 107, 156, 157, 159, 164, 171, 172, 174
urban challenges 8, 24, 25–27, 33
urban development 2, 8, 9, 12, 23–31, 33, 83, 89, 94, 95, 99, 101–103, 105, 108, 110, 160, 172
urban governance 23, 24, 26, 27, 29, 30, 171
urban logistics 151, 162, 163, 164
urban mobility 11, 12, 31, 32, 94, 96–98, **98,** 99–101, 105–108, 110, 123, 150–153, 155, 156, 158, 160, 164, 167, 172, 174
urban planning 2, 7, 8, 23, 27, 31–33, 44, 101–105, 121
urban spaces 8, 28, 90, 103, 172
urban stewardship 77–90
urban sustainable development 11, 12, 23–34
urban wind 70
urbanization 23, 25, 33, 59, 70, 73
USA 44, 46, 67, **141**

waste-to-energy technologies 64–65, 172